CONSTITUTING FEMINIST SUBJECTS

CONSTITUTING

CORNELL
UNIVERSITY
PRESS
ITHACA
&
LONDON

Feminist Subjects

KATHI WEEKS

Copyright 1998 by Cornell University

All rights reserved. Except for brief quotations in a review, this book, or parts thereof, must not be reproduced in any form without permission in writing from the publisher. For information, address Cornell University Press, Sage House, 512 East State Street, Ithaca, New York 14850.

First published 1998 by Cornell University Press.
First printing, Cornell Paperbacks, 1998.

Library of Congress Cataloging-in-Publication Data

Weeks, Kathi, 1958–
Constituting feminist subjects / Kathi Weeks.
    p.   cm.
Includes bibliographical references and index.
ISBN 0-8014-3427-0 (cloth : alk. paper). — ISBN 0-8014-8447-2
(pbk.: alk. paper)
    1. Feminist theory.   2. Subjectivity.   3. Subject (Philosophy)   I. Title.
HQ1190.W43   1998
305.42–dc21   97-52190

Printed in the United States of America.

Cornell University Press strives to utilize environmentally responsible suppliers and materials to the fullest extent possible in the publishing of its books. Such materials include vegetable-based, low-VOC inks and acid-free papers that are also either recycled, totally chlorine-free, or partly composed of nonwood fibers.

Cloth printing   10   9   8   7   6   5   4   3   2   1
Paperback printing   10   9   8   7   6   5   4   3   2   1

CONTENTS

Acknowledgments *vii*

INTRODUCTION *1*

CHAPTER ONE
Nietzsche, Foucault, and the Subject of
the Eternal Return *16*

CHAPTER TWO
Modernism, Postmodernism, and the
Logic of Paradigm Debates *48*

CHAPTER THREE
The Aspiration to Totality:
Identity, Difference, and Antagonism *70*

CHAPTER FOUR
Labor, Standpoints, and Feminist Subjects *120*

CONCLUSION
Beyond the Paradigm Debate *152*

Notes *161*
References *181*
Index *193*

ACKNOWLEDGMENTS

I am deeply indebted to Christine DiStefano, Nancy Hartsock, Dan Lev, and Michael McCann for the many ways they have inspired, supported, and encouraged me over the years. I am also grateful to Michael Hardt, Fredric Jameson, and Karen Stuhldreher for helpful comments on the manuscript and to my editor at Cornell, Alison Shonkwiler, for her guidance.

I want to acknowledge some of my colleagues at Fairfield University, Kevin Cassidy, Ed Dew, Don Greenberg, Alan Katz, Dennis Keenan, John Orman, and Sally Williams, for creating such a congenial environment in which to work. My special thanks to Marcie Patton for all her material and emotional support. In addition, a summer research stipend from Fairfield University provided some timely funding.

Brittany Faulkner and Julie Walwick saw this project through from beginning to end, and I am continually grateful for their love and friendship. Many thanks as well to Robert Adelman, Carol DiMarcello, Brian Henderson, and the rest of the humans and animals at 5251.

Finally, I dedicate this book to my parents, Lee Weeks and Hal Weeks, and my sisters, Regan Weeks and Diana Weeks.

K. W.

CONSTITUTING FEMINIST SUBJECTS

Introduction

In the wake of the postmodern critiques of the 1980s, feminists have been struggling to develop theories of the subject that are adequate to a feminist politics. Many of us want to move beyond models of the subject organized with reference to a natural core, authentic humanity, or enduring metaphysical essence and to trade the older focus on the unified subject of feminism for a multiplicity of feminist subjects. At the same time, we want a theory of feminist subjectivity that can acknowledge feminism's antagonistic force and cultivate its subversive potential, one that does not simply attach to a theory of social determinacy a vague evocation of voluntarist refusal. For us, then, the puzzle has been to understand how it could be that subjects so systematically constructed and well prepared to submit to the existing order of things can also collectively defy it. In other words, we want to endorse the critiques of humanism, functionalism, determinism, and essentialism without denying the possibility of agency.

This project, however, has been hampered by certain stubborn remnants of the modernist–postmodernist paradigm debate, a debate that helped to set this agenda but that also placed certain limits on our ability to pursue it. Although many will argue that the modernist–postmodernist debate that animated political theory and feminist theory throughout most of the 1980s is finished, having exhausted its potential, it lingers on nonetheless in the way we recall arguments from the past and conceive alternatives for the future. Here I focus on one specific configuration of this debate, a form that should be familiar to those of us reading in political theory and feminist theory over the years, wherein modernism and postmodernism are conceived as mutually exclusive theoretical paradigms. According to this particular conception of the debate (and of course, it is not the only way that the debate was conceived), the modernist tradition (with its wealth of differences) was equated with a paradigm that perhaps most closely resembled certain themes within Enlightenment modernism, poststructuralism (in all its heterogeneity) was identified with something called postmodernism, and the rest of us were compelled by the relentlessly oppositional logic used to maintain this dualistic framework to choose either one side or the other. By means of this formula, modernism was all too often effectively reduced to a caricature opposed to another caricature called postmodernism. This reactive dynamic left us with two equally unsatisfactory choices: a reaffirmation of the humanist subject in some form or the death of the subject *tout court,* a voluntaristic theory of political agency or a thoroughgoing social determinism. What now remains in the wake of this particular formulation of the debate (a formulation I refer to as the modernist–postmodernist *paradigm debate*) is a history of distortions and a continuing inability by many to recognize the potential of, and the nuances within, the rich traditions of thought that were subsumed into the category of modernism and the equally valuable theoretical frameworks confined by the category of postmodernism. The vestiges of this paradigm debate can also account for some of the defensiveness and dismissiveness that continues to characterize many of our exchanges. The modernist–postmodernist paradigm debate may be dead, but its legacy still haunts our analyses.

If we were to comply with the terms of this paradigm debate, the project of developing a nonessentialist theory of subjective agency would be a very difficult one indeed: too many potentially productive lines of inquiry would be closed to us. Thus my project is conceived in part as an effort to circumvent this propensity toward either/or formulas and to counter this inattention to the specificity of, and the potential affinities among, different theoretical undertakings. Here I present a nonessentialist theory of feminist subjectivity that draws upon a variety of resources, including "postmodernists" like Friedrich Nietzsche, Michel Foucault, and Judith Butler, as well as "modernists" from the Marxist and socialist feminist traditions. By staging their encounters on a different terrain, outside these paradigm categories, I believe that we can develop some potentially productive lines of dialogue among these diverse theoretical projects.

Feminist Standpoint Theory

I cast this reconfiguration of a feminist subject in terms of a version of socialist feminism known as feminist standpoint theory. The tradition of standpoint theory includes the contributions of many theorists who propose very different arguments.[1] This account is based on a selective appropriation and extension of a specific set of arguments from a limited group of texts. I do not, then, offer a detailed summary of the literature, one that explains my support for or quarrels with each of the different versions. Since my goal is not to present a faithful account of standpoint theories in all their difference and specificity, I make no claim to remain true to the methods, contents, or aims of any one author.[2] Rather than present a critical overview of existing standpoint theories, an endeavor that has already been admirably completed elsewhere, I intend to concentrate my efforts on constructing an alternative feminist standpoint theory, one that builds selectively on some of the fundamental themes of these original theories in a way that can render the basic project as I conceive it more compatible with a contemporary theoretical agenda.[3]

But why would I want to begin with standpoint theory? According to its critics, feminist standpoint theory is a relic of a bygone era in Anglo-American feminism: a throwback to an outmoded 1970s agenda, an archaic mode of theorizing anchored in the second rather than the third wave, a humorless operation in contrast to a playful gesture, in short, an obsolete approach situated within a modernist as opposed to a postmodernist horizon. If we accept the characterization presented by many of these reviewers, standpoint theory is so thoroughly mired in the pitfalls and conundrums of an older, irreparably foundationalist and essentialist brand of feminism that it can no longer speak to our concerns. There is, of course, some truth to this indictment: like the larger body of socialist feminist theory of which it is an instance, standpoint theory grew out of a particular historical conjuncture with its own specific openings for, and obstacles to, theoretical reflection; some of these we cannot recreate, others we would not wish to. The problem with this assessment, however, is that while it may serve to help us identify some of standpoint theory's failings (although, in this form, the critique is indebted to the modernist–postmodernist paradigm debate and, therefore, too often based on a caricature to provide many accurate critiques), it is blind to its distinctive strengths and potential contributions. While remaining alert to standpoint theory's weaknesses, I want nonetheless to argue for and expand upon its continuing promise and vitality. There are three fundamental reasons why I choose to enroll standpoint theory in this project of reconstituting a feminist subject, three sources of its enduring power and relevance. These can be encapsulated within three of its key concepts: totality, labor, and standpoint.

The concept of totality was one of the most frequently discussed under the auspices of the modernist–postmodernist paradigm debate and, unfortunately, one of the most often confused by its specifications. As I develop it here, the term "totality" designates an important set of theoretical and practical commitments. A notion of *gendered* subjectivity necessarily presupposes some conception of the social formation within which it is constructed and maintained, just as a notion of *feminist* subjectivity necessarily presupposes some conception of the complex relationships among the social forces it seeks to challenge. In the absence of some sense of the whole, some conception of the complex social formations that constitute and constrain subjects, we end up with an impoverished model of the subject that overestimates its capacities for self-creation and self-transformation, as well as a very limited understanding of the forces we must subvert in order to make possible the construction of alternative subjects. The project of totality—which I will try to distinguish from totalizing theory, or theories that reduce subjectivity to some functional effect of an abstract, determinable, and monolithic system of structures—refers to an attempt to locate some of the specific connections between our everyday lives and practices and the larger framework of social structures within which they are organized. The project of totality thus involves a methodological mandate to relate and connect, to situate and contextualize, to conceive the social systematically as a complex process of relationships. For example, capitalism, patriarchy, and white supremacy are not isolated forces, but rather systems that traverse the entire social horizon and intersect at multiple points. Standpoint theory cuts into this system by trying to make specific connections between certain modes of gendered subjectivity, women's laboring practices, the gender and racial divisions of labor, and global capitalism. How, standpoint theorists ask, are our practices both constituted by and constitutive of the structures that organize our experience? This "aspiration to totality"[4] that one can find in standpoint theory recalls some of the earliest and, I believe, strongest impulses of socialist feminism. Under the sign of totality, socialist feminism linked its interest in systemic analysis with a dedication to social transformation. Socialist feminists fashioned theories to help map the connections among the different social forces implicated in the construction of gender hierarchies; a feminist politics was conceived as a revolutionary politics, one that ultimately sought to transform the forces that maintain these systematic and institutional hierarchies. With this term, then, I want to preserve and develop two central commitments of socialist feminist standpoint theory: a theoretical commitment to understand the relationships between social structures and subjectivities and a political commitment to social transformation.[5]

Labor, as one of many mutually constitutive links between social structures and subjectivities, is the second source of what I see as standpoint theory's continuing appeal. Here I build selectively on those versions of standpoint theory that draw on, among other resources, the Marxist tradition to ground a feminist standpoint in some account of women's laboring practices in late capitalist social formations.[6] I focus most frequently on the work of Hilary Rose, Nancy Hartsock, and Dorothy Smith. These accounts begin with the assumption that what we do can have consequences for who we are and what and how we think, and that what we do is determined in part by a gender division of labor.[7] Critical of Marxism's narrow conception of production which fails to recognize the possibility of a standpoint grounded in women's laboring activity, these theories begin with alternative analyses of "women's work." The accounts differ depending on which types of practices are featured and the potential consequences the author wants to highlight. Thus, for example, in some accounts the practices for which women are disproportionately responsible are described in terms of "caring labor" or emotional labor, a set of practices that involves personal service.[8] Here we could include "maternal labor," the work of raising children,[9] and "kin work," the work of maintaining relationships among friends and extended family.[10] Women's labor is similarly characterized as "reproductive labor," a term designed to include many of the most common modes of women's labor not only in the home but also in the wage labor market, since women are so frequently channeled into those paid jobs that resemble their unpaid work in the household.[11] Finally, aspects of women's work have been conceived as "labor in the concrete bodily mode" to highlight those practices that give form to and provide support services for those engaged in more abstract conceptual practices or mental labor.[12] Note that in all these accounts, labor is not just activity that directly produces capital, but activity that produces society itself, including the networks of sociality and the subjects they sustain. These are constitutive practices that, whether waged or not, are socially necessary. Yet despite its importance, this labor is often invisible and many of the skills developed in and through these practices are naturalized and undervalued (Rose 1986, 165).

Regardless of whether particular women actually do this kind of work (and of course, many do not), women are generally (though differently) constructed to be the kinds of people who can perform these duties, and are usually (though variously) expected to be the ones who should (see Hartsock 1983a, 291). For this reason, theories of feminist subjectivities based on accounts of women's labor carry the potential to speak to broad audiences of women, and particularly to women outside the academy. However, it should be noted that this focus on labor is also what marks most clearly the specificity of this version of standpoint theory. Obviously one cannot claim that every object of feminist inquiry can be explained by reference to the gender division of labor. I do not, then, profess to offer a new feminist metanarrative or a General Feminist Theory of Everything that identifies labor as the fundamental source of women's oppression and the only site of feminist agitation. What I hope to present is a carefully delimited theoretical approach that aspires to help us think about and cultivate the possible consequences of a specific set of practices in a particular place and time.

Standpoint theories try to consider the ontological and epistemological consequences of these laboring practices. How might some of our laboring practices be suggestive of different ways of being in and knowing the world? How can they help us locate and develop alternatives to the existing configuration of social relations? What, in other words, is the subversive potential of women's laboring practices? I argue that—to the extent that these practices exceed the scope of current standards of cultural and socioeconomic valorization, to the extent that, for example, the labor of creating and sustaining socially necessary forms of sociality cannot be contained, cannot be accounted for, and cannot be valued adequately within the existing mode of production—they carry the potential to enable and to cultivate antagonistic subjects. Standpoint theories attempt to fashion from our everyday practices a chain of critical levers that can inspire our disloyalty and disobedience to the values of the larger social formation. By this interpretation, "women's work" is not just an instance of women's oppression and exploitation, it is also a site where alternatives can be constructed; women's laboring practices are not only constraining, but also potentially enabling. This potential power, these alternatives, are located not in some natural or metaphysical essence, but in our practices; more specifically, these possibilities of feminist subjectivity, of feminist political agency, are grounded in an ontology of laboring practices.

A standpoint, a collective project designed to affirm and pursue some of these possibilities, is the final element of this theoretical tradition that I want to highlight and affirm. Standpoints are constructed around the potential ontological and epistemological consequences of these laboring practices, around the subjectivities that emerge from these practices. A standpoint is constitutive of and constituted by a collective subject, in this case a feminist subject grounded in women's laboring practices and situated within the larger field of social relations that I call totality. In a time when some feminist theorists are reacting to the valuable critiques of essentialism by retreating from every theory of subjectivity, when some would seem to be translating the critique of humanism into the death of the subject, when some are responding to the oppressive and homogenizing focus on unity that has informed so many accounts and practices of feminist collectivities by committing themselves just as exclusively to the valorization of difference in a way that often simply recapitulates the logic of liberal individualism, standpoint theory points us in the direction of one possible alternative, toward models of collective subjectivity.

Once again, to locate the particular conception of a standpoint that is most in keeping with this project, we must be selective in our appropriation of standpoint theories. Here I focus on those accounts dedicated to the construction of *feminist* standpoints; that is, on those versions in which standpoints are conceived as political projects based on feminist reappropriations of women's practices. For this element I draw most frequently on the work of Hartsock and Rose, both of whom insist that the standpoint they propose is a feminist standpoint: it is a collective interpretation or reworking of a particular subject position rather than an immediate perspective automatically acquired by an individual; it is an ongoing achievement rather than a spontaneous attribute or consciousness of all women. For these theorists, a standpoint is neither self-evident nor obvious (Hartsock 1983a, 303); instead it must be derived from political practice (Rose 1986, 162). A feminist standpoint is, by this formulation, a collective project that is both a product and an instrument of feminist struggle.[13] When we put these last two dimensions together, the focus on labor and the feminist political project, we have the basic tenets of a political project based on the alternative ways of being, desiring, and knowing that can be developed from women's laboring practices.

Conceived as an achieved, constructed collectivity, I believe that a feminist standpoint can serve as an inspiring example of a collective subject, a subject that is neither modeled after the individual, and thus somehow unitary and homogeneous, nor conceived as spontaneous and natural community. Standpoint theory builds on an account of how women's subject positions are systematically constituted within a social field in order then to think about how antagonistic subjects—in this case, feminist collectivities—can be constructed on their basis; fashioned, as it were, from the same materials. Here I believe that we can find a productive account (though certainly not the only productive account) of the subjective bases of a feminist politics; here we can find the basic outlines not just of an ontology of practices, but of a political ontology of practices, an ontology that is inextricably bound to a politics.

Standpoint theorists have generally concentrated their attention on the potential *epistemological* consequences of the gender division of labor: these practices can suggest alternative methods or knowledges which, depending on the account, avoid the subject–object split, emphasize relational thinking, and revalue the concrete, everyday, and bodily dimensions of existence. Here I will focus instead on a relatively less accentuated dimension of these analyses—namely, the ontology that informs a standpoint and the constructions of subjectivity to which it gives rise. This is conceived, then, as an ontological rather than an epistemological project: whereas the primary goal of most of these original theories was to develop alternative epistemologies based on feminist cognitive practices, the primary focus of this account is the constitution of alternative subjects, feminist collectivities.[14] These projects are not incompatible; ontology and epistemology, being and knowing, are intimately related to one another and by no means do these theorists ignore this link. There are, nonetheless, some important differences between the two projects. For example, as a consequence of their focus on the epistemological possibilities of a standpoint in the original versions, the subject of standpoint theory tends to be cast as a knowing subject and, as a consequence, questions of subjectivity are often reduced to questions of consciousness. Here I will be less interested in what or how we know (and the controversies that attach to this epistemological question), than in what we are, or, better yet, in what we can be (and some of the issues of constitution that are involved in this question). To put it in different terms, it is not the possibilities of *becoming conscious* but rather—and here I anticipate a Nietzschean formula— the *being of becoming* that is my primary concern. The collective subjects of this account will be defined primarily not by the consciousness or knowledge they achieve but by the practices they enact and the desires and pleasures that they cultivate. This is where I find the most promising and timely contribution of standpoint theory: rather than an epistemological project, the political efficacy of which is linked to its claims about what or how feminists can know, claims that are supposed to legitimize the alternatives we seek, I believe that a feminist standpoint is more powerful as an ontological project dedicated to the construction of antagonistic subjects with dreams, passions, and interests at odds with the existing order of things, subjects with the will and the capacity to seek alternatives.

What I find valuable in the tradition of standpoint theory, then, is its commitment to make connections among what we are, what we do, and the larger framework of social relations we call totality; its interest in the subversive possibilities of women's laboring practices; and its efforts to assemble a collective feminist subject that is based on and dedicated to pursuing some of these possibilities. There are, however, several problems with these standpoint theories, problems that many different critiques informed by the discourse of postmodernism have helped identify. Among the most significant of these limitations is that the aspiration to totality, the ontology of labor, and the construction of a standpoint have, in some cases, been conceived in ways that betray a reliance on functionalist logics and humanist or otherwise essentialist formulations. First, the problem of functionalism turns up in those attempts to situate subjects in the context of a totality of social relations that deploy an insufficiently complex account of the multiplicity of social structures and subjects, and which limit their interaction to a closed and predictable logic. Second, the achieved and constructed character of a standpoint is not always rigorously attended to so that one can find residues of classic humanist formulations—gestures to some notion of a pre-existing, authentic humanity—in these accounts of a feminist subject. For example, labor, besides being frequently undertheorized, is often presented as the equivalent of a human essence, a universal creative potential from which we are estranged and to which we should be restored. Third, one can also find other forms of essentialist thinking (besides the classic humanist evocation of essence)[15] at work in the early conception of a single feminist standpoint, "the" feminist standpoint, rather than a multiplicity of feminist standpoints, a formula that reveals an inattention to differences among women. To help us move beyond these reductive and determinist conceptions of the social totality and falsely generalized and essentialist conceptions of subjectivity, I will draw on a variety of resources.

Marx and Nietzsche

Some of these correctives will be found in certain examples of Marxist theorizing beyond those that were deployed in the original versions of standpoint theory. This broader Marxist tradition was, unfortunately, one of the primary casualties of the modernist–postmodernist paradigm debate. Under the terms of this debate, the Marxist tradition was all too often equated with an orthodox version of the discourse that was then conflated with other modernist traditions, which were in turn reduced to a version of Enlightenment thought. Although my project is rooted in a Marxist tradition, it is not the tradition that some have described as an Enlightenment discourse predicated on metaphysical foundations, teleological narratives, and universal truths. Within this tradition one can also find historical materialisms that conceive life as a purely immanent social process, without an original human essence or a final telos, as well as methods of social inquiry that are suspicious of ahistorical, transcendental, and naturalizing analytical categories. These other Marxisms—the antideterminist, antihumanist, and antiessentialist versions of Marxism that were rendered invisible by the paradigm debate—confound the simple modernist–postmodernist opposition: they simply cannot be contained within either of its rigid categories. It is, thus, important to remember that Marxism is not a single monolithic discourse, but rather a heterogeneous tradition that encompasses lively debates and fundamental disagreements. There are, in fact, a multiplicity of Marxisms. One of my strategies will be to turn to some Marxist theories that were either not considered or not considered adequately by the original standpoint theorists to locate some conceptual resources that can help me construct an alternative feminist theory of the subject. The work of Antonio Negri is exemplary of this brand of Marxism (a poststructuralist Marxism, if you will) that can be used to develop some of standpoint theory's potential.

Although there are resources within the Marxist tradition to further this project, some of the most compelling sources of antideterminist, antihumanist, and antiessentialist thought can be found beyond its borders in the work of Nietzsche, as well as in the writings of some of the poststructuralists whom he inspired. However, if Marx was distorted as a consequence of being confined to the narrow terms of the modernist paradigm, Nietzsche was equally obfuscated by the limited purview of postmodernism. One would have thought that our understanding and appreciation of Nietzsche would have been furthered by the postmodernist popularization of "the new Nietzsche," and to some degree they certainly were. Nevertheless, while postmodernism routinely cites Nietzsche as founder and predecessor, that label not only fails to describe him adequately, it often obscures some of the most timely and valuable elements of his thought. One problem is that these interpretations tend to focus on the critical dimensions of Nietzsche's interventions and to neglect their constructive aspects. Of particular relevance to my project is not only Nietzsche's critique of the subject of humanism, but also the alternative theory of subjectivity that can be gleaned from his notion of the eternal return. It is here that I will find some of the basic specifications from which to construct a model of a feminist subject.

This is not an attempted "synthesis" of the Marxist and Nietzschean traditions. My goal is to develop a theory of feminist subjectivity, and I think that certain elements within both the Marxist and the Nietzschean traditions can contribute toward that end. It is not a "happy medium" or a "reasonable compromise" that I am after, but rather a selective engagement between these discourses, one that I hope respects their vital differences without discounting their moments of affinity. In other words, I am not proposing a marriage, just a truce. An unholy alliance? Perhaps. But to borrow a phrase from Raymond Williams, a phrase that seems particularly appropriate now that the rigid formulas dictated by the modernist–postmodernist paradigm debate are losing their force, "[i]f you're not in a church you're not worried about heresies" (quoted in Surin 1993, 62n3).

Overview

My argument proceeds as follows. In Chapters 1 and 2 I pursue two interwoven lines of inquiry. My primary goal is to locate in the work of Nietzsche and Foucault certain conceptual resources and critical standards that will aid my efforts in Chapters 3 and 4 to formulate an alternative theory of feminist subjectivity. At the same time, I seek to disengage these tools from the limiting terms of the modernist–postmodernist paradigm debate to which they have so often been confined.

In pursuit of the first goal, Chapter 1 explores Nietzsche's and Foucault's genealogies of modernity. I focus in particular on their similar critiques of totalizing theories of social systems and humanist models of the subject. These critiques of specific modernist theories of systems and subjects then serve as points of departure for my attempt in Chapter 3 to develop an alternative feminist account of the relationship between system and subjectivity. In addition to these critiques, I find in Nietzsche's thought of the eternal return an alternative conception of the subject that will guide my construction of a model of feminist subjectivity in Chapter 4.

Before these tools can be used for my project, however, I must confront the ways they have been framed in the context of the modernist–postmodernist debate, or, more specifically, the version of the debate that casts modernism and postmodernism as opposing paradigms. This brings me to the second strand of my argument in these opening chapters. It is often treated as a commonplace that Nietzsche, Foucault, and postmodernism are linked in a kind of linear progression: postmodernism carries the mantle of Foucault, who is the heir to Nietzsche. The first two chapters contest this narrative by marking distinctions among these discourses. Chapter 1 focuses on the first step in this supposed line of descent that leads from Foucault back to Nietzsche. Here I try to account for the relevant continuities between these projects as well as what I see as their crucial differences. Although Nietzsche and Foucault develop similar critiques of specific examples of modernist thought and practice, I argue that only Nietzsche locates a positive ground upon which to formulate an alternative model of subjectivity.

Chapter 2 then turns to the second step in the narrative and presents an analysis of the Anglo-American reading of Foucault as a champion of the postmodernist paradigm. Why, I ask, are Foucault's limited critiques of specific examples of modernist thought cast as a radical, total critique of modernism? How does Foucault's thought come to assume the form of a paradigm? I argue that postmodernism, as a global challenge to modernism, is, in part, the product of various attempts to insert Foucault's thought into contemporary debates in Anglo-American political theory and feminist theory by casting it as a complete departure from and fundamental challenge to existing approaches. While this paradigm debate between modernists and postmodernists has provided the impetus for many positive developments over the years, it is time to disengage our theorizing from the residues of this specular opposition. I find that for my purposes this debate has often obscured or blunted the particular Nietzschean and Foucaultian tools that I want to recover.

Having cleared a path and acquired some important resources for my project, in Chapters 3 and 4 I focus on the task of developing a theory of antagonistic feminist subjectivity. Chapter 3 takes on the concept of totality and focuses on developing an account of the relationship between structure and subjectivity that is adequate to my project. How, I ask, can we account for the coherence of a social totality without losing sight of our different positions within this order; how can we theorize structures of oppression in a systematic way without lapsing into functionalism; that is, how can we account for the general coherence of the social formation without losing a space for difference, contingency, and antagonism? How can I reformulate this Marxist project in a way that is responsive to these Nietzschean concerns? I begin with an archeology of socialist feminist systems theories—specifically the (early) work of Mariarosa Dalla Costa, Heidi Hartmann, and Iris Young—that excavates what is still productive in these accounts while also recognizing the limits of these initial efforts to theorize the relationship between capitalism and patriarchy. I then turn to the work of other Marxist theorists— including Georg Lukács, Louis Althusser, and Antonio Negri—in order to find ways to develop further a conception of the social field that is attentive to both the determinacy of social institutions and the relatively autonomous force of subjectivity. My goal is to construct a feminist account of a social totality or totalities that is open to the possibilities of contestation, a conception of a late capitalist socioeconomic formation that is both productive of and potentially disrupted by the feminist subjects I describe in the next and final chapter.

Chapter 4 presents a theory of feminist subjectivity that builds on what I contend is the antagonistic potential of women's laboring practices. How can we conceive a collective subject whose capacity to resist the forces that construct it is not sustained by a notion of free will? How can we formulate a theory of social construction that does not fall into the trap of social determinism? How, in other words, can we move beyond both voluntarist and determinist models of political agency? To begin, I must first distinguish the particular conception of labor upon which these feminist subjects are constructed from certain traditional notions of labor. As the concept is developed here, labor serves as an immanent, creative, and strategic ground from which to construct a model of subjectivity. Judith Butler's theory of gender performativity will provide both a source of inspiration and a point of contrast for this model of a laboring subject. The laboring subject must, however, undergo several permutations before it is transformed into a feminist subject, into a collective and subversive subject. To establish the terms for this process, I again invoke the Nietzschean theory of the eternal return that was recovered in Chapter 1. I then draw on Kathy Ferguson's work on irony as a feminist practice and Antonio Negri's concept of self-valorization to help me account for this subject's capacity for autonomy and its potential power. The feminist standpoint that finally emerges from this account, the alternative conception of feminist subjectivity towards which I have been building, is an achieved, selective, and politically engaged collectivity based upon an affirmation of women's laboring practices.

Nietzsche, Foucault, and the Subject of the Eternal Return

For decades after his death, Friedrich Nietzsche's thought occupied only a marginal position within the canon of modern philosophy. More recently, however, Nietzsche has become a dominant figure in a wide variety of theoretical debates. As William Connolly describes it, Nietzsche speaks "in a voice that strikes more responsive chords in readers living through the last decade of the twentieth century than it did for Nietzsche's contemporaries in the late nineteenth century" (1988, 12). Indeed, the recent proliferation of studies on Nietzsche is testimony to the timeliness of his thought. However, this new focus on Nietzsche tends to highlight not his participation in modern thought, but rather his explorations beyond its boundaries.[1] It is argued that "Nietzsche provides a model for philosophy which is so different from the model of Kant and other moderns that we are forced to call it postmodern" (Hoy 1988, 12). Today postmodernism claims Nietzsche as a foundational figure.

Here I want to problematize this lineage, to disrupt this popular narrative, by suggesting that postmodernism's reworking of Nietzsche is, in certain specific ways, inadequate. As a particular appropriation of neo-Nietzschean discourse, postmodernism is associated with several important poststructuralist thinkers. However, I will focus on the work of Michel Foucault as one of the more frequently cited links between Nietzsche and postmodernism. In these first two chapters I want to identify certain disjunctures in what is often presented as a smooth continuity or progression that joins Nietzsche, Foucault, and postmodernism. This chapter focuses on the first link in that chain, the relationship between Nietzsche and Foucault; the next chapter will concentrate on the connection between Foucault's neo-Nietzscheanism and the postmodernist paradigm.

Theoretical Selections and Specific Critiques

Foucault's contribution to this Nietzsche renaissance is most clearly distinguished by his efforts to construct a politicized Nietzschean methodology. According to Foucault's own account, political circumstances compelled him at some point to reassess the adequacy of existing theoretical orientations. The events of May 1968 had proven to Foucault that the French versions of orthodox Marxism were rigid, narrowly deterministic theories, unable to breathe life into their analyses or adjust to changing practices (see Foucault 1980a, 57, 116). Nietzsche's thought offered him a more useful set of tools. In particular, Foucault found in Nietzsche's theory of power a broader, more versatile, and more flexible analysis of the social relations of domination. Nietzsche, Foucault concluded, not Marx, is the true philosopher of power (ibid., 53).

Nietzsche seems, on the face of it, an unlikely resource for this kind of critical political theory, given his political sympathies. Although he never offers anything approaching a political program, he frequently valorizes the future role of a new cultural elite and consistently defends a vision of extreme social hierarchy. There is, however, a lively debate over the question of whether Nietzsche's political conclusions *necessarily* follow from his philosophical premises.[2] But Foucault is unimpressed with this kind of debate: "if commentators . . . say that I am being faithful or unfaithful to Nietzsche, that is of absolutely no interest" (ibid. 1980a, 54). These debates over the political status of Nietzsche's philosophy are, by Foucault's standards, unduly constrained by the philological issues at stake. Foucault seeks to formulate a selective recuperation or reoccupation of

Nietzsche's work; he sorts through and selects different aspects of Nietzsche's approach in order to fashion a discourse that might have a political effect. To achieve the kind of impact he wants, Foucault rejects the elitism of Nietzsche's perspective and focuses instead on the fate of those whom Nietzsche characterized as "the herd." In short, he reformulates a Nietzschean methodology and drafts it into the service of a critique rather than a celebration of domination. Edward Said captures this dual commitment to Nietzschean theory and anti-authoritarian politics in his description of Foucault "as perhaps the greatest of Nietzsche's modern disciples and, simultaneously, as a central figure in the most noteworthy flowering of oppositional intellectual life in the twentieth-century West" (1988, 1).

In keeping with this sense of Foucault's project, the criticisms I raise center neither on the claim that he is true to Nietzsche nor on the claim that he betrays him. I do not question Foucault's approach in making a selective appropriation of Nietzsche's thought; on the contrary, as we will see in subsequent chapters, I try to emulate it. Rather, I question whether the selections he makes are the most effective ones in light of this project of harnessing Nietzschean genealogy to a democratic political project. Foucault successfully develops Nietzsche's critiques, particularly his critiques of grand system theories and the rational, disembodied subject of humanism. These critiques play an important role in my attempt in later chapters to rework certain dimensions of feminist standpoint theory. Foucault does not, however, despite a promising shift in his late work, manage to incorporate what I see as the most central, the most timely aspect of Nietzsche's thought: his alternative model of subjective agency. This is not a simple omission but ultimately, I believe, a more fundamental consequence of Foucault's method. Although Foucault adopts many of Nietzsche's methodological innovations, he does not embrace a key feature of Nietzsche's ontology of the will to power and, as a result, is unable to propose a model of the subject that is adequate to contemporary feminist projects. Thus, whereas Nietzsche is typically cast in the role of Foucault's (and, by extension, postmodernism's) most important predecessor, he will emerge from the present chapter as, in certain respects, Foucault's (and in the following chapter, as postmodernism's) most compelling critic.[3]

This analysis depends on a reading of Nietzsche that emphasizes the constructive moment of his critique of the modern subject and refutes the conclusion that he only destroys existing values. For Nietzsche, critique involves not only negation, a destructive moment, but also affirmation, a constructive moment. It is Foucault, not Nietzsche, who tends to limit himself to the negative moment of critique, to the rejection of existing values. I argue that the theory of the eternal return, though cryptic and incomplete, contains within it a provocative alternative to existing models of the subject. With this constructive alternative, Nietzsche, not Foucault, opens up a space within which to theorize a model of subjectivity that is responsive to some of the central concerns of contemporary feminist theory.

Immanent Critique

Before considering Nietzsche's and Foucault's critiques of systematizing theories and humanist subjects, we need to examine the categories of will to power and power/knowledge that guide their critical studies of modernity. As we will see, although both theorists build their analyses around immanent notions of power, only Nietzsche provides a criterion for differentiating among our practices within this field of power.

Both Nietzsche and Foucault are critical of modern society and skeptical of modernist thought; "we moderns," they argue, pay a very high price for rationalization and individuation. Nietzsche argues that nihilism is the price we pay. This enervating sense of meaninglessness is the product of modernism's futile attempt to ground its values in a transcendental realm. Once the metaphysical conceptions of system, truth, and being with which we project value into the world are devalued, the world appears to be utterly without value: "the untenability of one interpretation of the world, upon which a tremendous amount of energy has been lavished, awakens the suspicion that *all* interpretations of the world are false" (Nietzsche 1968, 7). Nihilism is thus a "pathological transitional stage" (ibid., 14) between the devaluation and the transvaluation of modern values during which time we are unable to value life itself. This crisis of value is experienced in part as a crisis of agency, as an inability to give meaningful direction to one's will. Following Nietzsche, Foucault tries to uncover the price we pay for all this "progress": the debt that subjectivity owes to what is excluded, truth to subjugated knowledges, and order to the pettiest and most insidious mechanisms of control. Subjectification and subjection, he concludes, are the price modernity exacts. Foucault argues that modern society is best described as a disciplinary society, or, later, as a society constituted around the deployment of a normalizing bio-power. For both Nietzsche and Foucault, it is the theory and practice of the self as agent, one of modernity's most cherished ideals, that ultimately bears its costs.

Nietzsche and Foucault do not, however, trace the development of these crises of nihilism and subjectification from the same "origin" or along the same trajectory. Although power is the fundamental category of analysis for both theorists, each conceives power somewhat differently. Nietzsche's genealogy of modern nihilism traces the fate of the will to power. Characterized in a various contexts as a will to make, a will to overcome, or a will to difference, the will to power can be described in general terms as a kind of agonistic creative drive. As Michel Haar explains it, "[t]he will that is Will to Power responds at its origins to its own internal imperative: *to be more"* (1985, 11). This will can be expressed in ways that signify the health and strength of the willing subject, or in ways that signify its sickliness or weakness. Nietzsche suggests that the will to power expressed as the will to system, the will to truth, and the will to being, to the extent that these are constructed as transcendental ideals, are distortions or betrayals of the will to power because they deny its constitutive force and creative capacity.

The concept of the will to power serves at least two purposes in Nietzsche's thought: it functions first as a principle of ontological movement and second as an immanent standard of value. First, the will to power represents an attempt to formulate a minimalist originary principle. As a basic force in a theory that rejects teleology, it can be described as something on the order of an ontological dynamic or a principle of ontological self-assertion. The will to power, in other words, is a principle that animates being in history, or rather, a principle that renders this motion comprehensible. More specifically, it is a principle that makes the problem of nihilism intelligible (Warren 1988, 114), since nihilism, as we have seen, is a product of the disfiguration of the will to power, the denial of life. One of the tests of the utility of this concept—offered, as Nietzsche frequently insists, in the spirit of experimentalism—is its ability to help us make sense of the present. The will to power, then, can be seen as the key concept of Nietzsche's specific experiment in the immanent critique of nihilism. "Suppose," Nietzsche invites us to consider,

> nothing else were "given" as real except our world of desires and passions, and we could not get down or up, to any other "reality" besides the reality of our drives. . . . Suppose, finally, we succeeded in explaining our entire instinctive life as the development and ramification of *one* basic form of the will—namely, of the will to power. . . . [Then] [t]he world viewed from inside, the world defined and determined according to its "intelligible character"—it would be "will to power" and nothing else. (1966, 47–48)[4]

In other words, suppose that "*[t]his world is the will to power—and nothing besides!* And you yourselves are also this will to power—and nothing besides!" (1968, 550). The will to power is thus presented as an ontological category in the service of an experiment in rendering our lives—and being itself—intelligible in light of a specific historical problematic.

Second, the will to power, differentiated in terms of two basic qualities or directions, serves as a critical standard by which we can evaluate our values. In this way, Nietzsche proposes a standard of evaluation that is immanent to our practices. Life, he proposes, is the only standard of value that need not be estimated in terms of a prior standard of value (see Schacht 1973, 80–81). However, to be adequate to its critical task, this standard must be better specified; "Here we need a new, more definite formulation of the concept 'life.' My formula for it is: Life is will to power" (1968, 148). Finally, the critique of nihilism requires that we distinguish between a will to power that is active, or life (self)-affirming, from one that is directed reactively against life. According to Gilles Deleuze's reading of Nietzsche, these different qualities of will, one affirming and the other negating, are associated with the cultivation of different forces: active forces cultivate their own capacities, reactive forces merely respond to—react against—active forces. An active force "goes to the limit of what it can do" and "affirms its difference," making this difference "an object of enjoyment and affirmation"; a reactive force "denies active force" and "separates active force from what it can do," thus making active forces in some sense reactive too (Deleuze 1983, 61, 57).[5] The will to power can be constituted by different forces toward various ends with distinct effects, some of which affirm the existence and cultivate the strength of this will, while others deny and weaken it. On the basis of this rudimentary principle of evaluation, Nietzsche presents an immanent ground from which to launch both moments of the critique: the negative, destructive step (the devaluation of a sickly, nihilistic, fundamentally reactive subject—a subject separated from what it can do) and the positive, constructive step (the revaluation of a healthy, active, self-affirming subject). In other words, the active/reactive distinction provides Nietzsche with a basic normative criterion, which, he insists, is immanent to life itself, one that is contained within our social practices rather than imposed from outside.[6] Perhaps, then, the will to power is best understood as a "critical ontology of practice" (Warren 1988, 111) with utopian intent; not only is it designed to diagnose some of the maladies of a specific historical age, but to indicate some of the possibilities of the epoch as well. Thus the concept is also used to prescribe alternative directions for practice.

As stated earlier, Foucault diagnoses the illness from which "we moderns" suffer not in terms of nihilism but in terms of subjectification.[7] Unlike Nietzsche's genealogy of nihilism, which traces the fate of the will to power and the different qualities of force that can constitute it, Foucault's genealogy of subjectification centers on the deployment of power/knowledge. Like Nietzsche, Foucault aspires to view the world from the inside, and thus Foucault's genealogies trace the fate of historically specific deployments of power/knowledge. Translated into Nietzsche's formula, to posit the constitutive force of power/knowledge is to view our social life as the development and ramification of power/knowledge. One element that Foucault adds to the Nietzschean critique is a clearer focus on political and institutional relations; he explores the ways in which these discourses create and maintain hierarchical relations in society. With the concept of power/knowledge, Foucault can trace the different historical links between particular relationships of domination and the production of specific kinds of knowledge, revealing in the process, the artificial, contingent, and interested dimensions of our most self-evident truths. Like Nietzsche's principle of ontological self-assertion, power/knowledge is a creative, constitutive force that accounts for a specific form of life.

The most important difference between these two projects, for my purposes here, is that, while Foucault appropriates the immanent focus of Nietzsche's approach, he does not incorporate the evaluative qualities that Nietzsche claims for the will to power. In other words, Foucault's principle of immanent critique is not internally differentiated, either in terms of active and reactive manifestations (as in Nietzsche's distinction between those that affirm and those that negate the will to power), or, to consider another option, in terms of its possible negative and positive expressions (for example, as in the Marxist distinction between exploitative and nonexploitative relations of labor). Instead, power/knowledge is presented as a unitary force in which the active and the reactive are indistinguishable and in which power expressed as a will to create is completely subsumed under power expressed as a will to dominate. One cannot distinguish between power relations that are somehow better or worse. As a result, power/knowledge functions as a principle of ontological movement; that is, it puts being into historical motion without relying on a transcendental plan or natural essence, but cannot double as a critical standard of value because it lacks a criterion of evaluation. The significance of this particular difference between Nietzsche's and Foucault's projects will become clear when I consider how it figures into their attempts to construct alternatives to the humanist subject.

Both theorists suspect that certain modernist models of system or totality and conceptions of being are implicated in our current malady. Nietzsche argues that the will to power has been distorted in modern thought and practice, assuming such potentially life-denying forms as the will to system and the will to being. Foucault concurs with Nietzsche's critiques, which he then extends and updates in useful ways. In this chapter I discuss their critiques of modernist thought as represented by two of its most important models: the methodological distinction between system and subject used to construct a model of theoretical inquiry and the ontological distinction between being and becoming used to construct a model of the subject. First, both Nietzsche and Foucault reject systematizing or totalizing theories deployed by universal intellectuals from an archimedean vantage point that seek to fix the relationship between general systems and particular subjects by reducing subjects to their functional positions within the whole; and second, they refuse depth models of the subject, which oppose a natural or metaphysical essence or being to the more superficial layers of appearances or processes of becoming. Plato exemplifies that which they reject; Nietzsche then traces a line of development from Plato to Kant which Foucault extends to orthodox and humanist Marxisms. As we will see in the next chapter, some of Nietzsche's and Foucault's postmodernist proponents extend these critiques to a more global set of targets; that is, to modernism in its entirety. However, in contrast to those who find in these methodological and ontological dimensions of Nietzsche's and Foucault's writings a broad indictment of modernist discourse, this reading highlights the specificity of their critiques of certain examples of modernist thought—those, for example, that purport to be in some sense universal, objective, or absolute. Neither Nietzsche nor Foucault stands opposed to modernism in general. Instead their critiques are aimed at selected dimensions of or traditions within modernism.

Critiques of Systematizing Theory

Much has been made of the supposedly "unsystematic" quality of Nietzsche's philosophy; certainly his aphoristic style and use of metaphor make it extremely difficult to organize systematically, to unify, or to summarize his writings. Indeed, Nietzsche is explicitly critical of theoretical systems: "I mistrust all systematizers and I avoid them." According to Nietzsche, "[t]he will to a system," which seeks to fix, unify, and abstract in the service of truth, "is a lack of integrity" (1954a, 470). Nietzsche's analysis of systems theory is, however, more complex than this simple prohibition would indicate. In fact, he suggests to us both the costs and the benefits of these systems: how they distract our vision from one focus to direct it effectively toward another and how they discourage us from questioning some assumptions to encourage us to think critically about others.

Rather than oppose all forms of systematicity, Nietzsche rejects specifically the will to system that takes its direction from the ascetic ideal. As Nietzsche describes it, the ascetic ideal is a world-denying, life-inimical posture that denies the forces of becoming, contingency, and multiplicity. Conceptions of human nature or human essence can thus be seen as ascetic ideals in that they fix subjectivity to a preordained and determined identity. Perhaps the clearest example of an ascetic ideal is the notion of absolute truth. This conception of truth grounded in a transcendental realm is, according to Nietzsche, the product of the will to power turned against the processes and values intrinsic to embodied existence. When it takes the form of an ascetic ideal predicated on and dedicated to the denial of the essential features of the life process, including appearance, change, and the corporeal, the will to truth is a will in the service of nihilism. Modern science is, then, only one of the latest forms of the ascetic ideal; it is guilty of the very same "overestimation of truth" when it assumes "that truth is inestimable and cannot be criticized" (1969, 153). According to Nietzsche, theories of knowledge that privilege truth as that which is timeless, universal, and value-neutral devalue the social and historical processes within which the active contributions of human subjects are inscribed.

The notion of metaphysical essence and the ideal of transcendental truth are not the only forms of asceticism; comparable forms of ascetic denial can be located in any theoretical system that denies the dynamic, unpredictable force of multiple subjectivities and the constitutive role of the will. Ascetic approaches to theory building impugn the subjectivity of both knowers and known; they forswear the forces of subjectivity that construct both our modes of social existence and the linguistic and theoretical frameworks by which we claim to know them. By this reading, efforts to map the social totality that take their direction from the ascetic ideal include those which rely upon reified concepts to produce static and determinate models of social systems and dogmatic modes of inquiry.

Nietzsche's aphoristic and metaphoric style constitutes an alternative to ascetic modes of theorizing. His rhetorical method is designed to express certain claims about the world of "appearances" rather than the uncontested truth of some ultimate "reality" (Schutte 1984, 100). It thus serves as a counter to those who claim that by directing our attention above and beyond the sensual world, a battery of concepts linked together to form an abstract system could present us with a faithful model of an intrinsically and permanently ordered "real" world. As a method of exposition, then, it is consistent with his understanding and affirmation of reality as a product of the will to power: it denies or devalues neither the historical and material dimensions of human existence nor the constitutive role of will.

Nietzsche also doubts the integrity of system builders who build upon a foundation of fixed assumptions which they refuse to question (see Kaufmann 1974, 80). According to Nietzsche, every philosophy is a foreground philosophy; that is, "[e]very philosophy also *conceals* a philosophy; every opinion is also a hideout, every word also a mask" (1966, 229). What concerns him is the failure of these system-building philosophers to focus their critical gaze back on their own assumptions; they ask themselves too few questions. In the absence of a more reflective approach to theory building, systematic theories tend to ossify into unconditional, unambiguous, dogmatic formulas. Rather than present his own ideas as if they were, as in asceticism, "inextinguishable, ever-present, unforgettable, 'fixed,' with the aim of hypnotising the entire nervous and intellectual system with these 'fixed ideas' " (1969, 61), Nietzsche tries to restore and affirm the openness of theory by emphasizing the indeterminate and provisional status of his conclusions: "Objections, digressions, gay mistrust, the delight in mockery are signs of health: everything unconditional belongs in pathology" (1966, 90). Dogmatism is, according to Nietzsche, one more symptom of our failure to affirm our own creativity. From this Nietzschean perspective, the problem is that, in the absence of God's guarantee of an intrinsically ordered world, we find ourselves unable to organize it ourselves by delimiting its horizons, manufacturing collectivity, and positing meaning. The power of a theoretical framework should be measured in terms of its ability to provoke or inspire the reader to re-create the world, not in terms of its ability to paralyze the creative intellect.

None of this is to say, however, that Nietzsche categorically rejects all systems; rather, he rejects specifically those systems of valuation that authorize universal, permanent, and unconditional judgments. Although he rejects the will to system insofar as it takes direction from the will to fix, unify, and abstract, he suggests the value of open and dynamic forms of systematicity. First, Nietzsche's own ideas are linked together in a coherent fashion. The inability to recognize this coherence has been the source of some of the most troubling misappropriations of Nietzsche's work. "The reader is usually so impressed, whether favorably or not, by the expert 'miniatures' that he fails to look for any larger context, though this alone can indicate the meaning of a passage" (Kaufmann 1974, 94–95). Each aphorism is actually a skirmish in a larger war. Second, although Nietzsche rejects the model of a static, transcendental totality, he affirms the importance of the ability to describe society as a dynamic whole organized by human practices. Nancy Love, in her study of Nietzsche, argues that Nietzsche would be critical of contemporary attacks on totality, attacks that claim to be grounded in his work (1986, 94). Love understands Nietzsche to claim that "[a]lthough no cosmic whole exists (men have unconsciously created cosmologies to give their lives meaning within the universe), individuals and societies are organic wholes with characteristic tendencies and typical patterns of organization." Moreover, Love insists that in Nietzsche's account, the "inability to perceive societies as ordered wholes and the related inability to explain or to evaluate them in terms of man's expanding powers reflect real dislocations in modern society" (ibid., 92, 91). Our inability to conceive society as a systematic whole is related to our inability to affirm the creative powers of the will. While Nietzsche is critical of totalizing models, that does not mean that he rejects every effort to locate oneself in a larger system of social relations. The untenability of one approach to systematic theories of the social should not lead us to conclude that all forms of systematic theory are without value. By this reading, then, Nietzsche teaches us that both the will to system that takes direction from the ascetic ideal and the rejection of systematicity *tout court* demonstrate a lack of integrity.[8]

Foucault too is often described as an "antisystematic" thinker. According to John Rajchman, "his work lacks, and was devised to avoid, the coherence of a single method or doctrine" (1985, 2). However, like Nietzsche, Foucault's critiques of systematic theories and the universal intellectual do not lead him to reject all forms of systematicity, rather, it is specifically "the inhibiting effect of global, *totalitarian theories*" (Foucault 1980a, 80) and the intellectual as the "bearer of universal values" (ibid., 132) that Foucault rejects. What Foucault contributes to these Nietzschean critiques of "totalizing systems" is a closer attention to and a better understanding of the connections between social structures and subjective practices.

Following Nietzsche, Foucault is critical of abstract theories that are unable to account for, or speak to, the local level of everyday practices. According to Foucault, these grand theories of history and society carry the potential to draw our attention away from the specificity, materiality, and diversity of experience. Some of Foucault's most frequent targets are mechanical applications of a doctrinaire or orthodox Marxism. According to Foucault, these analyses employ a variety of strategies designed to neutralize inconsistencies and ignore anomalies in a way that allows them to extend the life of the theory and, by extension, the theorists whose work it legitimates. There are several operations designed to neutralize these challenges: for example, by means of theoretical reductionism a real experience can be reduced to a question of theory; by means of historicist reductionism the present effect of an existing force can be avoided by shifting our attention to the question of its historical origin; by means of utopian dissociation the purity of one's vision can be preserved by denying its affinity to any actual existing reality; and by means of a universalizing dissolution one can deny any specific responsibility for addressing a controversial aspect of one's own theoretical position by casting it as a more generalized objection to all theories rather than a specific challenge to one's own. These were the strategies, for example, that some orthodox Marxists have employed to respond to the "gulag question" (ibid., 135–137).

Foucault insists on the importance of a more vigilant attention to historical details and material effects by renouncing the claim to map accurately and permanently the totality of social relations. According to Foucault, "the attempt to think in terms of a totality has in fact proved a hindrance to research." To support this claim, Foucault unearths some of the "historical contents that have been buried and disguised in a functionalist coherence or formal systemisation" (ibid., 81). Instead of an analysis that explains a specific phenomenon or event by mechanically plugging it into an existing theory (for example, explaining the repression of certain modes of sexuality in terms of the interests of the bourgeois class), Foucault recommends that we do an ascending analysis of power relations, "starting, that is, from its infinitesimal mechanisms, which each have their own history, their own trajectory, their own techniques and tactics, and then see how these mechanisms of power have been—and continue to be—invested, colonised, utilised, involuted, transformed, displaced, extended etc., by ever more general mechanisms and by forms of global domination" (ibid., 99). Thus, for example, one-way models of causality should be discarded in favor of more complex models of multiple and mutually determining causality (see, for example, 1991b, 76). To the extent that existing models of the social totality divert our attention from the force of the local, the concrete and the specific, to the extent that abstract categories are used to shield the theorist from the singularity of events, they are without value. Thus, for example, the utility of discourses such as Marxism and psychoanalysis requires that we first curtail, put in abeyance, or caricature their tendency to harden into monolithic unities centered around simplistic formulas (see 1980a, 81); we must continually dereify our theoretical productions if we want them to remain useful.

Together with this model of "totalitarian" theory, Foucault also rejects the model of the "universal intellectual" who aspires to an archimedean vantage point and who assumes the role of "spokesman of the universal" (ibid., 126). Foucault singles out a "faded Marxism" as one of the more recent sources of this inflated conception of the role of the intellectual. As an alternative, Foucault proposes the more modest model of the "specific intellectual" who prefers the role of local participant to that of general director. According to this model, the role of the intellectual is to provide instruments of analysis that can help locate lines of strength and weakness in the present regime, not to provide a complete, ready-made analysis which commands, "Here is what you must do!" (ibid., 62).

To prevent his own theoretical project from suffering a similar fate, Foucault continually insists on the limited, provisional, and specific dimensions of his work. Like Nietzsche, Foucault's style is playfully polemical and purposefully enigmatic. He too insists on the open, conditional quality of his work with frequent claims that "this is what I would *seem* to be saying." And, again following Nietzsche, Foucault often reminds us of the experimental nature of his work. In a written note tacked on to the end of one of his particularly substantive interviews, Foucault claims that "[w]hat I have said here is not 'what I think,' but often rather what I wonder whether one couldn't think" (ibid., 145). The purpose of these gestures would seem to be the promotion of a practical approach as opposed to a reverential attitude toward theory; he advises us to think of theory as a toolkit rather than as doctrine: "If one or two of these 'gadgets' of approach or method that I've tried to employ . . . can be of service to you, then I shall be delighted" (ibid., 65). His work is not designed to provide us with a true history, but rather to present an experience that can change us (see 1991a, 36–37). In this way Foucault subverts attempts to turn his project into dogma and its author into a prophet.

Nonetheless, to claim that Foucault was not interested in elaborating a new dogma is not to say that the decentralized theoretical production he defends lacks a substantial degree of methodological, theoretical, and practical coherence. According to Foucault, while "[i]t is true that we have to give up hope of ever acceding to a point of view that could give us access to any complete and definitive knowledge of what may constitute our historical limits . . . that does not mean that no work can be done except in disorder and contingency" (1984, 47); systematicity need not be sacrificed along with an archimedean authority. Moreover, a focus on local events need not replace the consideration of more general patterns: "Localizing problems is indispensable for theoretical and political reasons. But that doesn't mean that they are not, however, general problems" (1991a, 152). Ultimately, what guarantees the systematic coherence of his analyses is precisely that which stands behind his faith in the adequacy of local resistance: the systematicity of the larger social framework. Foucault does not eschew the vocabulary of "the system"; rather, his critique is aimed at those who are too willing to ignore or even repudiate spontaneous, nonaligned, heterogeneous local movements of political action out of an allegiance to a *functionalist model* of the system. Foucault insists that we can't defeat the system through isolated actions; we must engage it on all fronts—the university, the prisons, and the domain of psychiatry—one after another since our forces are not strong enough for a simultaneous attack. . . . It is a long struggle; it is repetitive and seemingly incoherent. But the system it opposes, as well as the power exercised through the system, supplies its unity. (1977, 230)

The generality of the revolutionary struggles of women, prisoners, patients, homosexuals, and workers "derives from the system of power itself, from all the forms in which power is exercised and applied" (ibid., 217).

In short, Foucault does not categorically reject systematicity; rather, like Nietzsche before him, he finds fault with mechanical applications of reified, functionalist systems theories. These are, I want to emphasize, specific critiques aimed at particular targets. Both theorists reject the role of vanguard theorist and employ detotalizing techniques to demystify the production of theory in the attempt to render it more attentive to the multiplicity of social differences. Yet none of this should blind us to the fact that they also see societies as in some sense systematically organized wholes and affirm the importance of our attempts to make them intelligible as such. While they insist on the provisional nature and limited scope of various attempts to theorize these orders, neither endorses purely local research that ignores the relations between structures and subjects. The choice must not be between global theory and local analysis; the point is to examine the changing mechanisms by which the everyday world and larger systems are connected.[9]

Critical Ontologies

So far, I have indicated a substantial degree of compatibility between Nietzsche and Foucault. Neither Nietzsche nor Foucault rejects systematizing theory per se; rather, each is critical of the dualisms of system and subject, global and local, around which it can be organized. Neither one supports the simple rejection of systematicity as an alternative to ascetic or totalizing social theories; neither favors purely discontinuous and unsystematic or merely local approaches to theoretical inquiry. The point of both these projects is to help us move beyond the confines of this oppositional logic, this either/or choice. It is important to remember, however, that the methodological and epistemological critiques and recommendations documented above are, according to both Nietzsche and Foucault, of secondary importance; their central focus and fundamental concern is the question of the subject and the problematics of nihilism and subjectification.[10] Given this focus, much of the force and value of their contributions depends on the adequacy of their models of subjectivity. Here I want to elaborate Nietzsche's and Foucault's critiques of free will and metaphysical or natural unity and explore their alternatives to these humanist doctrines. Whereas the analysis up to this point centered on their destructive efforts and documented the similarities between their projects, this analysis of their theories of the subject focuses on their reconstructive efforts and reveals an important difference between their projects: although Foucault appropriates and develops Nietzsche's critique of certain models of subjectivity, he does not adequately develop Nietzsche's alternative. The distinction between the will to power and power/knowledge outlined earlier in part accounts for this dimension of Foucault's neo-Nietzscheanism.

Nietzsche makes clear his assessment of the humanist subject: "What is it that I especially find utterly unendurable? That I cannot cope with, that makes me choke and faint? Bad air! Bad air! The approach of some ill-constituted thing; that I have to smell the entrails of some ill-constituted soul!" (1969, 43–44). This remark, together with the other polemics that compose Nietzsche's critique of the rationally self-constituting subject, is directed primarily at the doctrines of free will and metaphysical or natural unity. Nietzsche insists that these doctrines are hollow ideals predicated on a devaluation of the embodied and historical dimensions of our collective existence.

Nietzsche's genealogy of "Man" presents us with an alternative account of the origin and development of this subject, an analysis that can serve to bring with it "*a feeling* of a diminution in value of the thing that originated thus" and prepare the way for a critical evaluation of it (1968, 148). In this account, the unified, rational, sovereign individual is presented as the fragile product of a long and painful training: "Ah, reason, seriousness, mastery over the affects, the whole somber thing called reflection, all these prerogatives and showpieces of man: how dearly they have been bought! how much blood and cruelty lie at the bottom of all 'good things'!" (1969, 62). According to Nietzsche, the autonomous constituting subject—the subject of free will and pride of Enlightenment humanism—is a particularly costly ideal. He claims that this fiction, the "doer" (spirit, ego, rational actor, will), is used to attach a conscious intention to our actions in order that we may be held accountable for our behavior. "Men were considered 'free' so that they might be judged and punished—so that they might become *guilty*" (1954a, 499). By this account, the pre-existing self is a point of access which is exploited by outside forces; the ideal of the self-constituting individual is one means by which we are enslaved.

In response to this overestimation of consciousness as a stable, unified force which is singularly responsible for our behavior, Nietzsche offers an alternative hypothesis: "The subject as multiplicity" (1968, 270). Nietzsche argues that "there is no 'being' behind doing, effecting, becoming; 'the doer' is merely a fiction added to the deed." In other words, there is no transcendental being, no natural unity to "that little changeling, the 'subject'" (1969, 45). The unification of identity is not natural or pregiven, "indeed, our body is but a social structure composed of many souls" (1966, 26). This "society" is organized by means of both education and punishment. Depth is literally drilled in as the will to power, given direction by these "instruments of culture," is discharged back on the self. Nietzsche claims that

[a]ll instincts that do not discharge themselves outwardly *turn inward*—this is what I call the *internalization* of man: thus it was that man first developed what was later called his "soul." The entire inner world, originally as thin as if it were stretched between two membranes, expanded and extended itself, acquired depth, breadth, and height, in the same measure as outward discharge was *inhibited*. (1969, 84)

This "inner world" is then reified into a transcendental essence which as our "sole ineluctable, irremovable reality" is supposed to guarantee the autonomy of our will.

Ressentiment, bad conscience, and ascetic ideals are the specific forces, or instruments of culture, responsible for Man's present constitution. Each is associated with the dominance of reactive forces and thus with the creation of "unhealthy" values that are the product of a will that is directed against others, against the self, and finally, against the world. As Nietzsche tells the story, the modern subject finds its genealogical origins in the values born of the ressentiment of the weak who are unable to discharge their will. The slaves' values are essentially reactive; that is, "slave morality from the outset says No to what is 'outside,' what is 'different,' what is 'not itself,' and *this* No is its creative deed" (ibid., 36). Christianity then alters the direction of this ressentiment by saying "No" to what is *inside,* different, and not itself: the body and the instincts. Guilt or bad conscience results when we measure the self against such an otherworldly ideal. Finally, ascetic ideals, as we have seen, expand the scope of the ressentiment by saying "No" to change and diversity in the world around us. In each case, our standards of value are external rather than immanent to the object of our evaluation; in fact, Nietzsche claims that "[w]e have measured the value of the world according to categories *that refer to a purely fictitious world*" (1968, 13).

The modern subject is ill constituted because the will, directed by these external standards, is turned against life itself. The modern subject, this crippled ascetic, expresses its will by creating values and meanings which are essentially opposed to life. The doctrine of free will denies our experiences as embodied, socially situated actors, while the valorization of a transcendental essence contradicts historical experience. Being, understood in this case as the rational soul, is constructed as a reaction against becoming, against the historical and material forces constitutive of life experience. This "horror of the senses," this denial of change and becoming, in short, this "rebellion against the most fundamental presuppositions of life" (1969, 162–163), constitutes the essence of this modern subject, a fundamentally reactive subject.

Foucault develops a similar critique of these models of subjectivity. After the publication of the first volume of his history of sexuality, Foucault claimed that the point of the project "lies in a re-elaboration of the theory of power" (1980a, 187). Sometime later, however, Foucault changed his mind: "it is not power, but the subject, which is the general theme of my research" (1983, 209). In fact, with the benefit of hindsight, Foucault could insist that the real objective and true significance of his research over the past twenty years had been "to create a history of the different modes by which, in our culture, human beings are made subjects" (ibid., 208). Like Nietzsche's, Foucault's genealogies present us with histories of these different modes by which we are made subjects that are designed to lead to a "diminution in value" of the rationally self-constituting subject. One of Foucault's distinctive (and, for my purposes, very valuable) contributions to this Nietzschean theme is his application of it to Marxist thought. Although it is not the primary target of Foucault's antihumanism, humanist Marxism, a version of Marxist discourse "which made the theory of alienation, in a subjectivist key, into the theoretical basis for translating Marx's economic and political analyses into philosophical terms" (1991a, 57), clearly must be included in its indictment.[11]

To combat the doctrines of free will and human nature, which ground the humanist model of the subject, Foucault assumes the position of a more rigorous, more thorough social constructionist. His work is centered around a basic working hypothesis: the subject is constituted in and through relations of power. There is no natural or transcendental essence (neither human nature nor spirit) that constitutes history:

> One has to dispense with the constituent subject, to get rid of the subject itself, that's to say, to arrive at an analysis which can account for the constitution of the subject within a historical framework . . . without having to make reference to a subject which is either transcendental in relation to the field of events or runs in its empty sameness throughout the course of history. (1980a, 117)

Following Nietzsche, Foucault decenters, denaturalizes, and historicizes the subject. These operations depend on an alternative understanding of the function of power: instead of the usual emphasis on the negative function of power (which mystifies, alienates, or represses), Foucault highlights its positive dimensions (which construct, organize, and direct). The subject in Foucault's texts is thus primarily the product rather than the agent of power relations. The constituting subject is replaced by a subject constituted by contingent mechanisms of discipline and normalization.

Foucault's work on the genealogy of sexuality, in which he presents a critique of the repressive hypothesis, is exemplary of his denaturalizing project. "What is peculiar to modern societies," Foucault concludes, "is not that they consigned sex to a shadow existence, but that they dedicated themselves to speaking of it *ad infinitum*, while exploiting it as *the* secret" (1980b, 35). Sexuality is not some pre-existing identity which is repressed; rather, sexuality is produced and exploited in different ways and for different purposes by a variety of mechanisms. The unique force of Foucault's presentation lies in his claim that sex itself—that essential, natural secret which the discourse of sexuality was supposed to mystify, alienate, repress or distort—is only "the most speculative, most ideal, and most internal element in a deployment of sexuality organized by power in its grip on bodies and their materiality, their forces, energies, sensations, and pleasures" (ibid., 155). The repressive hypothesis, deployed, for example, in analyses centered around the concept of alienation, inevitably identifies and defends an authentic, natural, permanent, universal, transcendental, or otherwise ahistorical essence.

For my purposes, the problem with Foucault's approach, at least in the middle period of his work through the first volume of *The History of Sexuality*, is that he only succeeds in replacing the autonomously constituting subject, the humanist subject, with its opposite: a subject that is utterly determined, a subject that is only subjected. Though Foucault suggests that we should resist these processes of normalization and pursue alternative modes of subjectivity, the sources of this resistance and the specifications of these alternatives are not developed. For example, returning to the genealogy of sexuality, Foucault claims that movements of "sexual liberation" built around a critique of sexual repression play well within the limits of the discourse of sexuality (see ibid., 131). To identify ourselves as sexually liberated people is to provide a new point of access for normalization and, ultimately, to enmesh us even more tightly in a web of power relations. Hence, what some may once have thought was a form of resistance is really just another moment in our subjection. As Foucault describes it in the first volume of *The History of Sexuality*, resistance seems merely reactive; there is no active will, no constituting moment in this process of subjectification.

What is it in Foucault's understanding of the subject that resists or directs subjectification? Nietzsche uses the internally differentiated notion of the will to power, which is constitutive of and constituted by individuals who have the potential to act in and to react against the world. Foucault lacks a similar evaluative criterion which can form the basis of an alternative to the disciplined, determined subject. As we have seen, the category of power/knowledge is not internally differentiated; there is no equivalent to the Nietzschean distinction between active and reactive forces. Foucault provides no way to evaluate different forms of practice or modes of existence within this determined world as being somehow better or worse.[12]

Although he valorizes resistance—which exists, he claims, wherever power is exercised—this affirmation alone cannot take the place of, or satisfy the need for, accounts of particular instances of resistance that are consistent with his rejection of normative standards of judgment and his analytics of power. Why is resistance to be affirmed over compliance? Moreover, how can this assertion of the fact of resistance be reconciled with his insistence on the thoroughly determinative force of power—what is it that resists? As a number of critics have observed, the repressive hypothesis (in this case, a moment of ahistorical naturalism) tends to emerge through the gap between his theoretical project (the critique of transcendental or natural foundations) and his political concerns (the critique of domination) (see Comay 1986, 114). To lend substance to his insistence on the inevitability of resistance Foucault takes brief refuge in "a certain plebian quality or aspect" (Foucault 1980a, 138) or in "bodies and pleasures" (Foucault 1980b, 157). The problem is, of course, that, according to his analysis, bodies, pleasures, and this "plebian aspect" are no more authentic, essential, or exterior to relations of domination than sex, rights, our laboring essence, or any of the other forces that have been posited under the auspices of the repressive hypothesis.[13] Of course, to argue that something is repressed, alienated, or mystified does not necessarily imply that this thing is somehow prior to or outside the processes of history, but Foucault did not pursue this Nietzschean line of thought in order to affirm an alternative model of the subject, at least not in this phase of his work. Resistance is undertheorized and the subjects of these genealogies remain subjected and docile.

Foucault, however, presents an intriguing shift in emphasis in his late work. The second and third volumes of *The History of Sexuality* and a short essay entitled "What Is Enlightenment?" develop a somewhat different analysis of the constitutive dynamics of an historical subject. In the context of a study of ancient Greek morality, a morality that he claims allows the individual more room to negotiate his or her understanding and execution of moral dictates (see Foucault 1986, 62), Foucault explains subjectivity as an individual's attempts to stylize his or her existence within the confines of these general cultural norms. According to the late Foucault, we can embrace what he describes as an Enlightenment "principle of a critique and a permanent creation of ourselves in our autonomy" without resorting to the humanist privileging of man (1984, 44). However, although he does suggest the possibility of a more dynamic conception of subjectivity than was presented in his earlier work, the analysis remains underdeveloped. First, he fails to account adequately for the source of the agency or the nature of the autonomy he describes. In her study of Foucault's late work, Lois McNay observes that

> by reducing the varying techniques of the self to the same effective level of self 'stylization', Foucault does not distinguish sufficiently enough between practices that are merely 'suggested' to the individual and practices that are more or less 'imposed' in so far as they are heavily laden with cultural sanctions and taboos. It is important to make this kind of distinction if we are to assess to what degree individuals act autonomously and in an innovative fashion, or to what degree they merely reproduce dominant social structures and inequalities. (1992, 74–75)

Foucault does not indicate how this process of self-constitution can be reconciled with the forces of determination that were the focus of his earlier work. Second, Foucault fails to develop, to select, the possible normative criteria by which we would judge one strategy of self-stylization, one model of the self, to be somehow better, more free, or healthier than another (see McNay 1992, 147). That is, Fou-

cault remains constant from the middle to the late period in his refusal to affirm alternative standards of value. Thus, although Foucault insists that "[w]e have to promote new forms of subjectivity
through the refusal of this kind of individuality which has been imposed on us for several centuries" (1983, 216), the sources of this
kind of resistance and the possibility of an alternative remain mysterious. My point is that the limitations of this attempt to construct an
alternative to the subjugated subject are built into his theory of
power; ultimately they can be attributed to the lack of an evaluative
criterion in Foucault's theory of power parallel to the active/reactive
distinction in Nietzsche's thought.[14]

Nietzsche in fact provides a helpful analysis of this dilemma. Like
Foucault, Nietzsche is critical of the model of the autonomously
self-constituting subject. However, unlike Foucault, he is better
equipped to formulate a principled critique of its standard alternative, the determined, constituted subject. Nietzsche writes: "Suppose someone were thus to see through the boorish simplicity of this
celebrated concept of 'free will' and put it out of his head altogether,
I beg of him to carry his 'enlightenment' a step further, and also put
out of his head the contrary of this monstrous conception of 'free
will': I mean 'unfree will,' which amounts to a misuse of cause and
effect" (1966, 28–29).

Indeed, the point of Nietzsche's critical efforts is to move beyond
the boundaries of this opposition in which humanity is either put in
the paradoxical position of an original cause that pulls itself "into
existence by the hair, out of the swamps of nothingness" (1966, 28),
or rendered a mere passive effect through an elimination of the will.
Nietzsche presents the doctrine of the eternal return together with
the model of the overman as alternatives to these dichotomies (cause
or effect, free or unfree, voluntary or determined), which are modeled
on oppositional formulations of the relationship between being and
becoming. The eternal return constitutes Nietzsche's response to
what many now describe as the central problem of post-Enlighten-
ment modernist thought: how can we reconcile two images of the
subject, one that sees the self as independent and self-defining, and
the other that sees it as historically situated and socially determined? With this doctrine, Nietzsche attempts to rework these two
models of the subject.

The Eternal Return

The eternal return appears in numerous aphorisms scattered throughout many of Nietzsche's texts and as the central, mysterious teaching of his most important work, *Zarathustra*. Yet, though he regarded the doctrine as the crowning achievement of his life's work, its meaning and significance are anything but clear. Commentators have approached it in a number of ways, most only to reject it as one of Nietzsche's more immodest and unfortunate proposals. In many cases, the theory that everything returns without alteration was dismissed as an insupportable empirical hypothesis regarding the nature of the physical universe.[15] However, the doctrine has since been revived, not as a cosmology but rather as something that can be characterized as an ethical teaching. Here I want to follow Deleuze in reading the eternal return as an ethical doctrine that builds on the normative element of the will to power described earlier.[16] As a "cultivating idea," the eternal return suggests that "in all that you will you begin by asking yourself: is it certain that I will do it an infinite number of times?" This, Nietzsche advises, "should be your most solid center of gravity" (quoted in Deleuze 1983, 68); whatever you will, will that it return eternally. With this simple command, Nietzsche is, I believe, telling us something important about both what we are and what we could become.

The revelation of the eternal return can be separated into two distinct moments. In the first moment, we are presented with the determined, constituted quality of our identity. In a flash of insight we recognize that: "[f]rom this gateway, Moment, a long, eternal lane leads *backward*: behind us lies an eternity. Must not whatever *can* walk have walked on this lane before? Must not whatever *can* happen have happened, have been done, have passed by before? . . . And are not all things knotted together so firmly that this moment draws after it *all* that is to come?" (1954b, 270). But this is a dangerous doctrine: if we believe that we are *only* the sum of our past thoughts, deeds, and experiences, what is to prevent us from succumbing to fatalism? What is to prevent the paralysis of the will? In this moment, the will is a prisoner. Certainly, Nietzsche agrees, "[w]illing liberates; but what is it that puts even the liberator himself in fetters? 'It was'—that is the name of the will's gnashing of teeth and most secret melancholy. Powerless against what has been done, he is an angry spectator of all that is past" (ibid., 251). Must we not respond to this understanding of our own historicity with resignation or despair? This is the central problem Nietzsche tries to confront with the doctrine of the eternal return: how can we affirm the determined character of existence without descending into nihilism?

The solution is to be found in the second moment of the revelation, when we learn that we must "will the past." Nietzsche teaches us that " 'The will is a creator.' All 'it was' is a fragment, a riddle, a dreadful accident—until the creative will says to it, 'But thus I willed it.' Until the creative will says to it, 'But thus I will it; thus shall I will it'" (ibid., 253). It is in the affirmation of this creative will that we can find our potential to exceed our past thoughts, deeds, and experiences. This is not to suggest that Nietzsche endorses our blind affirmation of everything in the past; such passive acceptance could never be reconciled with his affirmation of the will to power as a productive force. Rather, it is the deployment of a creative, evaluative will—one that says both "Yes" and "No"—that Nietzsche affirms. It is not the eternal return of the same that Nietzsche invites us to affirm. The eternal return is instead a selective principle: it teaches us to select those aspects that are the product of an active will and thus constitutive of a life-affirming stance, while rejecting those that are reactive and nihilistic. This selection is not the work of reflective thought but rather an achievement of practice.[17] In this way, the eternal return develops the evaluative dimension of the will to power into an ethics. As Deleuze describes it, "*[t]o affirm is not to take responsibility for, to take on the burden of what is, but to release, to set free what lives.*" The eternal return is one of the doctrines that teaches "not affirmation as acceptance, but as creation" (Deleuze 1983, 185). To will the past is to affirm what we have become as an ongoing achievement and a basis for action as opposed to a permanent fact and a source of resignation. It is, in Nietzsche's value scheme, a selective principle in the service of ontological health.

The eternal return is thus Nietzsche's enigmatic response to the central riddle of modern thought: how can we accept the reality of ourselves as embodied, historical processes without sacrificing agency? How can we affirm the world of becoming without paralyzing the will? The answer can be found in the reformulation of the relationship between being and becoming, or essence and appearance: "That *everything recurs* is the closest *approximation of a world of becoming to a world of being"* (1968, 330). As Deleuze explains it,

> all we need to do to think this thought is to stop believing in being as distinct from and opposed to becoming or to believe in the being of becoming itself. What is the being of that which becomes, of that which neither starts nor finishes becoming? *Returning is the being of that which becomes.* . . . It is not being that returns but rather the returning itself that constitutes being insofar as it is affirmed of becoming and of that which passes. (1983, 48)

Being in Nietzsche's account is torn away from its transcendental foundations. What returns, what we will to return, becomes being, becomes necessary, becomes essential. Being is not posited a priori as the guide, the directing force of becoming; being does not precede becoming nor does it remain unchanged by it. Rather, being is both the (contingent) product and the (changing) ground of social practice. We are that which we selectively and actively affirm. Although being and becoming are rendered meaningless as oppositions, the terms are preserved as "points of view" (Haar 1985, 34) that together can speak to our experiences and values as historically situated subjects who are both constituted by and constitutive of our world. That is, being, as the valuable experience of coherent subjectivity, of a self that wills, is devalued in the form of an otherworldly idol and then reconstructed, reinterpreted, revalued as a very real historical possibility (see Warren 1988, 115).[18] In short, Nietzsche's solution to the central dilemma of modernist thought is to renegotiate the boundaries between being and becoming after situating the distinction on an historical terrain.

The eternal return, then, represents an attempt to locate a ground immanent in the world around which we can organize our activity and constitute our subjectivity without relying on some transcendental or natural essence. Nietzsche insists that the subject can be organized, integrated, and autonomous without being conceived as a natural, rigid, or self-destructive unity.[19] He decenters the subject as a natural or pregiven unity and then recenters it around the project of constituting an active subject capable of expanding its own powers and projects, an alternative to the reactive subject which defines itself merely in terms of what it opposes. Thus, in Nietzsche we can find a model of the subject that carries some ontological weight; that is, the subject is centered around a notion of being, but this being is not conceived in opposition to becoming as a universal or timeless essence. Nietzsche's subject is, then, both autonomous and situated; there is a tension, but no necessary contradiction between the fact that we are both always already constituted and, at the same time, self-constituting.

Nietzsche beyond Foucault

Both Nietzsche and Foucault reject depth models of the subject that oppose natural or metaphysical conceptions of being to the historical and material processes of becoming. This is the basis for their indictments of models of the subject centered around theories of metaphysical unity, human nature, and free will. The difference is that where both theorists reject these models, Nietzsche is better equipped to affirm an alternative. Where Foucault opposes the model of the self-constituting subject by proposing its opposite, the constituted subject, which, as a subjugated subject is then devalued, Nietzsche transvalues existing models of being and proposes an alternative model based on standards immanent to a finite range of our historically specific experiences. Foucault continually resists the constructive project of developing alternatives. But contrary to what some have claimed, Foucault does not find precedent for this famous value-neutrality—this resistance to normative critique and aversion to utopian alternatives—in Nietzsche. In fact, by Nietzschean standards, Foucault's critique is inadequate precisely because it refuses to locate alternative standards of value; he prepares the way for a critique of dualisms, but, in the absence of critical standards, he cannot follow through with it.

What, from a Nietzschean perspective, does a critique entail? Two moments are required, one destructive, the other constructive. Certainly both theorists agree that it is only once we recognize the arbitrary origins and unfamiliar dimensions of the present social formation that we can prepare the ground for critical inquiry. Nietzsche insists on the importance of removing antitheses from the world after first discovering how we have projected them there (1968, 76). To dismantle these dualisms, Nietzsche first employs what I will call the method of reactive reversal, deprecating that side of existence which has been affirmed until now and affirming that which has been denied: thus, for example, the health of the noble is often opposed to the sickliness of the slave, or the pleasures of cruelty are affirmed in sharp contrast to the ideals of Christian propriety. We are presented with the same project when Foucault insists on emphasizing the productive mechanisms of power rather than the repressive ones, or when he focuses on the already constituted features of languages, social systems, and identities in contrast to the standard view that holds these to be the tools of a self-constituting agent.

Nietzsche, however, insists that a true critique requires something more. To propose only the opposite of what has been affirmed hitherto—to affirm, for example, pure becoming in the place of pure being—is ultimately insufficient by Nietzsche's standards. Certainly this kind of historical analysis "brings with it *a feeling* of a diminution in value of the thing that originated thus and prepares the way to a critical mood and attitude toward it." Nonetheless, "[t]he inquiry into the *origin of our evaluations* and tables of the good is in absolutely no way identical with a critique of them, as is so often believed" (ibid., 148). By this reading of Nietzsche's project, a critique requires a new ground from which standards can be crafted and alternatives weighed.[20] What standard shall we use to evaluate our current values and propose alternatives? Nietzsche offers a specific understanding of the forces constitutive of life: "My formula for it is: Life is will to power" (ibid., 148). Rather than limit himself to this polemical strategy, this simple reversal of "Yes" and "No," Nietzsche also attempts to transform these rigid dualisms into more subtle and earthly values.[21]

Foucault's interventions are, on the other hand, more narrowly focused on the destructive element of critique. Foucault's failure to adopt Nietzsche's constructive project grounded in the internally differentiated concept of will to power leaves him with little material from which to fashion alternative values that are also immanent to our practices. Consequently, Foucault's genealogy succeeds as a destructive project (a de-transcendentalizing, denaturalizing project), but not, ultimately, as a constructive project (a transvaluative project); the primary goal is one of devaluation not revaluation. Declaring that "I absolutely will not play the part of one who prescribes solutions" (1991a, 157), Foucault refuses the strategy of affirmation, along with the role of moralist and prophet, as if they were necessarily cut from the same cloth (see ibid., 172). According to Nietzsche's criteria, Foucault prepares the ground for a critique of subjugation but does not possess the critical tools adequate to its completion. In Foucault we find no criterion of evaluation, no eternal return; that is, no sustained discussion of how historical subjects are also constituting agents, no affirmation of an alternative model of subjectivity. Not only is there no allowance for the repression of some natural or pre-existing material, there is no notion of any kind of misdirection of an affirmative, constituting force such as we find in Nietzsche's work. Although the work of his late period is suggestive of an attempt to remedy this gap in his thought, it remains sketchy and incomplete. The problem is that Foucault does not carve out an immanent standpoint from which we can critically evaluate the quality of social relations and propose alternatives, as if to conclude that if we cannot stand outside history on some natural or transcendental ground, we cannot stand anywhere at all. Here I believe that because he cannot pose any alternatives, Foucault falls prey to the old oppositions. Thus Foucault follows Nietzsche in so far as he "anticipates experimentally even the possibilities of the most fundamental nihilism," but only Nietzsche points us beyond this to affirm new values in the place of the old (Nietzsche 1968, 536).

A word of caution is in order, however,: to say that Nietzsche takes us beyond Foucault is not to say that Nietzsche's thought provides a normative groundwork that is ultimately sufficient for the feminist theoretical project that I want to pursue. At the very least we have to consider another distinction, or rather, we should also investigate a further specification of the active/reactive aspects of the will to power. Some have identified two different conceptions of the will to power in Nietzsche's work: as it is embodied in our practices, the will to power can be expressed either as a force of domination or as a force of self-constitution and empowerment.[22] Yet Nietzsche himself was, for the most part, either unwilling or simply uninterested in distinguishing between these two expressions. Certainly there are many instances where he reduces the will to power to a will to dominate the self and others in order to emphasize the necessarily conflictual dimensions of individual self-assertion. There are also discussions in which the will to power is presented rather more amiably as a will to create the self and the world. Again, however, it is important to recognize that Nietzsche does not develop this distinction between the will to power practiced as a force of domination and as a force of creativity into a principle of evaluation that is separate from the active/reactive criterion. However, for those interested in developing the potentially democratic thrust of his teachings, for those who would take Nietzsche beyond Nietzsche, it is necessary to clarify and develop this more substantive distinction between constitution and domination and come to terms with Nietzsche's tendency to conflate power and domination.[23] The active/reactive distinction alone cannot suffice for the needs of a feminist (or any other progressive) political project. Thus, although I use Nietzsche's thought of the eternal return in Chapter 4 as a basis for constructing a model of a collective feminist subject, it is employed in the context of a project that also makes use of some specifically Marxist and feminist criteria of evaluation. Consequently, I assess the "health" of this subject not only in terms of the active/reactive distinction but in terms of its potential efficacy as a force for feminist, antiracist, and anticapitalist agitation.

It has not been my intention to present an account of the true Nietzsche or the true Foucault. Rather than confining my inquiry to the terms of a properly philological project, my investigation of these theorists has been guided by a different agenda: to glean from their texts specific conceptual tools that will help me in later chapters to develop an alternative theory of feminist subjectivity. These include Nietzsche's and Foucault's rejections of transcendental notions of order and essence and their use of immanent conceptions; their critiques of certain examples of ascetic or totalizing theories and their disavowal of humanist subjectivity; and finally, Nietzsche's alternative model of subjectivity suggested by the doctrine of the eternal return. The affirmation of the constitutive will demonstrated in the teaching of the eternal return represents Nietzsche's cure for nihilism: "To the paralyzing sense of general disintegration and incompleteness I opposed the *eternal recurrence*" (1968, 224). Despite the doctrine's rather enigmatic formulation, it succeeds, I believe, in opening up a space within which to develop an alternative to the either/or choice with which we are so often presented, the choice between either a freely self-constituting subject or a merely determined subject.

Before proceeding to questions of subjectivity, however, we must consider the context within which subjects are produced. Foucault's focus on the constitutive role of complex sociocultural formations (*dispositifs*) offers an important expansion of Nietzsche's alternative conception of subjectivity. An institutional focus is essential if Nietzsche's genealogy is to be developed as a political theory. Under what conditions can we achieve ontological health? What kinds of structural and discursive settings are compatible with this aptitude for self-constitution? Nietzsche's lack of attention to socioeconomic and political structures in general[24] and his refusal to theorize the institutional conditions conducive to the eternal return in particular pose serious limits to the political relevance and practicality of his teachings. Questions of structure and context, particularly as they have been posed within the Marxist and socialist feminist traditions, will be the focus of Chapter 3.

But before we can proceed to these structural problematics, there is one final set of issues to consider. To apply these Nietzschean and Foucaultian critiques and propositions, one must first examine their deployment in the context of contemporary debates. This detour refines these conceptual tools and clears a space for their application.

Modernism, Postmodernism, and the Logic of Paradigm Debates

Nietzsche's and Foucault's critiques of specific examples of systematizing theory and depth models of the subject that oppose natural or metaphysical conceptions of "self-constituting being" to the historical and material processes of "becoming constituted" add up to a strong indictment of certain themes within modern European philosophy. These specific critiques, however, are often presented as elements of a more global opposition to modernism that has taken the form of postmodernism. In this chapter I want to consider some of the consequences of reading the specific and limited critiques of universalizing theory, transcendental concepts and values, and natural or metaphysical models of the subject as part of a more general indictment of modernism. I focus here on the relationship between Foucault and postmodernism. How were Foucault's selective critiques transformed into part of a postmodernist opposition to modernism, and what is gained and what is lost with this formulation?

Let me clarify my use of categories here. The analysis that follows is based on a specific distinction—an admittedly rather arbitrary distinction—between postmodernism and poststructuralism. Before I define how I use those key terms, however, let me say something about a term that I will *not* use, the term postmodernity, which as I conceive it designates a historical period. Some argue we are witness to a series of changes in international socioeconomic relations the importance of which warrants this new label. I have nothing to say about postmodernity here, since I am dealing with a set of philosophical and methodological arguments which may or may not constitute a response to these new conditions. In the discussion that follows, the term postmodernism refers to an intellectual phenomenon as opposed to its possible social and historical correlates. More specifically, as I use it here, the term postmodernism refers to the *postmodernist paradigm* that is presented as an opponent and successor to another theoretical paradigm called modernism. The term poststructuralism, in contrast, is used here to designate a theoretical tradition (or, to be more accurate, a variety of traditions) that succeeded (though it was not directly opposed to) structuralism in France and which is generally associated with a certain reading of Nietzsche. According to this classificatory scheme, Foucault should be considered a poststructuralist. Postmodernism is then constructed around a particular interpretation of the work of poststructuralists like Foucault, an interpretation that poses their work as part of a coherent whole that is radically opposed to another coherent whole called modernism. Thus, under the sign of postmodernism, Foucault's neo-Nietzschean discourse is cast as a wholesale critique of modernism and a proposal for a paradigm shift.[1] So in the account below, the term postmodernism is reserved for the "paradigmatization" of neo-Nietzschean poststructuralism—in this case, for a particular conflation of Nietzsche and Foucault that is then posed as part of a paradigm opposed to another paradigm called modernism. Postmodernism could perhaps be described in these terms as the polemical life of poststructuralism. Confined to the boundaries of this paradigm debate, modernism is reduced to a homogeneous discourse to which postmodernism, posited as an equally unified position, stands radically opposed.

The paradigm debate between modernism and postmodernism had a substantial impact on both political theory and feminist theory in the Anglophone world throughout the 1980s and continues to inform many interpretations of poststructuralist theory, assessments of modernist discourses, and conceptions of their relationship today. But whereas this modernist–postmodernist paradigm formula played a productive role in revivifying some old debates and framing some new ones throughout the 1980s, today the value of this oppositional strategy is questionable: too many nuances are lost, too many potential affinities are ignored.

The Politics of Paradigm Building

Before we assess the possibilities and limits of the modernist–postmodernist paradigm debate, I want to investigate some of the rhetorical strategies that were deployed to establish the postmodernist paradigm in the 1980s, focusing on one case in which Foucault is the contested figure. Five essays will serve as examples of the substance and style of the emerging paradigm debate in the United States over the status of Foucault's relationship to modernism: an essay first published in 1983 by Michael Walzer entitled "The Politics of Michel Foucault," the three essays that make up the 1984–1985 exchange between William Connolly and Charles Taylor in the journal *Political Theory*, and Paul Bové's 1988 essay, which serves as the introduction to the English translation of Deleuze's book on Foucault and also takes up Taylor's argument. These essays were chosen not only because of their visibility but because I believe they represent some of the most compelling and sophisticated discussions of the significance of Foucault for philosophy and political theory. In reading these essays, however, my concern is not with the authors' fidelity or lack of fidelity to Foucault, nor with the merits of their various characterizations of Foucault's thought. Rather than take sides in this debate over Foucault's work, I want to take a step back—and I urge the reader to join me—in order to locate within these intellectual exchanges the terms of an emerging paradigm debate between modernism and postmodernism. What follows is not, then, a systematic review of the relevant literature on Foucault or an analysis of its exegetical merits but rather an attempt to isolate the logic behind this paradigm debate by focusing on some exemplary contributions.

To foreground this dimension of the arguments, I read these texts and the debate they helped precipitate through the prism of Thomas Kuhn's study of the strategies by which theoretical paradigms are constructed and contested. In *The Structure of Scientific Revolutions* (1970), Kuhn provides a useful analysis and some instructive examples of the methods by which scientific paradigms are built, preserved, and replaced. These insights into the politics of paradigm building and contestation can, I believe, both highlight certain characteristics of the modernist–postmodernist debate and bring the strategies by which this debate was constructed into sharper focus.

Although Kuhn's own use of the category was somewhat vague, a paradigm can be defined in very general terms as a "disciplinary matrix," or a set of values, questions, vocabularies, methods, and criteria of validity from which a coherent tradition, in this case of philosophy and political theory, evolves.[2] Paradigms serve to recruit new participants, as well as to direct and coordinate their research. One of the most important functions of a successful paradigm is to facilitate communication and promote solidarity among otherwise isolated researchers. But success is in some ways a mixed blessing; over time paradigms have a tendency to become rigid and resistant to change. Rather than question the authority of their fundamental assumptions, dominant paradigms tend to suppress novelties and obstruct paradigm change (Kuhn 1970, 64). Efforts to articulate a new paradigm to compete with one of the dominant paradigms can thus expect to meet with resistance as proponents of the prevailing paradigm defend their approach, refusing to see anomalies as counterinstances and devising "ad hoc modifications" of their theory where need be, in a way that stifles would-be challengers (ibid., 77, 78). To ensure its prospects of long-term survival a new theoretical model must, then, avoid assimilation at the same time as it strives to bolster its impact on the relevant intellectual community. Kuhn's discussion thus suggests that it may be prudent to present a successor paradigm, at least initially, in rather stark opposition to the dominant paradigm.

One paradigm cannot be falsified by another paradigm because the two do not share criteria of validity (ibid., 103, 148). In other words, a proper paradigm only accepts internal critiques of its claims. Presumably then, to establish its status as a credible alternative, a challenger must insist on the incommensurability of the competing paradigms' standards and values. Consequently, because every group "uses its own paradigm to argue in that paradigm's defense" (ibid.,

94), the proponents of competing paradigms "will inevitably talk through each other when debating the relative merits of their respective paradigms. In the partially circular arguments that regularly result, each paradigm will be shown to satisfy more or less the criteria that it dictates for itself and to fall short of a few of those dictated by its opponent" (ibid., 109–110). Given that the early debates across paradigms are formulated in such oppositional terms, it is probably not surprising that they tend to take on a combative tone.

Although in their early stages most new paradigms are formulated in rather crude terms (ibid., 156), over time the supporters of a successful paradigm will "improve it, explore its possibilities, and show what it would be like to belong to the community guided by it" (ibid., 159). New recruits may be attracted by its ability to solve puzzles and avoid problems, "[b]ut paradigm debates are not really about relative problem-solving ability, though for good reasons they are usually couched in those terms. Instead, the issue is which paradigm should in the future guide research on problems many of which neither competitor can yet claim to resolve completely" (ibid., 157). According to Kuhn, the transition to a new paradigm is experienced as a kind of conversion: "Just because it is a transition between incommensurables, the transition between competing paradigms cannot be made a step at a time, forced by logic and neutral experience" (ibid., 150). Eventually, professional allegiances begin to shift as more and more are "converted"; "[g]radually the number of experiments, instruments, articles, and books based upon the paradigm will multiply. Still more men, convinced of the new view's fruitfulness, will adopt the new mode of practicing normal science, until at last only a few elderly hold-outs remain" (ibid., 159). Ultimately, through collective effort, the successor paradigm is transformed into an increasingly complex and sophisticated tool which will, in time, face challenges from new would-be paradigms.

Many of these characteristics of paradigm debate are evident in the arguments presented by Connolly, Taylor, Bové, and Walzer about the status of Foucault's project. Kuhn's analysis suggests that one of the most important means by which an alternative paradigm is installed involves establishing clear, inviolable boundaries between the dominant paradigm and its would-be successor. As we will see, this is the strategy that Connolly and Bové pursue in their response to the kinds of readings put forth by authors like Taylor and Walzer who describe Foucault as an incoherent modernist. Connolly and Bové argue that Foucault stands outside the borders of the modern episteme and, hence, that modernist standards—in this case, the standard of coherence—do not apply.[3] In this way, Foucault becomes the object of a tug-of-war: one side (represented here by Taylor and Walzer) pulls him inside the borders of a more familiar discourse where his claims can be neutralized, only to have the other side (represented here by Connolly and Bové) pull him back out. Foucault's postmodernism as well as his critics' modernism (postmodernism and modernism understood here as paradigms locked in mutual opposition) emerge out of contests like these. The modernist–postmodernist debate as I understand it is in large part an artifact (though not necessarily an intended artifact) of the various strategies by which poststructuralist discourses—in this case Foucault's—were legitimized and delegitimized.

Taylor's own allegiance to the modernist paradigm is clear in these essays. In particular, an affinity for Enlightenment metaphors reveals his reliance on a particular standard of theoretical coherence. Measured against a standard of rational maturity, Foucault evinces an adolescent irresponsibility: "Rhetorical hijinks come just where we should be deploying the most responsible arguments" (1985, 381). Foucault shoots from the hip; with a few tricks of rhetoric he seems to "close down all the lights" (ibid., 383), leaving us to grapple in the darkness. Taylor sets himself apart as a more mature, more reasonable member of this intellectual community. Appealing to our common sense, he insists that "the fog emanating from Paris in recent decades" makes it even more necessary to clutch certain truisms as we would "a beacon in the darkness" (1984, 172). Taylor argues that we should see (perhaps with the aid of this common sense, these truisms) that "Foucault's shotgun remarks about truth as imposition and violence" are "a kind of obfuscation" (1985, 382). He then uses the language of "we," "us," and "our" in a way that implies that a single, unified modernist community stands behind his assessment of what a good theory entails: Foucault simply does not meet our requirements; he does not tell us what we want to know. This critical vocabulary helps to support Taylor's conclusion that because Foucault's explanation of the relationship between power and knowledge is ultimately incompatible with a specific understanding of the symbiotic relationship between freedom and truth, it is incoherent.[4]

Connolly reproaches Taylor for this assessment of Foucault's contribution. According to Connolly, Taylor simply *assumes* that Foucault is situated within the boundaries of the modern episteme and then judges him accordingly. Paul Bové concurs with Connolly's assessment of Taylor's interpretive strategy; Taylor, Bové claims, "is writing Foucault into the discourse of analytic Philosophy and so making him more available for discussion and correction" (1988, x). According to Bové, Taylor formulates a disciplinary reading of Foucault by reducing Foucault's statements to a *position*:

> For Taylor, "one's position" seems to mean just a "set of ideas" or an idea that one holds and tries to defend (often obscurely) by writing "arguments" or "telling stories" in an essay or book or collection of essays and/or books. I want to suggest that it is naive for Taylor to approach the text of a leading theoretician of writing, language, literature, and style as if his writing were merely a failed attempt at transparently presenting "positions," something merely unfortunately "obscure." (ibid., xiii)

Rather than try to understand him on his own terms, Bové continues, Taylor "arraigns Foucault before a rigged court that has prejudged him" (ibid., xvii). To put it in different terms (terms, it should be noted, that Bové and Connolly did not use), critics like Taylor read Foucault as a modernist when he is really a postmodernist.[5]

For proponents of the modernist paradigm to concede the incommensurability of these approaches to philosophy and political theory is, however, to risk elevating Foucault's alternative, his postmodernism, to the status of a potential successor. These particular proponents of modernism seem unwilling to hazard such an admission. Michael Walzer, for example, stubbornly refuses to concede the distance between his (modernist) and Foucault's (postmodernist) paradigms. Walzer's careful attention to issues of interpretation in this essay indicates that he is clearly aware of the postmodernist reading of Foucault and so, in response to these arguments about the radical difference of Foucault's thought, he begins his critique of Foucault's antidisciplinarian genealogies with a methodological confession. In evaluating Foucault's contribution to political theory he will assume two things: first, that since Foucault "makes arguments" he must operate "within the overall discipline of language" and according to "the rules of plausibility," and second, that uniting all of these genealogies is "a purpose." "So," he admits, "great minds are subdued" (1986, 52). Although he understands these to be contested assumptions, Walzer insists that they are all part of his standard interpretive procedure; "I will do what I always do with any book I read: try to puzzle out what the author is saying" (ibid., 52). Indeed, whereas Foucault, upon reading Borges's description of a Chinese encyclopedia,[6] is impressed by what "the stark impossibility of thinking *that*" suggests about the limitations of our own systems of thought (Foucault 1970, xv), Walzer makes the ironic observation that, presented with the same encyclopedia, he "would sit struggling to design a proper index" (1986, 52). Rather than marvel at the presence of this remarkable difference and let it lead him to question the sources of the present order of things, Walzer maintains a steady focus on the object of inquiry. In short, Walzer tacitly acknowledges the objections to his interpretive strategies, but insists on employing them anyway. Clinging defiantly to traditional categories of classification, Walzer considers a variety of labels for Foucault's political theory—infantile leftism, pluralism, anarchism, nihilism—and then, like Taylor, seems to conclude that Foucault's position is simply incoherent (ibid., 65).

Foucault's proponents, on the other hand, remain resolute. Suggesting to Taylor that "the limits of the modern episteme do not constitute the limits to possible thought as such" (1985, 372), Connolly attempts to extract Foucault from the perceived lethal grip of Taylor's assumptions. Connolly hopes that "those such as Taylor who seek to dismiss fundamental features of the project by showing it to be incoherent will find it more difficult to make that charge stick once they are not allowed to precede their critiques of Foucaultian genealogy by a translation of it into the very formulations it seeks to interrogate" (1985, 369). In order to defuse this charge of incoherence Connolly and Bové describe the incommensurability of, the paradigmatic difference between, Taylor's and Walzer's (modernist) and Foucault's (postmodernist) rhetorical strategies. They insist that Foucault's theoretical "hijinks" are an important part of his critical analysis and cannot be dismissed as mere delinquency. Foucault, we are told, offers genealogy not explanation, claims not arguments, gestures not positions, all of which must be judged by entirely different standards of validity. According to Foucault's proponents, Taylor's and Walzer's refusals to respect the autonomy of Foucaultian discourse represent attempts to domesticate, normalize, or discipline Foucault's radical difference.

In fact, according to these authors, Taylor's and Walzer's refusal to take seriously this proposal of an alternative to the modernist paradigm can be understood as a defensive posture: these modernists are guarding their intellectual and/or institutional turf. Connolly, for example, insists that Taylor underestimates the difference between modernist and Foucaultian discourses at Foucault's expense in order to preclude a potential challenge to his way of thinking: Taylor "seeks to evade the pressure Foucault exerts on his own theory of the subject by convicting Foucaultian theory of incoherence" (1985, 373). Having refused a defensive posture, Connolly goes on the offensive, insisting that the real burden is on Taylor to "defend his own affirmations from Foucaultian decomposition" (ibid., 365); why, he asks (to cite just one example), is Taylor's ontology more viable than Foucault's (ibid., 373)? Bové concurs with this assessment. Taylor, he claims, reduces Foucault to an incoherent modernist in order to avoid further debate. Modernists like Taylor object to Foucault because they refuse to recognize that their paradigm is only one among others.[7] Taylor, like many "humanistic intellectuals," misreads Foucault to "blunt the political consequences of his critique of their disciplines', their discourses', and their own positions within the knowledge/power apparatus" (Bové 1988, xi).

Foucault's critics seem frustrated by this sort of tenacious insistence on the paradigmatic difference of Foucault's work. Taylor, for example, clearly finds these classic paradigm-building strategies disturbing. He complains that the rhetoric his opponents deploy implies that we must choose between two different paradigms, and then, "when you want to challenge the rhetoric and ask for the argument, you are told that *you* are prejudging the question!" (1985, 382).[8] The borders between paradigms are inviolable. To cross them requires a kind of leap of faith, a conversion; one must be willing to work within an entirely different critical framework. According to both Connolly and Bové, Foucault's claims are neither coherent nor incoherent, and if commentators like Taylor (and we may add Walzer) want to judge Foucault's findings, they must do so on the basis of criteria immanent to his distinct, incommensurate (that is, in my vocabulary, postmodernist) perspective.

Although these authors do not cast Foucault as a postmodernist per se and do not for the most part employ the kind of reductive conceptions of modernism that we can find in other accounts, the strategies by which they defend and contest Foucault's work exemplify some of the means by which Foucault's work was, over time, linked to a postmodernist paradigm radically opposed to a modernist one. To avoid being absorbed by the dominant paradigm, to have the maximum impact on a broad audience, Foucault's selective critiques of certain aspects of the modern tradition are transformed in this North American discourse into a radical challenge to modernism itself. This postmodernist paradigm is not, however, built on an interpretation of Foucault alone, but rather, on a reading of poststructuralism more generally. A paradigm is a general framework and a collective project; as a successor paradigm rather than a single theory postmodernism is supposed to represent the agenda of a larger intellectual movement. As part of this broader postmodernist project, Foucault's work became linked to other poststructuralist critiques of totalizing metanarratives, foundationalist epistemologies, and ontological essentialism. Once linked to a more general project, once cast as part of a new intellectual paradigm, Foucault's specific critiques could be more easily understood as a general indictment of modernism. Thus, for example, interpreted as a contribution to the postmodernist paradigm, Foucault's critique of abstract, functionalist systems theories can be grouped together with Lyotard's more general indictment of metanarratives. Read as an example of postmodernist thought, Foucault's critique of absolute and universal truth can be seen as a version of Rorty's broader denunciation of epistemology. Finally, once Foucault's condemnation of naturalized models of the subject is expanded into a radical rejection of modernism, it can be conflated with other poststructuralist critiques of subjects, agents, and individuals. In short, once Foucault's limited critiques of specific types of modernist discourse are inflated into something consistent with postmodernism's more blanket indictment of and radical opposition to modernism—a feat that was accomplished collectively and over a period of time—Foucault's work can be presented as part of this proposal for a paradigm shift.

My goal in highlighting these techniques of paradigm construction and contestation is not to condemn this form of intellectual practice. On the contrary, these are some of the means by which innovative projects are organized and interjected into the field of intellectual debate; these are some of the ways that novel approaches to theoretical inquiry are formulated and disseminated as collective endeavors. Perhaps, given their polemical tone and combative spirit, the productivity of these strategies of paradigm competition are more evident when we do not measure them against a rationalist dream of academic "conversation"—an ideal of academic production that seems to me to be neither plausible nor appealing. The paradigmatization of a position, that is, the attempt to seal its borders and secure its autonomy, is an important way to enter new territory as well as to recruit members who can then further develop the framework. Part of the reason why Foucault's work, to cite one example, managed to have the energizing effect that it so often did is because of this vigorous insistence on the originality of its claims and the potentially transformative effect of its methods. Regardless of what one thinks of the accuracy or the utility of these readings of Foucault as a postmodernist, the point I want to emphasize here is that one cannot deny their effectiveness in gaining a broad audience and promoting sustained discussion and debate around a number of very timely issues. By continually pushing Foucault beyond the familiar limits of discursive practice, postmodernism established an important new agenda which had a stimulating effect on both political theory and feminist theory over the course of the 1980s.

There are, however, certain obvious problems with this paradigm debate between modernism and postmodernism. Over time, postmodernism's success is bought at a substantial price. Since the force of its arguments is acquired at the expense of precision and nuance, ultimately we are left with an unsatisfactory choice between opposing alternatives. Here I am particularly concerned with the way that the techniques used to transform Foucault's genealogy into an independent paradigm tend both to blunt the critical edge of Foucault's work and to reduce modernism to a straw figure, to a homogeneous model of Enlightenment thought.

Oppositional Logics and Reactive Reversals

The homogenization of modernism and postmodernism that is required for the paradigm debate is the product of a complex sequence of reductions. The complete strategy involves a series of conflations that reduce modernism to a single opponent which can be clearly contrasted to the postmodernist paradigm, itself constructed through a comparable series of conflations. The resulting paradigmatic conception of modernism is, it should be noted, an ideal type assembled from a variety of arguments; the complete series of conflations that gives rise to the most reductive conception of modernism is thus only partially replicated in the specific examples discussed below. As a paradigm, postmodernism is ultimately not the position of any one author so much as it is a discursive repertoire, a rhetorical strategy used to one degree or another in those analyses that are framed within and subject to the exigencies of this paradigm debate.[9]

Given my interest in exploring the possibilities of the Marxist discourse of feminist standpoint theory in subsequent chapters, what I find particularly disturbing in this debate is the inattention to the specificity of the Marxist tradition. That is, the modernist–postmodernist paradigm debate in both political theory and feminist theory is framed in a way that tends to make invisible Marxist alternatives to the Enlightenment. In discussions organized around this paradigm debate, when Marxist theory is not simply ignored, a quick paragraph or two is typically enough to suggest its association with the modernist paradigm and thereby secure its dismissal. As we will see, the strategy of conflation reconstructed below serves to establish Marxism's guilt by association.

First, in discussions informed by the modernist–postmodernist paradigm debate, the significance of modernism's own interparadigm distinctions are typically denied. Modernism originated, in part, in opposition to "antiquity," and this contrast played an important role in the development of modernism as a self-conscious project. Many of those interested in promoting the postmodernist difference insist, however, that this debate is obsolete: "The debate is now no longer between ancients and moderns, but between moderns and postmoderns" (Hoy 1988, 12). From the perspective of the postmodernist paradigm, ancient and modern thought are more similar than they are dissimilar, and this presumption of similarity is used to emphasize, by contrast, the dissimilarity between modernist and postmodernist discourse. As we have seen, for their part, defenders of the modernist paradigm often refuse to recognize the terms of this new debate, insisting instead on the continuing applicability of their own classificatory categories, their own oppositions. Habermas, for example, suggests that the label postmodernism is just a ruse when he claims that critics like Foucault are actually conservative *antimodernists* (1981, 13; see also Fraser 1989, 35).

Not only are modernism's interparadigm debates defused, its intraparadigm debates, particularly among Marxists and between Marxists and liberals, are also discredited. First, in political theory, differences within the Marxist approach to modernism are frequently obscured by conflating a variety of Marxist discourses with a version of orthodox Marxism. Marxism is thus associated with theories that privilege science over politics, laws of history over sites of struggle, exploitation over resistance. Rarely is the category "Marxism" further specified with the terms "Western," "structural," "orthodox," "autonomous," "Stalinist," and so on. In fact, seldom in the context of these paradigm debates is it admitted that alternative traditions of Marxist thought exist. In this way, a rich tradition of theory and practice can be dismissed along with its crudest representative. Allan Megill, for example, relies on an image of orthodox Marxism in order to magnify Foucault's radical alternative to the modern tradition. That is, he establishes Foucault's status as a "prophet of extremity" in part by contrasting him sharply to modernists like Marx who, he presumes, are committed to notions of universal truth and objective science (1985, 232, 249–250). "Marxism," Megill informs us, "has been the most durable remnant of that earlier [Enlightenment] dialectic, embodying a Cartesian faith in science, a Kantian faith in human nature, and an Hegelian faith in reason and history" (ibid., 341). While this may or may not be a fair characterization of a specific tradition of Marxist interpretation that shares with the Enlightenment a certain affiliation for objectivity and teleology, it is certainly not an adequate description of the tradition as a whole.

Mark Warren provides another example of this strategic disavowal of the differences within Marxism. Warren's discussion of Nietzsche is framed in terms of the modernist–postmodernist debate; that is, he contrasts what he describes as Nietzsche's (proto-) postmodernist position to a model of modernism that includes both liberalism and Marxism. He avoids disturbing his modernist–postmodernist formula by considering only "mainstream Marxism" (i.e., orthodox Marxism), which he likens in key respects to liberalism.[10] To retain this distinction between modernism and postmodernism as an organizing framework, Warren chooses to suppress the "anomaly" of Western Marxism. Only in a footnote does he acknowledge the existence of an alternative tradition of Marxist thought that does not fit so neatly into his classificatory scheme (1988, 153, 278n103).[11] This strategy of dealing with Marxism may or may not be problematic for these particular arguments; perhaps the contrast serves a useful purpose in these specific cases. The risk, however, is that as these examples accumulate and as the modernist–postmodernist paradigm categories are more frequently deployed in this purely oppositional and increasingly self-referential manner, the invisibility of alternative traditions of Marxist interpretation becomes more systematic; the reduction of all Marxisms to one broadly discredited representative becomes something that can be presumed by anyone who uses the categories rather than something that requires some kind of defense.

Once an orthodox version of Marxism is understood to represent the whole tradition, the second conflation, that of Marxism and Enlightenment liberalism, is somewhat easier to accept. To return to a previous example, Warren, having chosen to ignore the differences within Marxism, then underscores the similarities between Marxism and liberalism. From the perspective of the postmodernist paradigm, liberalism and Marxism are fundamentally similar doctrines rather than meaningful alternatives. To accentuate the difference between the modern and the postmodern, the differences between liberalism and Marxism are discounted in the same way that the differences between the modern and the ancient were made tenuous. And in the process, modernism is reduced to a single, homogeneous opponent. Of course, this approach to paradigm-legitimation is nothing new; modernism, for example, legitimated its own independence at the expense of a rich and varied description of antiquity as ancient and medieval thought were often reduced to the Socratic tradition as represented by Plato and Aristotle. Thus distinctions vital to the modern tradition's self-constitution are denied and a heterogeneous tradition of thought (including, for example, a variety of Marxisms) is reduced to its most vulnerable member (that is, a model of Enlightenment liberalism), which is then dismissed as inadequate in comparison to our new alternative (namely, postmodernism).

A similar fate befell Marxism and socialist feminism as the modernist–postmodernist debate made its way into and eventually became established within the field of feminist social and political theory. To characterize this strategy of conflation, I focus on a particular text, Susan Hekman's *Gender and Knowledge: Elements of a Postmodern Feminism* (1990). Hekman builds on the work of a number of poststructuralist theorists to criticize modernist feminism and defend postmodernist feminism on the grounds that postmodernist feminism offers a strong critique of and alternative to the dualisms of rational/irrational, subject/object, and nature/culture, around which she claims modernist epistemology is organized. This text is of particular interest to me because the nature of Hekman's project makes her use of conflation particularly noticeable. Hekman's objective seems to be to present a very sharp distinction between modernism and postmodernism in order to propose postmodern feminism as a new collective endeavor. Given the nature of her project one might expect to find more of these conflations presumed within the paradigm categories she uses, and indeed one does.

The modernist–postmodernist debate in feminism is typically constructed by conflating Marxist feminism with what participants frequently describe as Enlightenment liberalism, forming a unitary perspective which is then negatively contrasted to the postmodernist perspective. First, as we see in Hekman's presentation, Marxism is equated with an orthodox version grounded in notions of Reason and Truth, thus obscuring important controversies within Marxism over the credibility of these ideals (see, for example, 1990, 40).[12] Second, Marxist and socialist feminisms are then subsumed under Marxism, discounting the possibility of feminist innovation. Marxist and socialist feminists are accused of uncritically applying Marxist categories to the subject of women. According to Hekman, these feminists have "inherited" modernist epistemology from Marx and want only to bring women into unreconstructed male categories (ibid., 40). Marxist and socialist feminisms are thus dismissed as in every case a simple capitulation to, rather than potentially more creative reoccupations of, traditional Marxism. Finally, Marxist and socialist feminisms, now in the guise of orthodox Marxism, are merged with Enlightenment liberalism. Hekman suggests that Marxists are "the quintessential modernists because Marx's project is an attempt to complete the Enlightenment project of liberation that liberalism failed to achieve" (ibid, 40). The relationship between the Marxist and liberal traditions is certainly complex and multifaceted; the problem with this formulation is that it does not allow for the many significant differences between these discourses. Using this repertoire of reductions, modernism becomes a straw figure, a particular interpretation (a caricature, really) of Enlightenment thought, to which postmodernism is posed in sharp contrast.[13]

In a passage that presumes this triple conflation, Hekman argues that:

> Liberalism and Marxism will allow women into the public space of politics, but only if they renounce the "feminine" values that excluded them from this realm in the first place. This is due to the fact that the Cartesian, constituting subject that is the centerpiece of modernist epistemology is inherently masculine. The rational, autonomous subject of modernism is not only constitutive of modernist epistemology, it is also constitutive of the sexism that epistemology has fostered. (ibid., 188)

The most glaring problem with this claim is that this "Cartesian subject," this rational, self-constituting, and autonomous subject, is not the subject of most versions of historical materialism. Nonetheless, Marxism is reduced to an image of Enlightenment thought, labeled modernist, and then dismissed because it is masculinist. Thus, in feminist theory as in political theory, our options are limited to two: either Enlightenment modernism or postmodernism. According to Hekman, either we can employ rigid dichotomies and use ahistorical universals to search for the absolute truth of the essentialized Cartesian subject from an archimedean point, or we can construct a pluralistic, historically informed, materialist account of truth and agency.[14]

This oppositional formula, either modernism or postmodernism, played an important role in many fields throughout the 1980s. David Hoy, to cite another example, employs the same strategy when he reduces modernism to an ahistorical defense of an archimedean standpoint which he then contrasts to postmodernism's genealogical focus (see 1988, 33). According to Hoy's description, modernist analyses would seem by definition to involve metaphysical assumptions about the nature of man and truth, whereas postmodernist analyses do not (ibid., 36–37). Again, a variety of modernist discourses are collapsed into a specific representative which is then opposed to postmodernism. In this case, postmodernism then displaces historical materialism and assumes the position of *the* historically minded, materialist analysis of domination. In these accounts the postmodernist critique is presented as if there never was nor ever could be a radical critique of the Enlightenment generated from within the conceptual boundaries of modernism. This is precisely the point that Taylor makes when he complains that postmodernists present us with a false choice, which he understands as more or less a choice between Plato or Nietzsche (see 1985, 380, 382). Note, however, that while Taylor's formulation of these options is designed to suggest the problematic conflation of ancient and modern thought (i.e., all pre-Nietzschean thought is equated with Platonism), he does not recognize that it also presumes an equally suspect conflation of Nietzsche's, Foucault's, and postmodernist thought. It seems to me more accurate to describe the choice we are offered in this instance as either Plato (and the homogenized modernist tradition) or postmodernism (as the paradigmatization of Foucault's neo-Nietzscheanism).

To maintain this oppositional framework, one must continually emphasize the incommensurability of modernist and postmodernist discourses. Hekman, for example, enforces this rigid dichotomy when she argues that explorations of the territory in between or outside the Enlightenment and postmodernism are guilty of an "unten-

able" eclecticism (1990, 6–7, 81, 131).[15] Approaches that seek to retain the "good" aspects of modernity while rejecting its "bad" features do not recognize the fact that "[t]he epistemology of modernism is a unitary whole, not a piecemeal collection" from which
critics can pick and choose (ibid., 7). In this reading modernism and
postmodernism are mutually exclusive, coherent paradigms and any
attempt to subvert or "displace" this dichotomy is guilty of a sloppy
eclecticism. According to Hekman, such eclecticism "is precluded
by the radical nature of the postmodern critique" (ibid., 135). That is,
alternatives are prohibited by the fact that postmodernism disavows
any and every other possibility; whatever is not postmodernist is
modernist. The logic suggests that unless we repudiate modernism
in its entirety, assimilation is the only alternative. Either we can incorporate women into existing (patriarchal) categories, or, by adopt-
ing postmodernism as that which is not modernism, we can oppose
them absolutely. The possibility of a more creative or nuanced appropriation is dismissed by Hekman out of hand as an eclectic attempt to avoid the necessary either/or choice.

The most obvious problem with this modernist–postmodernist
formula is that too many differences are eclipsed and too many nuances are lost; what remains are often no more than straw figures.
Differences between, for example, Enlightenment and post-Enlight-
enment theories, liberalism and Marxism, and Marxisms of the orthodox, Hegelian and antihumanist variety are typically rendered
ineffectual once modernism is constituted as a unified and homogeneous position. While these accounts may present a provocative
juxtaposition, it is constructed at the expense of important—that is
to say, still vital, still productive—differences within the modern
tradition.

Poststructuralism suffers a comparable fate as serious disputes between, for example, Foucault and Derrida, are overshadowed by the
demands of paradigm coherence. Judith Butler suggests that the conflation of these different theoretical discourses into something called
postmodernism provides the reader an opportunity to disregard their
distinctive character and their unique force. Butler presents this
proposition in the form of a rhetorical question: "Is the effort to col-
onize and domesticate these theories under the sign of the same, to
group them synthetically and masterfully under a single rubric, a

simple refusal to grant the specificity of these positions, an excuse not to read, and not to read closely?" (1992, 5). Indeed, to the extent that these paradigms are locked in opposition to one another, the debates between modernism and postmodernism need not be grounded in specific textual references; once they become largely self-referential constructions, free of the constraints of any specific poststructuralist or modernist reference, the categories and the debates they enable take on a life of their own.

Such debates tend to evince a reactive logic. One paradigm is constructed as a reaction against a caricature of the other and is seen only as what the other is not, a mere reversal. Thus poststructuralism, conceived as postmodernism, is often presented as whatever modernism is not: for example, an irrationalist, relativist, or determinist discourse. As modernism's other, postmodernism is imagined so as to reflect a positive image of modernism rather than to serve as an accurate representation of the poststructuralist tradition. Postmodernism is reduced to antimodernism and modernism is transformed into anti-postmodernism. To the extent that they rely on these formulas, anti-postmodernist characterizations of postmodernism and postmodernist descriptions of modernism begin to sound equally fantastic. When these are the terms that inform our thinking and frame our exchanges, we will inevitably talk past one another.[16]

Presented as mutually exclusive alternatives locked in a reactive relationship to one another, modernism and postmodernism tend to become attached to and supportive of the dichotomies that so many of the participants hoped to deconstruct: global or local, objective or relative, being or becoming, voluntarist or determinist. Modernism is associated with one value and postmodernism with the other; one half of the dualism is valorized in order to deprecate the other. To the extent that postmodernism is defined in terms of what it rejects and these rigid borders between paradigms are enforced, there is a tendency among both some proponents and some critics of postmodernism to conceive it as a purely critical or destructive project. In such cases this binary formula is then implicated in what Connolly describes as "theoretical postponism": to the extent that some interpreters of poststructuralism see their task as "one perpetual assignment to 'invert the hierarchies' maintained in other theories," the project of developing alternative theories is deferred (1991, 56). The constructive dimension of theory is thus postponed by many "self-described postmodernists," who are immobilized by the prospect that any such positive claim could be deconstructed (1991, 53). Connolly suggests that this reading of poststructuralism, a reading that I attribute to the terms of the modernist–postmodernist paradigm debate, robs these discourses of much of their force.[17]

What are the consequences of this translation of Foucault's specific interventions into the terms of the postmodernist paradigm? I see two problems here. First, as I have already suggested, this paradigmatization of Foucault's neo-Nietzscheanism compromises its critical power. The postmodernist paradigm in political theory and feminist theory was, I have argued, constructed in a way that would lend weight, coherence, and legitimacy to poststructuralist critiques, including that of Foucault. Unfortunately, however, what was originally crafted by Nietzsche and Foucault as a sharp knife for cutting into specific problems is transformed by the terms of the paradigm debate into a relatively blunt instrument. More specifically, the selective nature of Foucault's critique of modernism is obscured by the exigencies of the postmodernist paradigm. One should not overlook the irony here: the means by which Foucault was forced onto center stage and that ensured his maximum impact also contributed to the inflation and ossification of his method into a paradigm opposed to a modernist paradigm, something he clearly condemns.[18]

Second, not only does this paradigmatization of Foucault's thought compromise its critical force, it can in some cases also reinforce the specific weakness of Foucault's appropriation of Nietzsche discussed in the previous chapter. The problem is that there is a tendency to focus on Foucault's value neutrality as evidence of his unyielding rejection of all modernist values, as that which locates him on the outside, in this case, outside the entire modern tradition. Hekman, for example, seems to suggest that what I characterized as Nietzsche's selective affirmation is ruled out along with other forms of "eclecticism" by the radical formulation of the postmodernist critique. When the postmodernist critique is formulated in such oppositional terms, creative alternatives to and selections of modernist thought tend to be dismissed as tainted or compromised. To the extent that postmodernism is sometimes confined to this critical, destructive project it constitutes a valorization of the most problematic feature of Foucault's reworking of Nietzsche; that is, its lack of evaluative criteria and alternative values. Indeed, this fundamental weakness in Foucault's thought, its potential Achilles' heel, is enshrined as its definitive quality and fundamental strength. In other words, reduced to a paradigm opposed to modernism, postmodernism promotes a Foucaultian strategy of reactive reversal at the expense of the Nietzschean project of selective affirmation. Thus, to the extent that it expands the limited focus of Foucault's critiques of modernism to include the whole of modernism and valorizes Foucault's destructive critique, postmodernism compromises the strengths and emphasizes the weakness of Foucault's reoccupation of Nietzschean thought. If for my purposes important aspects are lost in Foucault's appropriation of Nietzsche, much more is lost once Foucault is translated into the terms of the postmodernist paradigm.

I certainly do not mean to suggest that this captures all the relevant interpretations of Foucault, or that every reference to modernism or to postmodernism is implicated in these paradigm formulas. The literature on Foucault far exceeds these specifications, the terms modernism and postmodernism are used in a variety of ways, and the modernist–postmodernist debate is constructed along a number of different lines. Nonetheless, this version of the debate and these paradigmatic formulations of the categories of modernism and postmodernism have been frequently deployed and have had an important impact on debates in political theory and feminist political and social theory since the 1980s. This was by no means an entirely unfortunate development. As I argued earlier, the modernist–postmodernist debate was in many ways productive; although it closed some doors, it did force open some others. However, while it was perhaps appropriate at an earlier stage when, by recourse to simple oppositions and clear distinctions, new participants could be recruited and new agendas could be crafted, it has by now outlived its usefulness. At this point, maximizing the differences between modernism and postmodernism conceals the most difficult issues more than it helps to engage them. The ideal of absolute Truth, the pre-existing "Cartesian subject," the insistence that constructed subjects are necessarily passive subjects, or the claim that there is no reality outside of texts are more often than not, by now, red herrings. This is not to deny that there are substantial differences at stake in all this or to discount the important conflicts between, for example, Marx and Foucault, or feminist poststructuralists and socialist feminists. My point is simply that it is time to liberate these differences from the modernist–postmodernist paradigm debate so that we can see the nuances more clearly. At this stage, the terms of the paradigm debate serve only to cast important differences as reactive oppositions and to transform potentially productive conflicts into unproductive stalemates.

Marxist discourses in general and feminist standpoint theories in particular are, I believe, some of the most unfortunate casualties of this paradigm debate. Although the recent marginalization of both Marxism and socialist feminism is a consequence of a complex series of factors, it can be traced at least in part to the terms of this version of the debate between modernism and postmodernism. This dismissal is problematic, I want to suggest, because these traditions include some promising tools and potentially productive lines of inquiry that may be of interest to those of us searching for alternatives to the mutually exclusive categories of modernism or postmodernism. In the next two chapters I want to turn to the Marxist and socialist feminist traditions, among others, to locate some resources from which to develop a theory of feminist subjectivity that lies beyond the confines of these paradigm oppositions.

The Aspiration to Totality:
Identity, Difference, and Antagonism

Before reconfiguring a feminist subject, we must formulate an account of the social totality in which it is embedded. A theory of the subject that rejects its transcendental origins, metaphysical essence, and transhistorical continuity requires a conception of the social order within which subjects are constructed. Moreover, a theory of a gendered subject that conceives gender not as a role that can be discarded at will but as one constitutive element of subjectivity presupposes that gender is in part a systematic effect of a complex set of interconnected social processes. Finally, a theory of a feminist subject requires a conception of the social forces that we want to contest. "Totality" signifies this complex system of social relations, which is both the ground for and the target of feminist struggles.

Totality is, of course, a highly contested category. In recent years the term has been equated with various examples of reductionist, teleological, and universalizing modes of social analysis. For some, the term evokes as a normative ideal an image of social unity, a vision of the realization or restoration of harmony between the individual and the community. For others, it designates an equally problematic commitment to the abstract and general at the expense of the concrete and particular. The category of totality has thus been interpreted as a code word for metanarrative, a cover for totalizing theory, and an excuse to deny the force of specificity, difference, and contingency. By combining several of these formulations, some have even posited a clear and necessary path of evolution leading from the idea of totality to Stalin's suppression of internal dissent (see Kolakowski 1978, 303–304).

None of these characterizations, however, adequately describes the theoretical project of totality that I want to affirm and pursue in this chapter. As Althusser once noted in a discussion of the differences between the Marxist and the Hegelian conceptions of totality, the term may be the same across these varied traditions, "but the concept changes, sometimes radically, from one author to another" (1990, 203).[1] What they all share, as Althusser also noted, are certain theoretical opponents as well as some conception—though often very different conceptions—of the interrelatedness of social entities. As for its opponents, the Marxist concept of totality is clearly at odds with some typical procedures of traditional liberal inquiry. The focus on relations harkens back to the Marxist will to situate what liberalism seeks to separate: the private in the public realm, theory in practice, and the individual in society. The methodological mandate to relate and connect is fundamental to the Marxist project in the same way that the dictate to isolate and individuate is constitutive of traditional liberal inquiry. However, this minimal sense of the project of totality, this very basic methodological proposition, has been elaborated in many different ways. Although it need not culminate in a model of an all-encompassing and self-replicating system, a system in which differences are denied their effectiveness and subjects are reduced to role players, these are certainly dangers inherent in the endeavor to conceive a social totality. Before embarking on this examination of approaches relevant to this project, I want to consider certain potential traps.

Let me begin, then, with a brief review of Nietzsche's critique of the will to system and Foucault's critique of totalizing theories. As mentioned above, Nietzsche levels his methodological assault at abstract analyses that reduce the particular to a fixed function within the whole. From a Nietzschean perspective, attempts to deny the reality of specificity, to impugn irrecoverable manifestations of will to power and the inevitability of conflict, reveal a fundamentally ascetic or life-inimical impulse. Foucault takes up this Nietzschean critique and extends it to, among others, certain examples of Marxist theorizing in which universal claims, functionalist logic, one-way causal analysis, and the single-minded focus on abstract systems have all been found. However, to recall the earlier discussion of these critiques, neither author prescribes the wholesale repudiation of systematic theory or an affirmation of the purely local, specific, and contingent. Rather, their critiques can be read as an attempt to challenge us to build social theories that rely on neither essence nor telos, to build theories that create a space for difference, contingency, and antagonism.

Similar and similarly valuable critiques of abstract, functionalist, and universalizing models have been advanced in feminist theory as well. Nancy Fraser's and Linda Nicholson's critical consideration of Lyotard's recommendation to "wage war on totality" is one of the most well-known of these interventions. The authors conclude, however, that while feminists can learn from many of the specific analyses gathered under this slogan, this should not preclude the project of systematic theory per se. We must recognize, they argue, "that postmodern critique need forswear neither large historical narratives nor analyses of societal macrostructures. This point is important for feminists, since sexism has a long history and is deeply and pervasively embedded in contemporary societies" (1990, 34). Again, rather than constituting a case against the project of totality *tout court*, these critiques present a set of concerns, challenges, and correctives that will guide my attempt to reconfigure the project of totality in feminist standpoint theory, to move it away from what Nietzsche described as the ascetic denial of subjective forces.

What follows, then, is an exploration of different conceptions of totality that have been developed within both socialist feminism and the nonfeminist Marxist tradition. The Nietzschean themes suggested above are evoked to help me to recognize and, I hope, to avoid some of the characteristic shortcomings of these attempts to think the systematic organization of social arrangements. The point is not to elaborate a Nietzschean or a Foucaultian project; on the contrary, my goal is to rework the terms of specific Marxist and feminist projects. But this need not rule out the incorporation of certain de-ascetizing and de-totalizing techniques. My main concern is to develop, on the basis of these contributions, a conception of totality that is compatible with the project of feminist standpoint theory as I conceive it, that is; as a project dedicated to the construction of feminist subjects. What I want to develop is a conception of a complex totality of social forces that contains a multiplicity of subjectivities and is open to multiple sites of contestation and possibilities for rupture. In this chapter, then, what will be considered under the rubric of totality are the conditions of possibility for the construction of antagonistic standpoints.

An Archeology of Socialist Feminism

Feminist standpoint theory originally developed alongside, and in some cases in response to, another tradition of socialist feminism that I call systems theory. Here I trace one particular line of development within the tradition of socialist feminism that takes us through three specific examples of systems theory and then to standpoint theory.[2] By considering continuities and differences between standpoint theory and socialist feminist systems theory, we can gain a better understanding of standpoint theory as a distinctive contribution to a more general problematic and see more clearly which specific dimensions of standpoint theory could be productively cultivated.

The tradition of socialist feminist systems theory that I focus on here developed in part as a response to a specific agenda in feminist theory in the 1970s. One of the most pressing items on the agenda during this early period of theory building was the mandate to develop systematic theories of women's oppression. The aim was to theorize the systematic connections between what had been treated as isolated phenomena. Thus, for example, whereas early liberal feminism had tried to maintain the traditional boundaries between the public and the private realms, these radical and socialist feminists, armed with the slogan "the personal is political," fought to dismantle the borders between public and private spheres in order to eliminate the artificial division between a public world characterized by power relations and a private world in which relations are supposed to be either natural or voluntary, but in any case, politically inconsequential. The goal was to understand how specific phenomena such as rape, unequal pay, sexual harassment and poverty are connected to a larger system of social control—a system that does not honor the borders between the private and the public. This project was also seen by some to involve a search for explanatory models that could offer an account of the sources of women's oppression. In the words of one radical feminist, "[i]t became necessary to go to the root of the problem, rather than to become engaged in solving secondary problems arising out of that condition" (Koedt 1973, 318). For example, in one analysis, isolated acts like rape and abortion laws were explained as imperialist acts in a larger process of colonization (Burris 1973, 335).

For some—typically radical feminist in orientation—the point was to add explanatory breadth to feminist analyses by casting the conceptual net as far as possible. Thus in many of these early theories the universal and original or primary status of women's oppression was emphasized: women were the first to be oppressed (Burris 1973, 352; The Feminists 1973, 369) and are oppressed similarly through time and space, as, for example, in the claim that all women are a colonized group. Others, however, were unwilling to identify a single, primary model of oppression. Although socialist feminists were, like most radical feminists at the time, interested in developing systematic accounts of women's oppression, they were typically guided by different methodological criteria. For these theorists, the goal was to add complexity, not necessarily range, to feminist analyses. By situating women's lives in an institutional milieu, they hoped to develop better accounts of the pervasive forces that maintain the oppression of women. With the appropriation of a Marxist problematic, the emphasis on historical specificity tended to replace the commitment to universality and the interest in complexity replaced the search for origins. Thus, for example, both Heidi Hartmann and Zillah Eisenstein, two prominent socialist feminists, declared that they leave aside the question of the origins of women's oppression and focus instead on the question of why and how it happens in the here and now (Hartmann 1981a, 19; Eisenstein 1979, 43). In these early socialist feminist texts, women's oppression is presented as thoroughgoing and complex rather than primary or universal. For these theorists, the purpose of systems theories was to locate the complex connections between women's lives in a specific time and place and the larger system of social forces in which they are organized. It is this second approach that characterizes the three system theorists to whom I now turn.

Mariarosa Dalla Costa's Single-System Theory

No doubt a significant segment of Mariarosa Dalla Costa's audience in the early 1970s dismissed her as a heretic. "Orthodox Marxism," as Dalla Costa describes it, had marginalized "the woman question" by insisting that women's domestic labor was outside the realm of social production, and hence beyond the reach of Marxist economic analysis. Largely confined to the production of use values in the home, women were thought to play only an incidental role in the struggle between the true movers and shakers of history: capitalists and proletariat. In defiance of what was then the dominant Marxist line, Dalla Costa insists that domestic labor is productive labor and, as such, essential to the production of surplus value (1972, 31). The family is "the very pillar supporting the capitalist organization of work," and women, understood as a section of the working class, are well within the reach of traditional Marxian economic categories of analysis (ibid., 46). In response to Engels's argument that women are oppressed as women only to the extent that they are excluded from "productive labor" (i.e., wage labor), Dalla Costa argues that women are oppressed *in spite of* their (partial and temporary) exclusion from wage labor; as domestic laborers, women already participate in capitalist production in the "social factory." While it may not be recognized as such due to its more indirect relationship to the cash nexus, domestic labor—understood to be women's work—is another form of exploited labor. Dalla Costa urges women to refuse work and demand wages for housework in order to expose and condemn domestic work as a form of exploited labor.

Dalla Costa's historical contribution to socialist feminist theory should not be underestimated. Certainly her theoretical position is in many ways an improvement over the treatment of women found in the works of Marx, Engels, and their "orthodox" adherents. Dalla Costa's reconceptualization of domestic labor suggests to feminism the possibilities of a materialist analysis of gender relations; that is, women's oppression could no longer be conceived as a product of purely juridical or cultural forces. To Marxism, Dalla Costa offers a broader conception of production which includes forms of socially necessary labor not traditionally considered. Dalla Costa thus credits what had been posed within Marxism as "the woman question" with more credibility and importance in so far as it is now conceived as adding "a new dimension to the class struggle" (ibid., 39–40).

Nonetheless, as many critics have noted, Dalla Costa's feminism is subordinate to her Marxism, and both her feminism and her Marxism suffer as a result.[3] According to one critic, "[t]he rhetoric of feminism is present in Dalla Costa's writing (the oppression of women, struggle with men) but the focus of feminism is not" (Hartmann 1981a, 9). Class, not gender, is the primary category of analysis; capitalism, not patriarchy, is the primary object of critique. Capitalism is presented as a monolithic system and the sole force of determination. As the single system that organizes the field of social relations, capitalism is the force that is responsible for women's exploitation as "unwaged slaves," for the imposition of female passivity and, ultimately, for the "construction of the female role" (Dalla Costa 1972, 29). The analysis that would explain the specific mechanisms by which capitalist social forces could elicit these particular effects is weak; the argument remains abstract and reductive.

Dalla Costa's is an essentially additive, as opposed to a transformative contribution to Marxist theory: instead of revising Marxist categories to suit her feminist focus, Dalla Costa simply stretches their boundaries until they lose specificity. To claim, for example, that all women engaged in unwaged labor in the home are part of the working class is to discard any precision the category of class may have possessed. And little is gained in the process; we are left with a blunt tool that is incapable of helping us understand the distinctiveness of women's social locations. One of the problems here is that Dalla Costa subsumes too much within a Marxist analytical framework without substantially transforming the explanatory range of its categories. She simply adds an account of women's household labor to a largely unreconstructed appropriation of traditional Marxist theory.

Socialist feminist systems theory was developed during a period of intense political activity, a condition that accounts for some of the differences between these early texts and those produced today. One thing that leaps out at the contemporary reader is how focused the authors were on questions of strategy. Their theoretical frameworks were constructed within the context of specific social movements and were intended to intervene in particular debates about organizational forms and political strategies. Hence the practical political implications of the analyses were treated as absolutely central; a feminist theory should, among other things, be able to suggest productive new directions for practice. Dalla Costa, writing amid widespread and militant working-class struggles and in the very early period of Italian feminist activity, was attempting to address the relationship between the working class and feminist movements. According to Dalla Costa's analysis, feminism does not threaten the unity of working-class opposition to capital as many had feared, but instead expands it. Women's struggles are "inscribed" in working-class opposition to capitalist work (1972, 39). There is, then, no space in this single-system theory for an autonomous women's movement. Instead, the feminist struggle (and since women are described as a single, homogeneous group we can presume that the feminist struggle is, indeed, a single, unified movement) is assimilated within the working-class movement. What remains is the working class as the lone antagonistic subject.

Important developments in the women's movement and feminist theory separate early efforts like Dalla Costa's from my next three examples of socialist feminist theory. First, the emergence of a mass, autonomous women's movement provided a more solid (and more decidedly feminist) base from which to engage in both politics and theory. A movement emerged and a collective subject demanded that questions of women's subjectivity and issues of feminist political struggle assume a place of importance. Consequently, rather than examining yet again Marx's or Engels's discussions of "the woman question," or thinking about how to add feminism to existing Marxist paradigms, some feminists turned their energy towards more original efforts to place a Marxist method in the service of feminism. "[T]here is nothing about the dialectical and historical method that limits it to understanding class relations," insists one such theorist (Eisenstein 1979, 7). In these later versions of socialist feminist theory, a Marxist method is abstracted from Marxist theory and then

subjected to critical scrutiny by feminists increasingly eager to dis-
cover what Marxism could do for feminism rather than what feminism could do for Marxism. Second, later feminists also had an important new concept to work with: patriarchy. Just as one could
argue that it was the appearance in the nineteenth century of a new
proletarian subject that made it possible to see capitalism more
clearly, it was, perhaps, the emergence of a new feminist subject that
made it possible to bring patriarchy into sharper focus.[4] As the cornerstone of radical feminist theory, patriarchy refers to a system of
hierarchy, privilege, and domination exercised by men over women.
Although it is in and of itself analytically rather weak and descrip-
tively very general, the concept does succeed in focusing critical attention on power relations between the genders. Described as a synthesis of Marxism and radical feminism, this revived Marxist
feminism (now with a new name, socialist feminism, that signifies
the break with what came before it) claims that capitalism and patriarchy together organize social relations. The dual-systems theory of
Heidi Hartmann, benefiting from these developments in feminism,
represents the second stage in this archeology of socialist feminist
systems theory.

Heidi Hartmann's Dual-Systems Theory

Hartmann introduces as her alternative to single-system models a
mixture of Marxism and radical feminism. Whereas separately,
Marxist categories are gender-blind and radical feminist categories
are ahistorical and insufficiently materialist (1981a, 2), together they
complement one another. Hartmann offers a Marxist analysis of
class under capitalism supplemented by a materialist feminist analysis of gender under patriarchy to investigate what she describes as a
partnership between patriarchy and capitalism. Rather than one system, capitalism, under which women's oppression is conceived as an
aspect of class oppression, we have a dual system: capitalism and patriarchy. Hartmann presents a rich and provocative discussion of the
development of the family wage as a historical example of the way
that patriarchy and capitalism accommodate one another. Because
patriarchy divides the working class along gender lines, capital could

buy off working men with a family wage at the expense of the many women who, limited in their participation in the waged labor force and not paid on an equal basis, were driven back into the home: "Instead of fighting for equal wages for men and women, male workers sought the family wage, wanting to retain their wives' services at home" (ibid., 21). Capitalism supports patriarchy by limiting women's opportunities for economic independence, and patriarchy reinforces capitalism by providing socially necessary services in the home and by defusing certain forms of opposition to the system's failures (ibid., 22, 27–29).

Hartmann's dual-systems model, in which capitalism and patriarchy together organize social relations, offers several improvements over Dalla Costa's single-system model in which capitalism alone is held responsible for social order. Although it has several problems that I will not take up here, the materialist conception of patriarchy provides the model with more explanatory power. According to Hartmann's definition, patriarchy is "a set of social relations between men, which have a material base, and which, though hierarchical, establish or create interdependence and solidarity among men that enable them to dominate women" (ibid., 14). As a distinct set of social relations that change over time (Hartmann includes, among others, heterosexual marriage and female responsibility for child rearing and housework), patriarchy is based on men's control of women's labor power (1981a, 15). The point I find valuable in Hartmann's analysis is her view that (irrespective of their "control" over this situation) men (also) have a "material" interest in women's oppression (1981a, 9). Compared to Dalla Costa, Hartmann, by adding a second system, is better able to explain the links between certain gendered practices and historically specific socioeconomic structures. Moreover, in contrast to the single-system model, which recognizes one oppressed and antagonistic subject, the united working class, there is a space for two such subjects in the dual-systems model: women and working-class men. Hartmann's model thus recognizes certain differences in the social positions of men and women. Probably the most important advantage of adding a separate system of social forces is a practical one: in this way Hartmann could promote the legitimacy of an autonomous feminist politics. The practical implication of Hartmann's insistence that patriarchy and capitalism are independent but equal partners is that feminist and socialist or anticapitalist groups must be treated as separate but equal partners in the struggle against domination. This defense of an autonomous women's movement represents what was clearly a timely alternative to Dalla Costa's claim that women should subsume their interests under those of the working class.

Despite the many strengths of the analysis and the unmistakable timeliness of the argument, there are problems with this dual-systems model. The basic difficulty is that while it succeeds in giving patriarchy equal weight with capitalist relations, it fails to offer an adequate account of their relationship. Essentially, a feminist analysis of the oppression of women under patriarchy is attached to a Marxist analysis of the oppression of the working class under capitalism. The model thus tends to recapitulate the liberal distinction between the private and the public wherein patriarchal relations operate primarily in the "private" sphere of the family and capitalist relations obtain in the "public" realm of the economy (Young 1981, 48). According to the way that the two systems tend to be distinguished in this account, gender hierarchies organize us in one realm and class hierarchies in another. As a result, the dual-systems model cannot adequately explain the experience of women who work for wages (see ibid., 49), nor does it take into account the ways in which gender (not to mention race) hierarchies have played such an integral role in the historical development of capitalist social relations. As Hartmann herself admits, given the many points of intersection between these systems of domination, it is often quite difficult to isolate the workings of two distinct sets of relations (1981a, 29).

Several authors have called attention to the inability of dual-systems theories to account for other systems of oppression besides patriarchy and capitalism. Although Hartmann insists that—since the system she is considering is organized by class, gender, and race—it is more accurate to refer to it as "patriarchal capitalist white supremacist" (ibid., 18), rather than develop that insight, she slips back to more restricted references to a partnership between capitalism and patriarchy. In her critique of Hartmann, Gloria Joseph points out the weakness of this argument: "if one can claim that marxism is incomplete without a consideration of feminism, it is certainly true that neither is complete without a consideration of racial relations" (1981, 103).

The solution that remains faithful to the logic of the dual-systems model is a trisystems model. This remedy, however, only reveals the limitations of the separate-systems model itself. If patriarchy organizes relations in the private realm and capitalism in the public realm, where do we add the systemic forces that sustain race hierarchies? We encounter this same problem at the level of subject positions. Because of the logic of separate spheres that governs this dual-systems model, it becomes difficult to fathom the relationship between gender and class. We are men or women in one sphere and capitalist or wage laborer in the other. Every group is conceived as a homogeneous entity; the subject is either a worker or a woman, but not both. Thus dual-systems theory, while it registers certain differences between women and men, does not adequately recognize differences among women or among men. Consequently, as Joseph points out, Hartmann overestimates the solidarity among both women and men (1981, 101). The model suggests that women share a common position and feminists a united stance. Again, the limitations of the underlying logic are made clear when race is added to the list of subject positions. The model of separate spheres entails a model of singular subject positions; a trisystems model may add to the list—we are white or African American, for example—but would not lend itself to the development of an account of simultaneous oppression or of differences within subject positions.

Finally, I think we should add to this list of limitations the fact that dual-systems theory fails to challenge in a more direct and substantial fashion the classic tradition of Marxist theory. While Hartmann is willing to use Marxist tools to rethink feminist concepts like patriarchy, she does not in this account subject the Marxist analysis of capitalism to a comparable feminist reconsideration. In effect, then, despite Hartmann's interest in a healthier relationship between Marxism and feminism, she ends up with what resembles a more traditional marriage. As Young describes it, "not unlike traditional marxism, the dual systems theory tends to see the question of women's oppression as merely an additive to the main questions of marxism" (1981, 49).

Iris Young's Unified-Systems Theory

Rather than additional systems, the third contributor to this socialist feminist project proposes a reconceptualization of the interrelations among systems. Young claims that capitalist patriarchy is best described as a unified system in which both capitalism and patriarchy are presumed to be key components of the present functioning of the other.[5] By this account, then, the *"marginalization of women and thereby our functioning as a secondary labor force is an essential and fundamental characteristic of capitalism"* (ibid., 58). Capitalism and patriarchy are neither separate nor identical. On the one hand, Young insists that if patriarchy is grounded in men's control over women's labor power and access to economic resources, as Hartmann claims, "then it does not seem possible to separate patriarchy from a system of social relations of production even for analytical purposes" (ibid., 47). On the other hand, capitalism and patriarchy have also followed different historical trajectories. Thus, for example, like Hartmann, Young recognizes the existence of a feudalist patriarchy as well (see ibid., 61). Class and gender are preserved as distinct categories in order to focus on the specific situations of women in the context of a social formation that is simultaneously capitalist and patriarchal. In Young's unified-systems theory, capitalism and patriarchy are conceived as mutually determining distinctions within one system rather than as separate systems.[6]

Young proposes the gender division of labor as the central category in her alternative to dual-systems theory.[7] The problem with the more traditional Marxist category of class is that it does not register differences constituted along the axis of gender (or, I would add, along the axis of race). Hartmann remedied this with the addition of a second system that focused on gender relations. However, unlike the dual categories of gender and class that govern Hartmann's approach, the gender division of labor does not maintain the false boundaries between the private and the public realms by holding to the assumption that gender is operative in one realm and class in another. There is a gender division of labor in both the waged and unwaged sectors of the economy. "Use of the gender division of labor category," Young argues, "provides the means for analyzing the social relations arising from the laboring activity of *a whole society* along the axis of gender" (ibid., 52, emphasis added).

Not only can the gender division of labor be used to cut through a broader and more complex set of relations (at once capitalist and patriarchal), it can also be used to register certain connections between economic structures, on the one hand, and the actual laboring practices of women, on the other. The two categories are cast at different levels of abstraction: the division of labor "refers specifically to the *activity* of labor itself, and the specific social and institutional relations of that activity," whereas class analysis focuses our attention on the distribution of power throughout the system (ibid., 51). For this reason the division of labor holds certain advantages over the more frequently used category of class. Being at once more inclusive and less abstract, the division of labor recommends itself as a useful category for recovering specific links between what we do and the systemic forces that are constituted by and constitutive of these practices. As we will see, the gender division of labor also organizes standpoint theory's inquiry into women's laboring practices.

One of the most valuable aspects of an analysis organized around the division of labor is, according to Young, the fact that it does not disallow differences among women: "Gender division of labor analysis allows us to do material analysis of the social relations of labor in gender specific terms without assuming that all women in general or all women in a particular society have a common and unified situation" (ibid., 55). This ability to register difference and multiplicity is, I would argue, one of the virtues of the unified-systems model more generally. One of the problems with Hartmann's dual-systems model is that by positing patriarchy as a single system responsible for gender hierarchies, it tends, as we have noted, to assume that all women, as a consequence of their gender, find themselves in the same position. Although the trisystems model acknowledges the existence of differences along the lines of race, when we retain the model of separate systems, it becomes difficult to conceptualize ways in which race, class, and gender operate simultaneously; the model seems to presume that lives and identities can be neatly segregated, so that one's gender, or race, or class are important factors in one area of life and not others. The unified-systems model, by contrast, encourages us to conceive of patriarchy and capitalism as systemic forces, each of which traverses the entire social landscape and which negotiate relationships with one another. The subjects reproduced within these systems are, by implication, coded simultaneously by gender and class.

Although Young, like Hartmann, largely confines her focus to class and gender differences, there is nothing in the logic of the analysis that prevents the construction of a more complex model—for example, one that includes within this unified multiplicity the systemic forces of patriarchy, capitalism, white supremacy, and heterosexism. The forces included in these representations of the social system will, of course, change over time and according to focus. Some analyses will extend to the more global and others to a more local configuration of systemic forces[8]; some analyses will focus more exclusively on gender and others on race or on class. But whatever forces we include, we should presume, according to the logic of this model, that they play a role in every social effect and interact in complex ways with one another. The dynamics of this model move away from dual-systems theory's notion of separate systems and a single feminist subject toward a conception of simultaneous oppressions with a multiplicity of subjects. Thus, for example, at about the time when Young was developing her unified-systems model, The Combahee River Collective was explaining their socialist feminist perspective in these terms: "we are actively committed to struggling against racial, sexual, heterosexual, and class oppression and see as our particular task the development of integrated analysis and practice based upon the fact that *the major systems of oppression are interlocking*" (1979, 362 emphasis added). Presumably, then, to add to Young's account, one could also focus on the racial division of labor: whereas Young focuses on the gender division of labor to highlight the presence of gender differences, one could also focus on the organization of laboring practices along racial lines to examine the changing social relations that arise from the laboring activity *of a whole society* along the axis of race. Regardless of the particular ways that one may decide to cut into this unified multiplicity or the particular forces one chooses to emphasize, the point is that the various structures of social determination are not confined to particular realms of effective action.

As Young recognizes, a feminist theory can be judged not only in terms of its theoretical merits but also in terms of its implications for practice (1981, 62). Whereas Dalla Costa's single-system theory prescribed the assimilation of feminist politics into the working-class movement and Hartmann's dual-systems theory was consistent with a political strategy in which separate groups made specific and contingent coalitions with one another, Young's unified-systems theory corresponded to a vision of a unified movement of oppressed groups. Although she insisted that she did not want to challenge Hartmann's defense of an autonomous women's movement, "[t]here are urgent practical reasons," Young argued, "for rejecting the notion that patriarchy and capitalism are separate systems entailing distinct political struggles" (ibid., 64). Nothing in the logic of dual-systems theory would encourage other components of the left to take up feminist concerns or incorporate feminist analyses or, by the same token, encourage white feminist groups to consider the concerns and analyses of women of color. Young suggests an alternative to Hartmann's political strategy, using the example of the feminist issue of reproductive rights to illustrate the ways in which the struggle against patriarchy must also be, at some level, a struggle against capitalism and racism (see ibid., 63). By this logic, an adequate movement for reproductive rights must be responsive to the potentially distinct priorities of differently configured groups—for example, middle-class white women, poor women, lesbians, and women of color. The unified-systems model, which encourages us to be attentive to the ways in which the different axes of oppression intersect with one another, also urges us to consider the ways in which our struggles against these conditions should be informed by one another.

Despite the compelling alternatives it offers to Hartmann's dual-systems theory, however, Young's political prescription and the unified-systems model in general have a problem that centers around the question of the precise nature of this "unity" that the theory proposes. Young's model suggests that to confront a system that is simultaneously capitalist and patriarchal, a political movement must be simultaneously socialist and feminist. Socialist feminist practice emerges as the singularly competent form of practice. Compared with Dalla Costa's assimilation and subordination of feminism within the working class, the logic of Young's analysis suggests a different type of unity of the oppressed. Practically speaking, if the system one confronts is a unified multiplicity, then presumably the movement that would challenge it must be similarly coherent. As Hartmann notes in a response to Young, the unified political struggle that Young defends discounts the many tensions and conflicts among these groups (1981b, 365–366), not to mention their specificity; the problem is, in other words, that the unity presupposed here seems to disregard the force of difference that the model had, in other places, confirmed. The possibility of multiple subjects is occluded by Young's particular conception of unity. Despite her interest in defending the role of an autonomous women's movement, Young does not leave an adequate space for autonomy in this model of a seamless, coherent, unified system of forces. I develop this point further when I consider some of the more general limitations of systems theory.

One of Young's most valuable contributions to the project of socialist feminism stems from her ability to rethink and rework the tradition of Marxist thought. Because "traditional marxian theory will continue to dominate feminism as long as feminism does not challenge the adequacy of the traditional theory of production relations itself" (1981, 49), Young argues that feminists must transform Marxist theory. According to Young, "we need a theory of relations of production and the social relations which derive from and reinforce those relations which takes gender relations and the situation of women as *core* elements. Instead of marrying marxism, feminism must take over marxism and transform it into such a theory" (ibid., 50).

Whereas Dalla Costa asked the question what feminism could do for Marxism, and Hartmann asked what Marxism could do for feminism, Young insists that the proper question is what each could do for the further development of the other. Rather than remaining content simply to add to or supplement Marxist theory, feminists must be willing to transform its methods and models. By these means, Young insists, we can construct a thoroughly feminist historical materialism (1980, 181).

The Possibilities and Limits of Systems Theories

There is much of value in this tradition of feminist systems theory. The efforts to expand the conception of production, the project of making connections between women's laboring practices and the larger socioeconomic structures within which they are situated, the attention to the economic dimensions of gender identities and relations and the gendered dimensions of economic identities and relations, and the increasingly creative appropriations of Marxist theory constitute just a few of their most important contributions to a variety of feminist projects. For my purposes, the line of development traced here culminates in Young's unified-systems model. As a system composed of multiple systemic forces, of mutually determining distinctions within a unity that together organize the production of subjectivity, the unified-systems model suggests the rudimentary outlines of a model that can map the workings of systemic forces like capitalism, patriarchy, white supremacy, and heterosexism while simultaneously enabling us to conceive the subject positions organized by these forces as complex pluralities.

Despite these accomplishments, however, the project of socialist feminist systems theory as it is conceived in these examples tends to rely on a functionalist model of power. In each case, we are presented with rather abstract and reified systems—whether single, dual, or unified—that are secured through a basically functionalist relationship with their constituent elements. Patriarchy and capitalism work together as partners to secure the smooth running of the system. As one participant and critic recalls the project,

> in that functionalist conception, "capitalism" and "patriarchy" were seen as interdependent and abstract systems, each with its own inexorable needs, together forming a seamless web of "capitalist patriarchy." We saw capitalism as functioning to reinforce and support patriarchy, and patriarchy functioning to reinforce and support capitalism, not as the result of historical contingency, but by necessity: the logic of capitalism demanded the patriarchal nuclear family and the free labor of the housewife. (Van Allen 1984, 82)

Although the systems theorists suggest certain lines of conflict and potential tensions in the relationship between capitalism and patriarchy, the emphasis in these accounts is on explaining the system's solidity and longevity.[9] In an exaggerated though nonetheless telling characterization of the logic that she associates with this early socialist feminist systems theory, Barbara Ehrenreich recalls that, according to some of these analyses, "[e]verything women did in the home was in the service of capital and indispensable to capital. When a mother kissed her children goodnight she was 'reproducing labor power'" (1984, 52).

Part of the problem is that these analyses tend to rely on a reductive causal analysis wherein a few independent variables (for example, capital and patriarchy) generate effects in entirely dependent variables (for example, the family and gender identity). Foucault warned us about these kind of reductive analyses that isolate causes from effects and posit a one-way flow of power from the top down.[10] The "system" is credited with a kind of monolithic force that seems to guarantee its ability to recover from potential challenges to its power. At least in some cases this is accomplished by attributing a certain level of intentionality to the systems. Hartmann's description of the relation between capital and patriarchy as a "partnership" seems to evoke just this sense of conscious collusion, a contract negotiation between two clever and farsighted conspirators.[11] Thus agency is effectively denied to oppressed subjects and transferred instead to a set of social structures.

But regardless of whether conscious control and intentionality is ascribed to the system, its apparent ability to recuperate contingencies effectively discounts the potential for rupture. Thus both patriarchy and capital are, in Hartmann's scheme, "surprisingly flexible and adaptable" (1981a, 27, 24); capital adjusts to the evolving needs of patriarchy (for example, by accepting the family wage), and patriarchy adjusts to the evolving needs of capital (insofar as it seems capable of surviving any potential—and, in Hartmann's estimation, unlikely—threat to its contemporary power base, the traditional family [ibid., 27]). The system thus appears to be total and closed.

How can we conceive the possibility of resistance and transformation? Where can we find the openings in this system? The problem is not just that these theorists do not focus enough on structural contradictions within the system, as if by these means the system itself could produce its own demise,[12] but that they do not attend to the role of active subjects. As Ehrenreich describes these systems theories, "[t]he world of capitalism plus patriarchy, endlessly abetting each other to form a closed system with just one seam, was a world without change, a world without a subject" (1984, 50). Again, this is, in part, a consequence of the fact that these examples of the project were designed to focus on the question of how certain structural forces are maintained over time rather than on the question of how subjective forces disrupt them. Nonetheless, when subjects are reduced like this to role players, there is little space in the analysis for agency and hence few resources with which to conceive possibilities for social change. The irony here, as Jean Bethke Elshtain has noted, is that "functionalists devoted to social equilibrium and Marxists or socialists devoted to social change have met on common theoretical terrain" (1984, 22).

Returning to Young's unified-systems theory, the version of systems theory that I found to be in many ways the most compelling, we can now see the limitations of the model more clearly. Although it is the most cogent model, one that acknowledges the complex connections among the various social formations and the simultaneity of oppressions experienced by those situated within, one could say that Young pays a price for this sophistication, simply because the most highly developed model is also that which most completely eliminates the possibility of rupture. Consider one of Young's typical formulations of her basic thesis that capitalism and patriarchy are integral to one another: "The specific forms of the oppression of women which exist under capitalism are essential to its nature" (1981, 61). The problem is that there is no room for slippage here, nothing that is in excess or potentially subversive of the determinist power and functionalist coherence of this unity of social forces. The system seems to preclude the process of history, or, if history does proceed, it moves according to a fixed and predetermined logic. In the absence of social subjects—that is, without the space for relatively autonomous active subjects—systems theories are unable to account adequately for change. While these theorists were all driven by the practical concerns of social movements, the force of these movements, their subjectivity, seems to be crushed under the weight of the determinations of the system. The creative capacities and subversive potential of feminist subjects tend to be deemphasized in these accounts, which tend to focus instead on the victimization of women.

Standpoint Theory and the Reinsertion of Subjectivity

The relationship between socialist feminist systems theory and feminist standpoint theory is marked by both continuity and rupture. Like Young's systems theory, standpoint theory—at least the examples of standpoint theory that I focus on here—begins with the role that the gender division of labor plays in Western capitalist societies and considers some of its consequences for women's lives.[13] But standpoint theories then take off in another direction. There are two fundamental differences between these socialist feminist projects that I want first to identify and then in the course of my investigation to develop further. First, whereas systems theories focus primarily on the system as a whole, standpoint theories shift the focus to the positions of subjects constituted by and constitutive of these systemic relations. It is the potential power of these subjects rather than just the effectiveness of the system that is the primary concern. Second, whereas systems theory is primarily concerned with how the system is maintained, the tradition of standpoint theory that I draw on here pays more attention to how it can be transformed. Taken together, these tendencies within standpoint theory can disrupt the propensity toward functionalist equilibrium that we found in systems theories.

Dorothy Smith provides a clear example of the first contribution of standpoint theory. Smith, it should be noted, is also critical of the functionalism that she sees pervading certain examples of Marxism. In a description that may also be apropos of socialist feminist systems theories, Smith laments the fate of subjects in many adaptations of Marx's work:

> As his theories have been developed, subjects have been seen as totally subdued to the driving historical dynamic of capitalist forces and relations. In the thinking of some notable contemporaries they have been wholly displaced, surviving on the ontological margins, inhabiting the fox-holes of functional positions, subjected to the massive on-rolling of structures lurching toward obscure destinies. (1987, 142)

Smith, by contrast, focuses on the active participation of subjects in the reproduction of their social relations. As Smith describes it, our social relations—for example, our gender or class relations—are not constructed by outside forces, but rather are constituted in and through our everyday practices: "Such relations exist only as active practices" (1987, 135). Thus, for instance, where systems theories treated gender identities as the artifacts of structural forces, standpoint theories insist that they are also the practical accomplishment of subjects situated within these structured spaces. The first remedy for functionalism is thus a more dialectical conception of the relationship between system and subject, one in which women are not just passive products of social forces but also active participants.

Hilary Rose adds to this insistence on the role of interactive subjects an appreciation of their potential to become antagonistic subjects. Rose is, like Smith, critical of the functionalist tendency within socialist feminism, but suggests that the problem with these theories is that they do not include along with their critique of the status quo a theory and vision of change, an affirmation of alternative possibilities (1986, 173). The remedy for functionalism involves not only the reinsertion of subjective agency but a recognition of the potential for these subjects to become agents of social change who are capable of disrupting the smooth workings of the system. Thus one of the distinctive traits of standpoint theory is that it focuses not only on the exploitative dimensions of the gender division of labor but also on the potentially positive dimensions of women's laboring practices, on the alternative ontologies and epistemologies that these practices may be able to sustain.

Here standpoint theory departs from the tradition of systems theory, which was typically less likely to recognize the distinct possibilities associated with the gender division of labor. Dalla Costa, for example, appears to exclude from her analysis the subversive potential of women's laboring practices. Capitalism alone is endowed with agency in her account; women are only its passive victims. As a result of this emphasis on the agency of the system rather than on the subjects who respond to the range of options available to them, Dalla Costa is unable to find anything of value—any potential alternatives—in women's domestic labor: "As it cuts off all her possibilities of creativity and of the development of her working activity, so it cuts off the expression of her sexual, psychological and emotional autonomy" (1972, 28–29). Hartmann, on the other hand, devotes some attention to the possibilities as well as the limitations of these practices. In a suggestive passage Hartmann explains that

> we think the sexual division of labor within capitalism has given women a practice in which we have learned to understand what human interdependence and needs are. While men have long struggled *against* capital, women know what to struggle *for*. As a general rule, men's position in patriarchy and capitalism prevents them from recognizing both human needs for nurturance, sharing, and growth, and the potential for meeting those needs in a non-hierarchical, nonpatriarchal society. (1981a, 32–33) [14]

However, rather than proceed to develop this insight, Hartmann, like most systems theorists, tends to treat women's labor as a force of constraint, a set of practices that merely reproduces gender hierarchies, whereas standpoint theorists are more interested in exploring the ways that women's laboring practices might also be enabling. The point of standpoint theory's different focus is to see women not merely as victims but also as potential agents. Standpoint theory as I delimit it here thus combines a critical project, that of identifying the exploitative character of women's labor and the social relations it sustains, with a project that affirms the ontological or epistemological possibilities, the seeds of the future, that can be located there as well.

From the point of view of this rendition of standpoint theory, with its focus on interaction and rupture, one shortcoming of socialist feminist systems theory is that, because of its focus on system maintenance, it is insufficiently attentive to the historical force and potentially creative role of subjectivity. As the tradition of feminist systems theory has pointed out, we need a conception of how subjects are constituted by social systems, but we also need to recognize how collective subjects are relatively autonomous from, and capable of acting to subvert, those same systems. These are different, overlapping projects: one takes the point of view of structures and their equilibrium, and the other focuses on collective subjects situated within and against the system. Conceiving this dialectical relationship between system and subject is, however, no simple task. How, for example, can we understand the relationship between system and subject in such a way as to register the differences between them—

their conflicts, disjunctures, and contradictions, their *dysfunction*—without relying on a humanist conception of the subject to account for these differences? How might we rethink the "unity" of the unified multiplicity we recovered from Young's systems theory in such a way as to render it open to the potentially subversive force of multiple subjects?

In the next section I turn to the nonfeminist Marxist tradition and consider how I can further the project of conceiving a totality of social forces that is open to the possibility of antagonistic subjectivity. Many of these Marxist theorists have also struggled with this relationship between system and subject, and there is much to learn from their successes and their failures. In the course of this inquiry I add to the complexity and depth of my problematic. These explorations will be confined to the three theorists whose work, I believe, carries the most relevance for this project: Georg Lukács, Louis Althusser, and Antonio Negri. Rather than present exhaustive studies of these thinkers, I offer a highly selective discussion of their extensive theoretical projects. In each case I consider how the theorist can help us rethink, first, the nature of the system and, second, the place of subjects situated within and potentially against this system. This also provides opportunities to flesh out the characterization of standpoint theory outlined above and to continue the evaluation of its problems and possibilities. More specifically, these analyses will help to locate what is valuable in standpoint theory, highlight what is problematic, and in some cases provide resources with which to address those concerns.

Georg Lukács: The Total Subject

Given my interest in developing a dialectical conception of subject and totality, the work of Georg Lukács is an obvious place to begin. In his major work, a collection of essays entitled *History and Class Consciousness*, Lukács asserts the importance of the concept of totality within Marxism and insists on the role of subjectivity within the social totality. In these essays, Lukács attempts to rescue Marxism from the reductive analyses and political fatalism brought to prominence by a resurgence of the kind of mechanical and functionalist Marxism usually associated with the Second International (see Arato and Breines 1979, 173). Lukács returns to Hegel to retrieve a more dialectical conception of the relationship between system and subjectivity, to reclaim the historical force of human agency. In Hegel's dialectical method Lukács finds an antidote to determinist brands of Marxism. To reassert the role of subjective forces in history, he argues, we must replace static and determinist models with analyses that can better account for the complex interactions between subject and object; "the *totality*," Lukács insists, "is the territory of the dialectic" (1972, 140). Although, as we will see, this infamous "return to Hegel," this selective reappropriation of Hegelian dialectics provides the inspiration for some of the most productive dimensions of Lukács's project, it is also implicated in some of its most notable failures.

Lukács's dialectical conception of totality stands opposed to reified forms of thought, both bourgeois and Marxist, that are unable to conceive society and history as processes. Included in this list of reified forms of thinking are those that conceive the parts as existing within a purely functional relationship to the social whole. (As I have argued, feminist systems theories are susceptible to this critique.) The problem with these formal and abstract systems models is that they imagine that every element exists in a calculable, predictable, and supportive relation to the "laws" that govern the internal dynamics of the system. Also included under the heading of reified forms of thinking are those modes of inquiry that fetishize the parts at the expense of any credible sense of the whole. According to Lukács, dominant forms of thinking will intersect with dominant forms of social organization and practice, with the consequence that in capitalist social formations, conceptual practices that seek to isolate, separate, and individuate serve as the prevailing methodological standard. So-called "facts" are the stock in trade of these ahistorical and undialectical approaches to social inquiry. In neither example, whether it is a matter of reifying the whole or fetishizing the parts, do we find a compelling conception of the role of the subjective, a sense of process or insight into the dynamics of social change. Humans are either completely subsumed by these objective forces or presumed to be somehow exempt from their determinative power. Consequently, these forms of thinking pose as our only alternatives

either complete social determinism or ethical utopianism: "The reified consciousness must also remain hopelessly trapped in the two
extremes of crude empiricism and abstract utopianism. In the one
case, consciousness becomes either a completely passive observer
moving in obedience to laws which it can never control. In the other
it regards itself as a power which is able of its own—subjective—vo-
lition to master the essentially meaningless motion of objects"
(1971, 77). In practical terms one is left with either political fatalism
or humanist voluntarism, both of which, he insists, support the status quo.

The category of totality is the key to an alternative way of conceiving reality that is not beholden to the fetishism of static "facts"
or the predictable force of social "laws." A totality is not the mere
aggregate of its parts; it implies rather an entirely different conception of reality. The category of totality signifies the whole of society
seen as a process. Lukács's insistence upon the distinction between
the notion of sum, on the one hand, and whole or totality, on the
other, is indicative of the difference he wants to underscore (ibid., 9,
25n20); whereas a sum suggests a result that stands apart from the
internal relations among the parts, a whole or totality implies a
purely immanent context in which the internal relations among the
parts are both constituted and constituting. Beginning with Marx's
claim that the "[t]he relations of production of every society form a
whole" as his methodological point of departure, Lukács insists on
the importance of developing dialectical models of the totality of social relations that can help us to make sense of and participate in its
changing internal relations (1971, 9). As Lukács explains it, "the objective forms of all social phenomena change constantly in the
course of their ceaseless dialectical interactions with each other. The
intelligibility of objects develops in proportion as we grasp their
function in the totality to which they belong. This is why only the
dialectical conception of totality can enable us to understand *reality
as a social process*" (ibid., 13).

The fundamental contribution of Lukács's dialectical perspective
is its insistence that "a one-sided and rigid causality must be replaced by interaction" (ibid., 3). Citing one of the better known pas-
sages from Marx, a passage that is also repeated in the feminist
standpoint literature, Lukács reminds us that "[a] cotton-spinning

jenny is a machine for spinning cotton. Only in certain circumstances does it become capital. Torn from these circumstances it is
no more capital than gold is money or sugar the price of sugar"
(quoted in ibid., 13). Thus, as Lukács reminds us, "[t]he interaction
we have in mind must be more than the interaction of *otherwise unchanging objects"* (ibid., 13). This interaction includes not just objects but subjects as well. This insight provides the grounds for
Lukács' critique of humanism: the problem with humanism is that it
refuses to make man "dialectical" (ibid., 187); that is, both thoroughly constituted by and constitutive of social relations. As Lukács
understands it, humanism simply places humanity in transcendent
space, a space outside history and beyond the reach of social forces,
once reserved for God; it exempts subjectivity from this process of
social constitution. Humanity too, Lukács wants us to understand,
is a process.

Subjectivity is a force of dereification, an element that dethrones
all forms of objectivism and absolutism. As we have seen, it transforms facts into processes; in Lukács's account *processes* replace
facts as the fundamental unit of social analysis (ibid., 184).[15] In a similar move, the *tendency* is advanced as the subjective equivalent of
and alternative to the *law.* In contrast to laws of history, historical
tendencies do not unfold automatically and necessarily according to
some rational plan or transcendental telos, rather they are historical
potentials that may be made into actualities through practice (see
ibid., 204). Tendencies, in contrast to the closed and determinative
power of laws, are open to the unpredictability and contingency in-
troduced by the subjective (see 1972, 141). Lukács's repeated insistence on the constitutive force of subjectivity challenges the kind of
reified systematicity that one can find in some examples of feminist
systems theory: rather than merely a force to which we are subjected, a social system is also the product of our practices.

By establishing connections among the various aspects and realms
of the social totality, Lukács clearly does not wish to suggest that
they be reduced to a kind of identity:

> We repeat: the category of totality does not reduce its various ele-
> ments to an undifferentiated uniformity, to identity. The apparent
> independence and autonomy which they possess in the capitalist
> system of production is an illusion only in so far as they are in-

volved in a dynamic dialectical relationship with one another and can be thought of as the dynamic dialectical aspects of an equally dynamic and dialectical whole. (1971, 12–13)

Given the contradictions and antagonisms that the totality of social relations embodies, the connections among forces are not predictable, nor are they obvious or immediate; any kind of adequate understanding of these connections requires an ongoing collective effort and a complex process of mediation (ibid., 155).

Fredric Jameson's reading of Lukács locates some of the most positive and productive dimensions of Lukács's project. Jameson argues that Lukács's notion of totality should be understood not as a normative ideal but rather as a *methodological aspiration*. There are two parts to this proposition: the focus on method and the significance of the term aspiration. First, Jameson contests the popular understanding of Lukács that identifies in his concept of totality a utopian vision of a unified society cured of all conflicts, contradictions, and even difference itself; a kind of totalitarian vision in which all apparent differences are resolved into some ultimate, essential identity; a vision that conflates some vaguely Hegelian concept of Absolute Spirit with a vaguely Marxist conception of communism (see 1981, 50–51). Rather than the expression of a longing for unity, perhaps in the form of a Hegelian synthesis ordered by the state, the Lukácsian project of totality is, by this reading, the product of a theoretical commitment to internal relations and dynamic processes. Lukács, Jameson argues, presents the concept of totality as a methodological imperative to situate and contextualize, to locate the links between our more immediate encounters with specific phenomena and the complex social and historical forces that shape them (see 1988a, 55).

Jameson's second contribution to my reading of Lukács is his insistence upon the significance of Lukács' phrase, the *aspiration* to totality (see, for example, 1988a, 60). By emphasizing the term "aspiration," Jameson suggests a more modest rendition of Lukácsian epistemology. Rather than expect to know the totality in all its plenitude, we should aspire to grasp the complexity of systemic social relations, even though, as the term suggests, reality will always be in excess of these attempts to represent it (see Jameson 1981, 55). Totality here functions as an interpretive horizon. Although it amounts to more of an innovation than a simple clarification—since Lukács himself did not for the most part adhere to this more modest conception of the epistemological capacities of the proletarian standpoint—Jameson's formulation presents what is for my purposes a very useful reworking of Lukács. Described as an aspiration to totality rather than something that can be presupposed or achieved, the incompleteness of our representations of this dynamic totality, representations that are continually in flux and necessarily provisional, is more clearly acknowledged. Of course, to do justice to this particular question of representation, I would need to embark on a much more sustained and systematic exploration of a number of difficult epistemological controversies. While these epistemological debates and concerns are beyond the scope of my project, we can nonetheless find here a valuable corrective to the presumption—one that many have discovered within the tradition of socialist feminist systems theories—that the full complexity of the totality of social forces can be represented adequately. For my purposes, then, Jameson's emphasis on the phrase "aspiration to totality" can be used as a reminder that the project of mapping the totality must be conceived as an open-ended process rather than as a concretely realized or realizable goal.

As Jameson also notes, echoes of this dimension of Lukács's project can be found in some of the most important and productive methodological commitments of feminist standpoint theory (1988a, 66–71; see also Shaw 1990). For example, this emphasis on process, interaction, and change is an prominent aspect of Hartsock's work. Hartsock, who draws explicitly on Lukács's Marxism, insists that the social whole should be conceived as a complex set of interrelated processes, "structures of relations in process—a reality constantly in evolution" (1981, 37). Social forms, events, and meanings change constantly in the process of their interaction with the totality of social relations. To understand the specific phenomena that have an immediate effect on our lives, they must be seen in the context of these larger social forces.[16] "For example," Hartsock explains, "in order to understand increased wage work by women in the United States, we need to understand the relation of this work to the needs of capitalism. But we must also look at the conditions of work and the kind of work prescribed for women by patriarchy and white supremacy as *different* aspects of the same social system" (1981, 37–38). This Lukácsian/Marxist conception of reality as a social process is also consistent with Smith's project. Smith describes her method as one that attempts to account for the complex relationship between the everyday world and the social relations of contemporary capitalism, to understand "[t]he determination of our worlds by relations and processes that do not appear fully in them" (1987, 99). Social entities, events, and meanings are ongoing social processes that are linked with other social processes; they must be understood in the context of a dynamic interactive system of relations.

But as I have already noted, standpoint theory also wants to break with those accounts of the system of social forces that would deny the constitutive force and potentially antagonistic role of subjectivity. The point is to develop theoretical accounts of the social world that do not suppress the existence and vitality of the subjects who bring these relations into being. Hence, in a move that parallels Lukács's efforts, these standpoint theorists refocus the socialist feminist effort to understand the relationships among the construction of gender, the oppression of women, and patterns of capitalist development to the point of view of subjects who reproduce these relationships. Thus Smith explains that, like Marx, she begins "with the activities of actual individuals whose activity produces the social relations that they live" (1987, 90). As in Lukács's Marxism, social reality is conceived as a process that is reproduced and potentially subverted in and through the practices of active social subjects. These potentially subversive subjects, however, do not stand outside the process of social constitution; to recall Lukács's formulation, "the interaction we have in mind must be more than the interaction of otherwise unchanging objects." Through our practices we continually change and are continually changed by the system of social forces; subjectivity is an ongoing social process. Consequently, our fate as subjects is linked to the structures that through our practices we reproduce: "We can transform ourselves only by simultaneously struggling to transform the social relations that define us: self-changing and changed social institutions are simply two aspects of the same process" (Hartsock 1981, 37). This basic methodological commitment to reality as a social process signals one of the most valuable dimensions of Lukács's theory of totality, an impulse that I too affirm as one of the most productive aspects of feminist standpoint theory.

However, despite these valuable methodological elements of Lukács's reading of Marx, there are other aspects of the project that limit its ability to recognize multiple subjectivities. These weaknesses of Lukács's contribution to my understanding of totality and subjectivity emerge most clearly in his conception of the proletariat as the "identical subject-object of history." To understand this concept of the identical subject-object of history we must begin with Lukács's account of the development of a revolutionary proletarian subject, which hinges on the development of class consciousness. Lukács begins with the simple claim that, as social beings, we are both the subjects and the objects of history; we are both the producers and the products of a totality of social forces. However, our consciousness of ourselves as social beings and of reality as the artifact of our practices is undermined by the forces of reification under capitalism: "Man finds himself confronted by purely natural relations or social forms mystified into natural relations. They appear to be fixed, complete and immutable entities which can be manipulated and even comprehended, but never overthrown" (1971, 19). Our consciousness of the origins of social forces in human practices can only be achieved through constant struggle. But this revolutionary consciousness is the achievement not of an individual but of a class: "For when the individual confronts objective reality he is faced by a complex of ready-made and unalterable objects which allow him only the subjective responses of recognition or rejection. Only the class can relate to the whole of reality in a practical revolutionary way" (ibid., 193). Whereas the collectivity has the potential to grasp the social genesis and implications of its labor, for the individual, as Lukács explains it, "reification and hence determinism" are inevitable (ibid., 193). Only a collective is capable of understanding and changing reality in a systemic way; social transformation is necessarily a group project, a cooperative undertaking. This affirmation of the power of collective subjects, in this case a proletarian subject, is, I believe, one of the most valuable dimensions of the Marxist tradition and one that I build on in my construction of feminist subjects.[17]

The problem with Lukács's account is his claim that the standpoint of the proletariat is privileged because the proletariat is the identical subject-object of history. Once he conceives the proletariat as the identical subject-object of history, the proletariat is no longer a collective, it is a "totality." The proletariat in this account is not just, like any class, the subject and object, maker and product of history. The proletariat is distinguished by its unique historical status and mission: it alone can represent all subjects and objects. "The self-understanding of the proletariat is therefore simultaneously the objective understanding of the nature of society. When the proletariat furthers its own class-aims it simultaneously achieves the conscious realisation of the—objective—aims of society" (ibid., 149). As a totality, the proletariat does not express the collective will of the class but the "general will" of humanity. When Lukács describes the proletariat as a totality, he does not mean that it is all of us, but rather that its will, its consciousness, its singular historical mission is that of all of us,[18] a collective individual cast in the role of "Subject of History." Here Lukács introduces a transcendental element that negates the immanence, materiality, and plurality of the collective; this proletariat-as-totality is a mystification of the category of class. Although, as I noted earlier, Lukács is explicitly critical of humanism, humanism seem to be at work in this conception of proletarian subjectivity. That is, Lukács appears to attribute to the class what he denied the individual: the proletariat may be a social construction rather than a pre-existing will, yet it possesses the same kind of unity, force, and authority as the transcendental forces that his own materialism should preclude.[19]

As was the case in the exploration of feminist systems theories, where the theory of the political subject or subjects they propose often served to clarify the limits of the framework itself, Lukács's conception of proletarian subjectivity suggests certain weaknesses with his model of totality. Despite some of the other tendencies and commitments Lukács has presented, the model of social forces presumed within this account of the proletarian subject is, to use his own phrase, highly unified (ibid., 70). Lukács thus contradicts his own insistence, in other sections and in other texts, on the irreducible complexity of the totality of social forces. Consider the following description of a conception of totality that defies the kind of unity he presumes when he presents the proletariat as the identical subject-object of history:

> The materialist-dialectical conception of totality means first of all the concrete unity of interacting contradictions . . . ; *secondly* the

systematic relativity of all totality both *upwards* and *downwards* (which means that all totality is made of totalities *subordinated* to it, and also that the totality in question is, at the same time, *overdetermined* by totalities of a higher complexity . . .) and *thirdly*, the *historical relativity* of all totality, namely that the totality-character of all totality is changing, disintegrating, confined to a determinate, concrete historical period (quoted in Mészáros 1970, 66).

This thoroughly immanent and highly complex conception of totality (taken not from *History and Class Consciousness* but from a later text, written in a very different historical context) is, unfortunately, not that which underpins the concept of the identical subject-object of history. This ideal of a single, unified subject of history is simply inconsistent with such a complex web of social and historical forces. One must presume a highly unified social formation in order to imagine that the "general will" could be concentrated within the will of one group that could then represent the rest.

Although feminist standpoint theories do not posit women as the identical subject-object of history, there are, I would argue, residues of the same formula in some versions of this feminist project. In particular, the affirmation in some of the original feminist standpoint theories of a single feminist standpoint, "the" feminist standpoint, resonates with Lukács's idea of the subject-as-totality. That is, the notion of a single feminist standpoint suggests that it in effect contains within itself the "general will" of all feminists, or perhaps even the unrecognized interest of all women. Conceived in these terms, unity takes precedence over multiplicity and the project is conceived in terms of the construction of a single feminist standpoint rather than multiple, overlapping standpoints.[20] The concept of a single feminist standpoint conflates what are, from my perspective, two contradictory conceptions of the subject, both of which we found in Lukács: a subject as group or collectivity and a subject as unity modeled after the figure of the individual. Before I can build on the former notion of a collective subject, I must first eliminate all traces of the latter formulation of the total subject. This requires an alternative conception of the totality of social forces, one that can recognize the presence of a multiplicity of subject positions from which a multitude of feminist subjects could emerge.

Lukács presents his project as an attempt to separate out and release that which is still living in Hegel (1971, xlv). What he found
and tried to reclaim was a dialectical perspective, one that restores to
Marxism a conception of reality as a process constituted through the
interaction between collective subjects and the structural and historical terms of their social existence. Although this is, I would argue,
part of the remedy for those forms of thinking that would exclude
the constitutive force of subjectivity, such as the various forms of
positivism, determinism, and functionalism, Lukács unfortunately
did not restrict his return to Hegel to this limited conception of dialectics. As his problematic analysis of the potential role of the proletarian subject suggests, he was not as selective in his reappropriation of Hegel as we might wish. In addition to—and even in
contradiction to—that more minimal conception of dialectics that
focuses on mutually constitutive interactions among social forces,
Lukács also recovers certain dimensions of the Hegelian Dialectic,
that grand narrative of history with its closed, predetermined dynamic and its transcendental subject. In this case the role is played
by the proletariat, cast as the identical subject-object of history,
which Lukács himself later characterized as an "attempt to out-
Hegel Hegel" and an "edifice boldly erected above every possible reality" (ibid., xxiii). Thus, in certain crucial moments, Lukács compromises the most valuable dimensions of his project. Despite other
promising tendencies in his work, tendencies that Jameson amplifies
and standpoint theory replicates, Lukács nonetheless falls into the
trap of rendering Marx's proletarian subject into something akin to
Hegel's absolute spirit.

Louis Althusser: Processes without Subjects

Althusser accuses Lukács of a "guilty Hegelianism" (1990, 114n29).
Although Althusser's reduction of Lukács's work to a rather self-
serving image of Hegelian Marxism is in many respects unfair, certain problems with Lukács's account of proletarian subjectivity
could be attributed to too close an allegiance to Hegelian logic. Althusser proposes a more radical break from Hegel than that allowed
by the materialist "inversion" thesis; that is, the traditional claim
that Marx simply stands Hegel's idealist dialectic on its feet. While

driving the "phantom" of Hegel back into the night (ibid., 116), Althusser makes two important contributions to my project of developing a conception of the social totality that is open to the force of multiple antagonistic subjectivities. First, Althusser provides conceptual resources with which to rethink the nature of the unity of social forces, to render it consistent with the forces of multiplicity, contingency, and difference. Althusser's efforts to recover a non-determinist Marxism can build on what I identified as the more productive dimensions of Lukács's work by enabling us to perceive both the complexity and the openness of the social totality. Second, Althusser presents a more thorough antihumanism that can remedy certain fundamental weaknesses of Lukács's account.

Of Althusser's important conceptual innovations, I want to single out for consideration a closely related pair of constructs that are central to Althusser's project of combating determinism: the concepts of overdetermination and relative autonomy. Together they yield a richer and more complex account of the dynamics of social forces within which feminist standpoints can be situated.

Althusser presents his model of a structural totality as an alternative to what he describes as the Hegelian totality.[21] Whereas the Hegelian model, which Althusser labels an expressive totality, presupposes a simple unity of forces such that every permutation and development can be reduced to an original, essential dynamic or contradiction, Althusser proposes that we view the Marxist model as a structural totality that cannot be explained by reference to an original essence, a final goal or a unity of forces organized around a single contradiction; plurality and complexity are affirmed in what he describes as "*the ever-pre-givenness of a structured complex unity*" (ibid., 199). Within this complex unity or structural totality, social phenomena are overdetermined by a complex configuration of economic, political, and ideological forces. Every social phenomenon is the product of multiple determinants, each of which has its own specific effectivity. In the context of this analysis, then, one could say that gender identity, to take one example, determines and is determined by a multiplicity of social processes, including the gender and racial divisions of labor, ideologies of racial identity, heterosexual romance and femininity, and the institutions of marriage and "The Family," each of which has its own distinct and variable impact.

Gender identity is, thus, not determined but overdetermined: it is the unstable effect of multiple and potentially inconsistent forces of determination which are themselves overdetermined.

There are four possible implications of Althusser's notion of over-determination that can benefit my project. First, the logic of this account, if not the content of it, affirms the possibility of a multiplicity of subject positions. Part of what Althusser is contesting with this notion of overdetermination is the traditional Marxist conception (derived, Althusser insists, not from Marx so much as from Hegel) of a single, general contradiction between productive forces and the relations of production, embodied in the struggle between two classes. There are in fact multiple contradictions, multiple lines of conflict, and presumably multiple subject positions. To situate this once again in the context of my feminist problematic, the complex set of forces that overdetermine gender identity could presumably produce many different variations depending on how they interact with, for example, the forces that produce class and race identities. A multiplicity of causes makes possible a multiplicity of effects. While Althusser himself did not develop this potential implication of the logic of overdetermination, presuming instead that this accumulation of contradictions and their various modes of embodiment would fuse, as they had in the past, into a "ruptural unity" (see ibid., 99), the concept can be used to raise the possibility.

A second implication of the concept of overdetermination relevant to my project has to do with the way that revolutionary processes are conceived. Given the complexity of a social formation, the plurality of contradictions, and the unevenness of their development, we must think about social transformation as a more multifarious and drawn-out affair; we must, in other words, reject the Hegelian logic of "supersession" (ibid., 116; see also Freedman 1990, 321). To push once again Althusser's conclusions somewhat beyond the limits of his own formulation, a social formation is not a unity to be transformed all at once in its entirety, but a decentered totality of practices with multiple fault lines and possibilities for destabilization. To those who rightly disparage readings of the social totality that deny the effectivity of local movements and partial challenges (see, for example, Gibson-Graham 1993), this conception acknowledges the presence of multiple sites of contestation and the micropolitics of resistance while affirming the politics of coalition as the most effective, though of course not always the most feasible, strategy.

A third and closely related benefit of the idea of overdetermination is that it allows for the systematicity of social forces without precluding the force of contingency. The outcomes of the interaction among these multiple and ever-changing causes cannot be predetermined. As Althusser conceives it, history is a process without a goal, a dynamic without a telos; there is nothing prior to or outside of the complex totality of social forces. This refusal of simple determinism and the affirmation of complexity serves to open up the system, to render it to some degree unpredictable.

Finally, Stephen Resnick and Richard Wolff identify an important epistemological implication of the concept of overdetermination. Given the complexity of the processes of social determination that the concept of overdetermination is designed to register, how we can possibly hope to develop adequate explanations of social phenomena? "The answer to this problem," they argue, "lies in the recognition that all explanations are inherently and unavoidably incomplete. All theories of society—forms of explanation—are partial; each takes up only some of the factors influencing the object of its theorizing. With those factors it fashions an explanation, a necessarily partial explanation reflecting the particular subset of overdetermining factors that it favors" (1993, 65).

Again, I do not want to depart on a long detour into this epistemological terrain. What I do want to note, however, is that this formulation effectively affirms and expands on a point gleaned from Jameson's discussion of the significance of the term "aspiration" in Lukács's understanding of totality—namely, that the attempt to grasp this totality is an ongoing and always incomplete project. The concept of overdetermination introduces more complexity into conceptions of the social totality and corresponding models of subjectivity and forces us to recognize the necessarily partial and provisional status of our theoretical enterprises.

Althusser's concept of relative autonomy is closely related to overdetermination; primarily, it is part of his attempt to develop an alternative to reductive explanations of the relationship between structure and superstructure. In contrast to those formulas that reduce political and cultural phenomena to the merely dependent effects of economic forces, Althusser insists that structure (productive forces and relations of production) and superstructure (the state, law, politics, and ideology) be conceived as distinct and relatively autonomous forces that are mutually conditioning. "The superstructure is not the pure phenomenon of the structure, it is also its condition of existence" (1990, 205). Superstructural forces have their own effectivity, their own capacity to elicit palpable effects that, while dependent on their changing articulation within the whole, cannot be reduced to mere epiphenomena of the economy. Thus, for example, the state cannot be understood as merely the executive committee of the bourgeoisie; state power cannot be reduced to a simple expression of economic power. The noneconomic forces are relatively autonomous from and reciprocally related to the economic forces in society.

Althusser's explorations of structure and superstructure provide an opportunity to think about how to draw these categories and how to think about their relationship. These questions are obviously important for anyone engaged with Marxist inquiry, but are particularly relevant to socialist feminists who understand patriarchy as a simultaneously economic, political, and cultural phenomenon. As Hartmann explains it, "what the attempt to analyze patriarchy fully has brought about is a questioning both of the marxist view of what is material and of the dominance of the 'material base' over the 'ideological superstructure' in marxist theory generally" (1981b, 371). Althusser's theory of ideology complicates formulations of these categories even further by refusing to present the distinction in terms of a division between the material and the ideal, or between what we do and what we think. Ideology, this imaginary relation of individuals to their real conditions of existence, is a material force; ideas, derived from cultural and political institutions and inscribed in our practices, are constituted by and constitutive of "material" existence (see Althusser 1971, 169).

Rosemary Hennessy presents an instructive adaptation of this insight in her reworking of standpoint theory, arguing that "[s]uch an understanding of the materiality of ideology reformulates the empiricist notion of materiality based in an objective reality outside discourse by including the discursive within the materiality out of which the social is produced" (1993, 75). Althusser insists that noth-

ing lies outside ideology; as part of the process by which we make reality meaningful, ideology is an integral part of any social formation.
As Hennessy reminds us, "[t]his means that 'reality,' whether in the
form of 'women's lives' or the feminist standpoint, is always social"
(ibid., 75).

Thus the distinction between structure and superstructure should
not be conceived as a division between the "material" and the
"ideal," between "reality" and "language," or between "experience"
and "meaning." Labor, for example, cannot be conceived as something we do that can be separated from how we understand and value
that activity, how we make that activity meaningful. Rather than attempt to distinguish between the material and the ideal, Althusser
conceives this as a distinction between different kinds of practice:
economic practices, on the one hand, and political and ideological
practices, on the other.

The question then becomes how to understand the relationship
between these modes of practice. Again, Althusser argues that structural and superstructural practices are mutually determining but relatively autonomous. Here we find some agreement with socialist
feminists who also point to the reciprocal relationship between
structure and superstructure. Indeed, few feminists would deny the
constitutive force of cultural practices or the mutually determining
relationship between superstructural modes of practice (ideologies of
femininity, for example) and economic relations (such as the gender
division of labor). Thus Hartsock credits feminism for calling attention to the forces of cultural domination and insists that ideological
and political forces are in some sense a part of the process of production (1979, 70–71). The real question here is what if any priority to
attribute to these mutually conditioning practices.[22] This is, as we
will see, one of the more difficult problems Althusser faces, and his
response is not completely satisfying.

Althusser does not want to suggest that the totality of multiple determining forces is governed by a pluralist logic, that each is effectively equivalent to every other. Instead, the social totality is a
"structure in dominance" in which the mode of production plays a
privileged role: the economy, as Althusser describes it, is determinant, but only "in the last instance." This does not contradict his opposition to the logic of economic determinism, Althusser insists, be-

cause as he explains it the last instance never comes (see 1990, 111–113). How can we interpret this simultaneous affirmation and negation of the classic Marxist assertion of the primacy of economic forces? As his collaborator Étienne Balibar explains it, in the capitalist mode of production the special force of the economy has to do with its role as arbitrator: "*the economy is determinant in that it determines which of the instances of the social structure occupies the determinant place*" (Althusser and Balibar 1979, 224). The economy plays an indirectly rather than a directly determining role (see Freedman 1990, 318); it sets certain limits on the development of a particular social formation.

At the same time, Althusser wants to insist that while economic forces are primary in this sense, they can never be isolated from noneconomic forces: "in History, these instances, the superstructures, etc.—are never seen to step respectfully aside when their work is done or, when the Time comes, as his pure phenomena, to scatter before His Majesty the Economy as he strides along the royal road of the Dialectic" (1990, 113). There is never some original or final moment when economic forces act alone in some pure form; there is only the "given-ever-pre-givenness" of an existing complex, structured unity (ibid., 208).

Given the way he sets up the problem, Althusser finds himself trapped between what he sees as two untenable positions on the question of priority: either he affirms the pluralist position that, for example, economic and cultural forces are always equally (if differently) effective, or he affirms a form of economic determinism. To avoid the pluralist model, Althusser instead evokes, in very tentative and ambiguous terms, a form of economism. There are, however, other ways to work through these propositions, to move beyond or at least displace this impasse, that affirm neither the pluralism that the notion of a structure in dominance sought to correct nor the residual determinism that the rather enigmatic last instance formula (not to mention his insistence on the priority of class struggle) reinvokes.

In a particularly useful formulation, Jameson presents the question of priority as a problematic. That is, Marxism is characterized "not by specific positions (whether of a political, economic or philosophical type), but rather by the allegiance to a specific complex of problems, whose formulations are always in movement and in historic rearrangement and restructuration, along with the object of study (capitalism itself)." By this reading, then, the concepts of structure and superstructure designate a problem rather than a solution, an open series of questions rather than a predetermined answer (Jameson 1993, 175). As one part of the Marxist problematic, the distinction between structure and superstructure can be formulated "as the imperative to find relationships between culture and consciousness on the one hand and the impersonal socio-economic processes on the other" (ibid., 180). What is left is not a problem to be resolved and a formula to invoke, but a project to be investigated and a question to pose. The categories of structure and superstructure are retained but there is no presumption that the relative effectivity of economic and cultural practices can be explained according to some predetermined law.

Smith provides an instructive example that can help to make this problematic of structure and superstructure more concrete. In an inquiry that exemplifies many of the strengths of her basic project—that is, the investigation into how our everyday practices both organize and are organized by larger social processes, an investigation in which the active role of subjects is always foregrounded—Smith examines the complex interrelationships among the fashion industry, the textually mediated discourse(s) of femininity, and women's practices. It is a rich analysis that refuses to give priority to any one complex of forces. The discourses of femininity are grounded in but not determined by economic relations and the everyday practices of women are both constitutive of and constituted by these cultural texts (see 1990, 204). In Smith's formulation,

> Rather than an image of superstructure balanced over the layers of relations of production rather like the frosting on a cake, the concept of a discourse of femininity, as developed here, envisages a web or a cats-cradle of texts, stringing together and coordinating the multiple local and particular sites of the everyday/everynight worlds of women and men with the market processes of the fashion, cosmetic, garment, and publishing industries. (ibid., 167)

This metaphor of a web is perhaps more appropriate to the notion of the problematic than the classic metaphor of the building (or, as

Smith prefers, the cake), which is, as Althusser notes, designed to represent the determination in the last instance by the economic base (1971, 135).

Althusser's first contribution to this revised feminist standpoint theory can thus be summarized as a more complex account of the internal dynamics of a totality. By this account, the social totality can be conceived as a set of mutually determining and relatively autonomous systems of practice, each of which is overdetermined. It is a system that contains multiple contradictions and multiple points of contestation. With these concepts, one can continue to develop the complexity of interactions that was the centerpiece of the feminist unified-systems model, while also loosening or decentering the unity of forces it presented. One can rethink the nature of this unity, this totality, including within its purview the force of contingency, difference, and (relative) autonomy without resorting to a model of separate spheres of influence. The result is a conception of the totality of social forces that is more open and porous than we have yet encountered.

Althusser's second contribution to my project is his insistence on an antihumanist reading of Marx. The critique of humanism, a centerpiece of the Nietzschean and Foucaultian problematics discussed earlier, can lead to development of a more rigorously immanent model of the social totality. However, although this provides a corrective to the residual humanism that can be found in some forms of Marxism and certain examples of standpoint theory, Althusser's alternative, his notion of a process without a subject, is, as we will see, an ultimately unsatisfactory substitute for Lukács's identical subject-object of history.

Perhaps more than any other Marxist, Althusser has identified Marx's antihumanism as one of his most important contributions to contemporary theories and practices. Unfortunately, this antihumanist tendency has not been consistently promoted within the Marxist tradition. According to Althusser, humanism is not only inconsistent with the strictly immanent focus of Marxist theory, but also obstructs the most productive possibilities of Marxist practice. There are two forms of humanism that have played important roles in certain Marxist discourses. First, we can find a classic form of the doctrine wherein the subject is conceived as a self-constituting, essential subject that precedes the social world of which it is a part. For example, Marxist analyses that center around the problem of alienation often presume this conception of a subject prior to the social world. In this genre of Marxist humanism, the critique of capitalism revolves around the assertion that it alienates us from our essence as humans, that it makes us into something we are not; communism is affirmed by contrast as that which would reunite us with this fundamental attribute, this creative essence. There is, in other words, a transcendental moment—an essence from which we are alienated and to which we should be restored—that grounds both the critical analysis and the utopian project of this variation of Marxism.

However, this is not the only form in which humanism, this fetishism of "man" (Althusser 1976, 51), has been preserved in the Marxist tradition. In addition to the transcendental subject, there is what he describes as a historicist version of the doctrine, according to which human subjects—those who make history—are also always already its products (see Althusser and Balibar 1979, 139–140). What this historicist humanism shares with the nonhistoricist version that we found ensconced within some versions of the theory of alienation is that they both begin with humans (as active, world-creating subjects) rather than with an existing set of social structures. Humanity is placed in the role of cause rather than effect of an existing social formation.[23] Lukács provides us with a clear example of this formulation. The identical subject-object is a humanist subject not because it is pregiven—Lukács is insistent upon the subject's immanence in history—but because he attributes to this historical subject, the proletariat, a place in the analysis otherwise reserved for a transcendental subject, a role in history that is beyond the scope of any historical collective. This subject of history plays the part of a "human god," regardless of whether that subject is supposed to be transcendental or historical in origin.[24]

The affirmation that "Man" is the active force that makes history—which was in many ways the heart of Lukács' project—is, by Althusser's estimation, highly problematic. We should recall, Althusser argues, that the claim that humans make history was a rallying cry of the revolutionary bourgeoisie against the idea, a centerpiece of feudal ideology, that God is the author of history (1976, 46n9). But this claim, which may have been revolutionary at one time, today only affirms what has become a cornerstone of bourgeois culture. Once again, paralleling humanism in its classic form, the human subject is cast in the role of creator, as cause, as a free individual. We thereby reinforce the ideology of individualism that obscures the fact that it is really the masses who make history. The claim that it is "Man" who makes history "serves *those* whose interest it is to talk about 'man' *and not* about the masses, about 'man' *and not* about classes and the class struggle" (ibid., 63). Not only does this divert attention away from the structural sources of power, the means of production and the state, it also blinds us to the structural forces of insurrection and the possibilities of subversive practice; namely, working-class collectivities and organizations (ibid., 64).[25] Presumably this critique could apply to Lukács insofar as he presents the proletariat as a totality rather than as a collectivity.

Althusser's antihumanism provides a much needed opportunity to assess critically the legacy of socialist feminist theory. There are many examples where, despite the commitment to the Marxist conception of socially constructed subjectivity, both systems theories and standpoint theories lapse into humanist formulas. This is often apparent in, though certainly not confined to, those analyses that include the concept of alienation in their critical apparatuses. For example, Eisenstein grounds her systems model in a conception of human essence that she locates in Marx's theory of alienation. According to Eisenstein, our "species-being," this creative and social essence, serves as both the touchstone for the critique of capitalism and the source of revolutionary will: "Without the potential of species life we would have Aristotle's happy slaves, not Marx's revolutionary proletariat" (1979, 8). Although I can certainly appreciate the importance of finding alternatives to capitalist forms of organization, I see no reason to locate these outside our practices in some purely metaphysical notion of human essence.[26]

Similar gestures toward humanism can be found in the work of standpoint theorists. Hartsock, for example, while insisting that an individual is the ensemble of her social relations, a social and historical construction, nonetheless resorts to a humanist problematic when she asserts that "we cannot be ourselves" in a capitalist and patriarchal society (1979, 64) and when she describes her alternative to this "inhumanity" as a "fully human community" (1983b, 123,

247). Again, the critique of capitalist patriarchy and the conception of an alternative is tied to a notion of a true, authentic, original, or otherwise essential humanity. Not only is the constructedness of the human subject—its immanence in the social world, its status as a social process—compromised by these references to an authentic humanity that is somehow outside history, these formulations could also feed into and serve as support for the discourse of the true and free individual (and potentially its corollary, the real woman).

However, whereas Althusser's critique of humanist Marxism serves as a valuable contribution to this project of reworking feminist standpoint theory, his proposed alternative to the logic of humanism, the notion of a "process without a subject," is clearly inadequate for my purposes. The problem is that in order to assert the constitutive power of structural forces, the creative force of subjectivity and the relative autonomy of antagonistic subjects are occluded. The subject is, by Althusser's reading, the effect of ideological practices which transform individuals into subjects who accept their subjection and "work by themselves" (1971, 181–182). Subjects are the embodiments of structural forces, the bearers of functions within a mode of production. According to Althusser, "the structure of the relations of production determines the *places* and *functions* occupied and adopted by the agents of production, who are never anything more than the occupants of these places, insofar as they are the 'supports' (*Träger*) of these functions" (Althusser and Balibar 1979, 180). The subject is no longer the central point of the analysis; it is, thus, decentered. History does not have a subject but rather a motor: class struggle. Yet this dynamic is described as the historical embodiment of a structural contradiction rather than as relations between two classes-as-subjects (1976, 48, 49n12). The role of subjectivity is displaced in favor of the efficacy of social structures.

Althusser thus falls into the same trap as Foucault. Instead of developing a theory of class collectivity as an alternative to humanism, instead of developing the claim that the "masses make history," he chooses instead the path of anti-subjectivity. Although the rigorous insistence on attending to the forces that constitute historical classes is valuable as a corrective to humanism, the reactive response, the refusal of subjectivity itself is for my purposes clearly problematic. Decentering the subject is one thing, eliminating subjects quite another. In my earlier discussion of Foucault I considered some of the limits of an antihumanist project that also refuses subjectivity. The major problem with Althusser's account is this: in the absence of relatively autonomous subjective agency, his analyses slip into a kind of functionalism. Thus, for example, in his study of the role of ideological state apparatuses Althusser suggests that the process by which subjects are constituted as functionally adequate role players—subjects that "work by themselves"—is uncontested by the apparently passive materials from which these subjects are fashioned (see Honneth 1994, 92). Despite Althusser's interest in exceeding the limited and predictable logic of the Hegelian totality, in creating a space for difference, he ends up with a systems model in which the subjective manifestations of difference are easily and systematically recuperated. As one reader of Althusser describes it, "[t]he emphasis throughout is on what forces tend toward systems maintenance rather than toward systems change" (S. Smith 1984, 166). Again we are left with a systems model of functional equilibrium. If one problem with Lukács's account is that he presents one exclusive subject, The Subject of History, the problem with Althusser's approach is that he delivers subject positions but no subjects; he refuses the project of developing antagonistic subjectivities.

Antonio Negri: Totality and Antagonism

Although I have acquired some useful ways to conceive the internal relations of the social formation, I have yet to find a compelling understanding of the place of subjectivity; that is, I have yet to encounter a concept of totality that is open to the possibility of a multiplicity of collective subjects. I turn to the work of the Italian Marxist Antonio Negri, specifically his *Marx beyond Marx: Lessons on the Grundrisse*, to help in this quest to locate and develop an antihumanist theory of collective subjectivity adequate to my feminist project.

The relationship between Althusser's and Negri's Marxism can be expressed in terms of their choice of privileged texts. Althusser proposes *Capital* as the ultimate Marxist text and the basis for an alternative to those brands of Marxism that focus on the earlier "humanist" texts. It is through his reading of *Capital* that Althusser develops

his antihumanist theory of structural forces. Negri, by contrast, privileges the *Grundrisse* over *Capital* and his rationale for this emphasis indicates how his project compares to that of Althusser. Although
he appreciates many of the achievements of *Capital*, Negri argues—
in what could be read as an attack on structural Marxisms like Althusser's—that *Capital* is also the text "which served to reduce critique to economic theory, to annihilate subjectivity in objectivity, to
subject the subversive capacity of the proletariat to the reorganizing
and repressive intelligence of capitalist power" (1991, 18–19). The
Grundrisse, on the other hand, is a text that highlights the potential
of relatively autonomous subjective actors, an analysis that never
seeks to contain the forces of antagonism within the simple logic of
dialectical opposition or the predictable formulas of economic deter-
minisms. This is a Marxism centered around a theory of crisis rather
than a theory of equilibrium. As Negri explains it, "[t]he originality,
the happiness, the freshness of the *Grundrisse* rest entirely with its
incredible openness." And what is the source of this openness? "The
paradoxical *non-conclusive character* of the science is derived necessarily from the fact that it contains a subjective determination"
(ibid., 9). I turn to Negri's reading of the *Grundrisse* to find an antihumanist theory of subjectivity situated within the social totality
that moves beyond the structuralist tendencies found in Althusser's
reading of *Capital*.

Both Althusser and Negri are critical of totality conceived as an
Hegelian synthesis governed by a closed logic that renders its internal relations—between, for example, base and superstructure or capitalist and worker—necessary and predictable rather than open and
contingent. Althusser uses the concepts of overdetermination and
relative autonomy to carve out a space for difference within his
structural totality. Negri takes this a step further: not only is the
identity of the elements reconceived as a different kind of unity, a
unity of differences, but these differences are then transformed into
the subjective equivalent of difference, that is, into antagonism
(ibid., 46). The antagonistic forces that reek such havoc with the
functionalist logic of a closed systematicity are the potential subversive practices of collective subjects; that is, the collective subject effects of the different forces of determination. These antagonistic subjects are situated both within and against the system. By Negri's

reading of Marx's method, "[w]e can see in it the passion for totality, but only in the form of a multiplicity of sequences and leaps, never in a monolithic sense; we can find in it, above all, a dynamic which has the plurality and the same diversity of subjectivity, and is nowhere closed" (ibid., 13). Even more than Althusser, Negri succeeds in distancing Marx's historical and materialist method from the "all-resolving logic" of the Hegelian dialectic. To make room for "the delirium of the material," we must not only open our conceptions of totality to the force of difference and contingency, to the relative autonomy of different social forces and the possibility of multiple subject positions, we must conceive these as spaces within which relatively autonomous subjects can be cultivated, as spaces within which these subjects, in my case feminist subjects, are fleshed out. It is the focus on antagonistic subjectivities that makes the system fully open and porous.

There is no place in Negri's account for a narrative that features the loss and recovery of an original, authentic human essence. Like Althusser, Negri also develops an antihumanist reading of Marx. Unlike Althusser, however, Negri rejects the eclipse of subjectivity as an alternative: "In avoiding humanism some would also seek to avoid the theoretical areas of subjectivity. They are wrong. The path of materialism passes precisely through subjectivity" (ibid., 154). To displace the determinism, the functionalism, the all-encompassing logic of the dialectical synthesis that leaves no room for agency or for resistance, a space must be created for the constitutive force of collective subjects. The working-class subjects of Marx's texts are not only exploited; they are also potentially revolutionary. "To want to reduce subjectivity to exploitation is to avoid the definition of subjectivity in Marx which is presented as subversion and transition" (ibid., 11). Within a Marxist logic, effects can also be causes; subjects are constituted by but also constitutive of the changing totality of social relations. It is possible, Negri maintains, to recognize the role of active subjects in history without lapsing into humanism. From this perspective, Negri stands in relation to Althusser in the same position I earlier cast Nietzsche in relation to Foucault: Negri too follows the critique of the humanist subject with an affirmation of alternative modes of subjectivity.

In a sense, Negri brings us back to Lukács's project, that of presenting a conception of totality that is attentive to the role of subjective factors, but on new terms. First, where Lukács returns to Hegel to find a way of conceiving a mutually constitutive relation between the subjective and the objective, Negri, like Althusser before him, retreats from Hegel to avoid some of the additional baggage Lukács may have picked up as well, including the conception, reminiscent of Hegel, of a single subject of history that effectively subsumes all others. Rather than a single, unified subject, the proletariat emerges from Negri's analysis as a plurality of antagonistic forces constituted along multiple lines of conflict. Negri's account is open to the possibility of a multiplicity not just of subject positions but of subjects. In this context, then, we must recognize the prospect of multiple proletarian subjects or, to translate this into terms more directly relevant to my project, multiple feminist subjects.

Second, Negri suggests an important corrective to Lukács's tendency to reduce subjectivity to cognition. As Lukács conceives it, the production of revolutionary subjectivity is a matter of achieving a critical and revolutionary consciousness. Within this model of the knowing subject, consciousness is accorded a kind of sovereign authority whereby a subject's ideas will necessarily determine a subject's deeds. Rather than one among many perhaps conflicting dimensions of subjectivity—including desires, pleasures, interests, and will—consciousness is presented as having the final word, as effectively ruling these other forces. In Negri there is no comparable emphasis on consciousness. The development of a revolutionary consciousness is, one may surmise, a necessary but insufficient achievement; the complex process of becoming cannot be reduced to (although it is certainly not exclusive of) the process of becoming conscious.

This conception of multiple and powerful feminist subjectivities is central to the project of standpoint theory as I conceive it here. In the following chapter I shift my focus to the questions surrounding the construction of one such subject, a feminist collectivity based on labor. There "laboring subjects" will supplant the "knowing subject" of Lukács's account. In the course of that discussion I turn once again to Negri, among other theorists, to consider how some of the system's victims could also conceivably emerge as its saboteurs.

Totality is, above all, a project: a dynamic social configuration that, in feminist terms, certain feminist subjects aspire to conceive for specific purposes from a particular set of locations. The project of totality as it is developed here involves the aspiration to grasp a complex, overdetermined totality of social processes. From this selective tour through socialist feminist systems theories I located a model of a unified plurality of mutually articulated systemic forces. The problem with this project was not its insistence on the systemic force of capitalism and patriarchy in our lives, but rather the ways that this systematicity, its coherence, and the role of subjectivities were viewed. From the work of Lukács, Althusser, and Negri I gathered tools with which to reconceive this unity so that it would be consistent with the participation of a multiplicity of subjects and vulnerable to their potentially subversive interventions. Totality thus conceived does not subsume differences within the closed and predictable logic of a seamlessly unified system nor deny the force of will, contingency, and conflict; it is not, then, necessarily just another guise for the ascetic ideal.

Labor, Standpoints, and Feminist Subjects

One objective of the discussion so far has been to prepare the ground for the construction of an alternative theory of feminist subjectivity. The preceding analysis located some conceptual resources, cleared a path, and established a context for this project. First I investigated the work of Nietzsche and Foucault and identified critical standards to use in developing a model of a social system and in moving away from humanist models of the subject. Nietzsche, in addition, offered an instructive means of conceiving subjectivity with his idea of the eternal return. However, before these tools could be utilized in the context of a project centered around the discourse of feminist standpoint theory, particularly around a version of that discourse so heavily indebted to Marxist thought, they had to be disentangled from the remnants of the modernist–postmodernist paradigm debate, which through its insistence on reactive oppositions had rendered them increasingly ineffective. I thus sought to develop a more nuanced conception of the field of theoretical perspectives than the specular alternatives of modernism and postmodernism would permit. Having removed these obstacles, I then turned to an exploration of the relationship between structure and subject, a necessary backdrop to any theory of subjectivity.

Specifically, I tried to develop a conception of a social totality that would be consistent with a theory of multiple, antagonistic, feminist subjects. Equipped with these tools, freed from these hindrances, and provided with this context, I am now prepared to focus in on the problematic of feminist subjectivity.

My goal in this chapter is to develop a nonessentialist model of a feminist subject.[1] Two kinds of essentialism concern me here: those that pose the subject as a pre-existing, self-constituting agent, and those that conceive the subject as a passively constituted effect of social forces. The essence of one is a will that is free; the essence of the other, its exclusively, thoroughly, and uniformly defining social position. The first is associated with voluntaristic models of political agency and the second with theories of social determinism. This dualism of voluntarism and determinism has figured in a number of recent feminist debates. Like many feminist theorists, sharing a dual commitment to the philosophical concept of immanence and the political projects of resistance and subversion, I am interested in moving beyond the opposition between voluntarism and determinism, beyond these mutually exclusive alternatives and an all-or-nothing choice.[2] In this chapter I attempt to develop the ontological specifications of a feminist standpoint or, more specifically, to articulate the relationship between the ontology of labor and the constructions of subjectivity to which it gives rise in terms that move beyond the orbit of this opposition between voluntarism and determinism.

The Ontology of Labor

Labor is the basic building block of this model of feminist subjectivity. But before describing what the role of labor is, I should clarify what it is not. First, the notion of women's labor proposed here is not a set of practices allocated to women by nature (that is, it does not entail a biological essentialism). The gender division of labor is the product of culturally and historically specific determinations, not the inevitable product of sex differences. The laboring practices that figure in these versions of feminist standpoint theory—caring labor, kin work, labor in the concrete bodily mode, and so on—have no necessary connection to women's specific biological capacities.[3] Neither is women's labor tied to some conception of an essential humanity (that is, a metaphysical essentialism), as is the case in some versions of humanist Marxism that privilege the concept of alienation. Rather than an original, authentically human essence from which we are estranged and to which we should be restored, labor refers in this account to variable practices that are constitutive of ever-changing forms of existence and modes of subjectivity. In contrast to both these approaches, labor is posited here as an immanent and creative force of social production and historical change.

An instructive formulation of this conception of labor can be found in the work of Marx and Engels. These authors explain the premises from which they begin (in highly polemical terms) as "real individuals, their activity and the material conditions under which they live, both those which they find already existing and those produced by their activity" (1978, 149). These premises are then separated for analytical purposes into four specific claims. The first premise of history is that human beings—those who collectively "make history"—must meet their basic subsistence needs. If we can presume life as a fundamental fact, then we can also presume that life can be sustained. The second premise is that the satisfaction of these needs leads to the production of new needs; necessity, they suggest, is for the most part a historical construct. Third, they presume that humans reproduce one another and, fourth, that social relations of cooperation develop in the process. According to Marx and Engels, this mode of cooperation is a "productive force": "As individuals express their life, so they are. What they are, therefore, coincides with their production, both with *what* they produce and with *how* they produce. The nature of individuals thus depends on the material conditions determining their production" (1978, 150).[4]

Along these lines, then, labor is conceived in my account as an immanent ontological dynamic. As Marx describes it, "[l]abour is the living, form-giving fire: it is the transitoriness of things, their temporality, as their formation by living time" (1973, 361).[5] In other words, labor serves as a basic causal force or principle of the historical motion of being. Dorothy Smith describes the ontological assumptions of her standpoint theory in very similar terms: "These practices, these objects, our world, are continually created again and again and are already social. Because they arise in actual activities, they are always coming into being as a local historical process, falling away behind us as we move forward into the future. They are being brought into being" (1987, 125).

When deployed in the context of a Marxist analysis that rejects all notions of necessary developments and predetermined ends, the category of labor, as it is elaborated here, leads to a field of constitutive practices, forces of assertion, or lines of movement that provides a particular angle of vision on and site of intervention into the social construction of subjectivities.

To clarify certain aspects of the reading I propose, I want to suggest some instructive parallels between the place of labor in Marxist thought and that of will to power in Nietzschean thought. By reading labor through the lens of my interpretation of will to power, the immanent and creative dimensions of labor are brought to the fore. Like the will to power, labor functions as a principle of internal genesis or as an ontology of practice.[6] Like the will to power, labor is a claim about existence, about the constitutive force of practices, rather than a claim about the essence of things. By this reading, then, labor serves as an immanent creative principle in the service of specific historical problematics.

The category of labor is also intrinsically strategic; that is, its philosophical attributes—in this case, its immanence and creativity—cannot be separated from its practical value. Marx, of course, deployed the category of labor as part of his effort not only to understand the world but to change it. There are practical reasons for concentrating on labor. Thus, as Marx explains it at one point, rather than inquiring into the role of private property in the alienation of labor, he focuses instead on the relationship between labor and its self-alienation. Private property, he claims, is not the cause of alienated labor, but rather "the product, the result, the necessary consequence, of *alienated labor*" (1964, 117). He then offers the following explanation for this unexpected conclusion: how, he asks, do we come to alienate our labor?

> We have already gone a long way to the solution of this problem by *transforming* the question of the *origin of private property* into the question of the relation of *alienated labor* to the course of humanity's development. For when one speaks of *private property*, one

thinks of dealing with something external to man. When one speaks of labor, one is directly dealing with man himself. This new formulation of the question already contains its solution. (1964, 118–119)

Again, the philosophical and political dimensions of Marx's project cannot be separated. In this example Marx privileges an account of the experience of producing at least in part as a strategy to incite and empower revolutionary agency.

Here I want to highlight this strategic aspect of the focus on labor, but in a somewhat different way. For my purposes the practical dimension of the category can best be accentuated by characterizing labor as value-creating activity.[7] Obviously, the determination of what counts as a value-creating activity is never fixed; it is an unstable social judgment of enormous consequence and can be contested. Thus, when the claim is made that women's laboring practices create value, a specific political problematic is framed: Why and how are the practices in question recognized and rewarded? What is the social value of these activities and the subjectivities they engender? The point of focusing on women's labor is neither to glorify work nor to extol the realization or lament the loss of some genuine mode of being; the point is to create sites of contestation over the social construction of specific constitutive practices and thereby to raise questions about what we can do and who we can become. (Consider, for example, how feminists have contested the ways in which the labor of child care is organized and valued.) That is, what is at stake here is not the alienation from or restoration to our essence as humans, but rather, the economic, political, and cultural value ascribed to various practices. In this way the category is pulled away from the more abstract problematic of a humanist Marxism and its discourse of interiority and attached to a more practical problematic that focuses our attention instead on struggles over the institutionalization of our practices. Thus, rather than resting on philosophical claims about essential selves, the category of labor can be deployed to provoke political debate over questions of social value.

My contention is that by highlighting the immanent, creative, and strategic dimensions of this ontological principle we can move beyond both the metaphysical logic of voluntarism and the mechanistic logic of determinism. When we build models of subjectivity around labor, we do not presume to identify the voluntary source of an only superficially determined identity, but rather attempt to isolate a mechanism of and a point of entry into the larger process of gendering that can double as a means to or a site of resistance to this procedure. By this reading, labor is a category that enables us to acknowledge our historical immanence and to recognize the determined dimensions of social life while simultaneously affirming the creative force of the will. However, my response to the difficult problem of determinism is not yet sufficient: the connections proposed in this version of feminist standpoint theory between what we are and what we do have not been adequately specified. A complete response must await the conclusion of the final portion of this account, in which we move from the ontology of labor to the politics of a standpoint. But before proceeding to that discussion, I want to continue this exploration of the laboring subject—this subject position or identity effect—which will constitute the ground of this feminist standpoint, the basis for this collective subject.

Performativity, Labor, and Subjectivity

The work of Judith Butler, which proposes an antiessentialist theory of subjectivity, provides an important opportunity to take another look, from a somewhat different angle, at the subject of feminism and the problem of determinism. Butler takes her cue not from a Marxist but from a Nietzschean problematic. As we have seen, Nietzsche was also occupied with the project that seeks an exit from the opposition between a metaphysical voluntarism and a fatalistic determinism. For his part, Nietzsche rejected both transcendental and mechanistic models, neither of which are able to conceive an immanent form of human agency. Butler's theory of gender performativity takes up this Nietzschean agenda—often drawing on its Foucaultian reformulation—and attempts to develop a theory of the social construction of gender that is not trapped within the familiar terms of either free will or determinism. Butler argues that gender identity is the effect of a compulsory reiteration of gender norms; gender discourse is, thus, performative: it creates and sustains the identity it is purported to name and describe.[8] By considering the specific strategy by which Butler disengages from conventional approaches in light of the model of laboring subjectivity sketched above, I can accentuate—in the sense of both recording and encouraging—certain productive affinities as well as some crucial differences between our two projects.

In contrast to those feminist theories that assume that "there is a 'doer' behind the deed" (1990, 25), including those that presume a natural core identity or an a priori agent responsible for adhering to or rejecting the conventions of femininity, in *Gender Trouble* Butler reformulates Nietzsche's statement that there is no doer behind the deed, saying that "[t]here is no gender identity behind the expressions of gender; that identity is performatively constituted by the very 'expressions' that are said to be its results" (ibid., 25). This model of culturally constituted subjectivity rules out any recourse to a standpoint outside the constitutive field from which to launch a pure opposition to the mechanisms and effects of social production, "There is no self that is prior to the convergence [of discursive injunctions] or who maintains 'integrity' prior to its entrance into this conflicted cultural field" (ibid., 145). Resistance cannot be conceived as a simple rejection, a clear break, an absolute refusal, a complete denial, or a pure opposition on the part of a choosing subject, because the subject is the effect of the very norms that it seeks to resist (see 1993, 15). Gender performativity—that is, the claim that a gendered subject is an effect of the reiteration of exclusionary norms—is thus Butler's constructionist alternative to transcendental and naturalized models of the subject and the voluntarist conception of politics that they sustain.

In *Bodies That Matter*, the follow-up to *Gender Trouble*, Butler extends and develops this aspect of her argument. Here Butler insists that she has never said that one is radically free to choose one's own performance of gender norms. The reiteration or repetition of norms by which a subject is constituted is not freely chosen but rather forcibly compelled. Performativity should be understood as "a ritualized production, a ritual reiterated under and through constraint, under and through the force of prohibition and taboo, with the threat of ostracism and even death controlling and compelling the shape of the production, but not, I will insist, determining it fully in advance" (ibid., 95). Often-cited or hegemonic discourses are not easily displaced or challenged; their considerable constitutive force is attributed to and sustained by the accumulated reiterations of their conventions. "No 'act' apart from a regularized and sanctioned practice can wield the power to produce that which it declares" (ibid., 107). Thus the historical density of discourse supports the performative force of its norms, while its various enforcement mechanisms induce (but do not ensure) our compliance.

The central insight and key contribution of Butler's project is not, however, this critique of the metaphysics of free will and the politics of voluntarism, but rather her refusal simply to substitute in their place a model of cultural determinism. The problem is, as Butler reminds us, that social forces can be seen to produce an identity that is as fixed, intractable, and predictable as that which is attributed to nature, and thus a disabling determinism can follow from theories of social construction as readily as it can from theories of natural or metaphysical subjectivity (see 1990, 7–8). As Butler repeatedly insists, "[t]here is no subject prior to its constructions, *and neither is the subject determined by those constructions*" (1993, 124, emphasis added). Butler's alternative to the apparent determinism of thoroughgoing conceptions of social construction is to insist that this construction is an activity rather than an act; the subject is not a final product but an ongoing, always incomplete series of effects of a process of reiteration. The fluidity and instability of this artifact ward off fatalism; contingency is the antidote to determinism. The tenuousness of gender performativity opens up the field of political possibilities and affirms the potential for resistance. If gender identity is established through "a *stylized repetition of acts*" as "a constituted *social temporality*" (ibid., 140, 141) rather than a pre-existing essence or a deep and intractable construction, then it follows that we can intervene in and hopefully disrupt this process through strategies of subversive resignification. We cannot simply refuse to comply with the norms, but we can perhaps alter our performance of them in ways that call into question their status as natural and necessary foundations. Agency, Butler argues, "is to be located within the possibility of a variation on that repetition" (ibid., 145).

The theory of gender performativity and feminist standpoint theory thus share a specific problematic: how can we develop a theory of gender construction which in rejecting the metaphysics of voluntarism does not then lapse into determinism? For both, identity is a practice that cannot be adequately conceived in terms of the conventional models of the humanist subject or the determined subject. Both develop alternatives that combine a rigorous immanentism with an affirmation of agency, insisting in each case that the refusal of any transcendental "outside" enables rather than precludes agency. The question is not where to locate a standpoint prior to or outside the field of power from which we can launch our opposition; the central problematic for both projects is, as Butler puts it, "how to acknowledge and 'do' the construction one is invariably in" (ibid., 31). Butler responds to this challenge, to the problems of immanent resistance and subversion, with a conception of gender identity as both constituted *and* indeterminate. Given these points of convergence, I believe that standpoint theorists can benefit from a careful consideration of Butler's problematic.

There are, however, at least two limitations of the performative model, both of which derive from Butler's specific formulation of this indeterminacy. Although, as we have seen, Butler does not rely on a pre-existing, choosing subject to found and direct subversive acts and sustain her optimism about the possibilities for social change, the performative model cannot adequately account for the forces that compel us to "do" gender. It also underestimates the effects of this process of engendering. One weakness of the project, then, is that it does not adequately connect the processes of subjectivization to a larger institutional framework. A second—and related—limitation of the performative model is that it does not recognize the substantial quality of the subjective residues of these compulsory repetitions. Consequently, Butler cannot sufficiently account for the intransigence of gender.[9] I maintain that in both cases standpoint theory can provide the means to address these weaknesses and thus can present an improved account of both the regime of power and its effects.

The first limitation of Butler's theory of performativity is that while she insists that gender performativity is compelled, she does not adequately account for the forces that induce our practices. This relates back to Butler's linguistic model of power, in which signifying practices are privileged as the primary constitutive forces that produce, restrain, and enable their subject effects (see, for example, 1990, 145). The problem is that Butler fails to situate these compulsory discursive practices within a socioeconomic matrix: language is attributed a determinative power that isolates and exaggerates its constitutive force.[10] The relations between socioeconomic and political institutions, on the one hand, and everyday signifying practices, on the other, are invisible in her account. The limitation of this proposal from a Marxist perspective is not that it is idealist rather than materialist, but rather that it does not engage the problematic of theorizing the complex relations between ideas and institutions, the cultural and the economic.[11] Discursive categories and cultural norms are, in and of themselves, insufficient mechanisms of force; that is, they cannot adequately account for the manner in which gender practices are compelled or how they can be most effectively challenged. As Teresa Ebert explains it: "To disrupt, undo, or exceed the gender binary requires a collective social struggle not only on the level of ideological constructions but, more importantly, against the systematic socioeconomic relations requiring and maintaining the specific forms of gender and sexual difference" (1992–1993, 39).

I argue that if we take laboring practices, rather than signifying practices, as our point of entry into these configurations of gendered subjectivity, we can better account for the coercion through which gender is embodied; few would mistake labor for a practice that can be freely taken up or easily refused. Thus, by privileging labor, we are better able to keep sight of the constitutive links between systematic socioeconomic relations, on the one hand, and collective modes of practice and forms of subjectivity, on the other.[12]

A second potential weakness of the performative model is related to the rather ambiguous status of the subject effect in Butler's account. Although Butler is somewhat unclear on this point, it seems often, that in order to maintain the subject's indeterminacy, the subject is rendered underdetermined. For example, when Butler claims that "the appearance of an abiding substance or gendered self . . . is . . . produced by the regulation of attributes along culturally established lines of coherence" (1990, 24), how are we to understand the ontological status of this "fictive production"? How does the term "appearance" function here: in an anti-ontological opposition to reality or in the more ontologically neutral mode of being visible, intelligible, or otherwise apparent? In claiming that genders are produced as "truth effects" (ibid., 136), Butler sidesteps the issue of the ontological significance of these epistemological artifacts. When Butler describes the idea of a true gender identity as a fiction, it is not clear whether it is the notion of truth that merits this status or if any lasting gender effect can be described in these terms. The question is, then, what is the status of this effect? It seems that Butler herself may be ambivalent in her response to this question. The texts can support at least two possible answers which, for lack of better terms, I will refer to as the ontological and the anti-ontological alternatives.

According to the first reading, the ontological alternative, the subject effect is a substantive artifact with a certain relative autonomy. Consider Butler's Nietzschean formulation of her basic claim: namely, that "there need not be a 'doer behind the deed,' but that the 'doer' is variably constructed in and through the deed" (ibid., 142). Although the idea of a doer *behind* the deed is clearly a fiction, an illusion, we could still maintain that there is an immanent doer *in* the deed; that is, we can reject the a priori subject without rejecting the subject altogther. Butler's use of the terms "sedimentation" and "materialization" (1993, 15) to describe these constructions of subjectivity is perhaps suggestive of a moment of being in this process of becoming. Consider another passage in a different text in which Butler discusses the question of what it means to be, or to play at being, a lesbian: "To say that I 'play' at being one is not to say that I am not one 'really'; rather, how and where I play at being one is the way in which that 'being' gets established, instituted, circulated, and confirmed. This is not a performance from which I can take radical distance, for this is deep-seated play, psychically entrenched play, *and this 'I' does not play its lesbianism as a role*" (1991, 18). As she claims in another context, identity as an effect is "neither fatally determined nor fully artificial and arbitrary" (1990, 147). One could thus conclude that it is a substantive—though certainly precarious—being-effect that is performatively produced. By this first reading, then, the subject does carry a certain ontological weight.

This first possibility, however, tends to be eclipsed in Butler's texts, in part as a consequence of a specific textual practice or rhetorical strategy that is best exemplified in what she presents as a "crucial" distinction between expression and performativeness (ibid., 141). According to Butler, those who hold to an expressive model of gender identity presume a pre-existing subject, a real or true gender identity as interior depth, that is then expressed in speech and action. Natural and metaphysical models of the subject are the clearest but not the only examples of this approach. The performative subject is presented in sharp contrast to this expressive model as a purely contingent effect of gendered practices. This distinction between expression and performativeness is actually the culmination of a series of similar analytical devices and rhetorical strategies deployed throughout the text. Consider, for example, the traditional dichotomies that are invoked to support the oppositional framework and to distinguish the performative model from those she critiques: gender identity is described as an effect rather than a cause; gender as corporeal style is distinguished from traditional notions of gender as metaphysical substance; gender is presented as a surface rather than a deep phenomenon; gender identity as becoming or "doing" is proposed in contrast to gender identity as being or "a doer." Most importantly, the opposition between the expressive and the performative is grafted onto the opposition between the necessary and the contingent. Even in its constructivist mode, the expressive subject is founded upon a necessary core that then negotiates its gendered constructions (see ibid., 143), whereas performativity is always linked to contingency. The general effect of these devices is to collapse a variety of different theories into a single category, the expressivist model, to which the alternative, the performative model, is counterposed; thus a neat dichotomy, a mutually exclusive opposition, is established to highlight the radical difference and originality of the proposed alternative. These divisions effectively reduce our choices to two: gender identity as necessary cause or gender as contingent effect. Thus, as a rhetorical strategy, the oppositional frame functions to maintain a radical difference between an absolute necessity and a pure contingency. Note that, when posed within the terms of this opposition, my first reading of the subject as a substantial artifact, the ontological alternative, tends to be associated with the discredited expressive models and thereby effectively dismissed.[13] The problem is, of course, that this kind of oppositional logic works against the elaboration of more nuanced distinctions.[14]

Hence, although there is some evidence for the first reading of But-ler's project in her texts, the ontological model is more often rejected as merely a version of the expressivist model in favor of a second ap-proach, the anti-ontological model, presented as the performative al-ternative. By this second reading, the independent ontological status of the artifact or effect is denied, or rather, put under erasure: "That the gendered body is performative suggests that it has no ontological status apart from the various acts which constitute its reality" (ibid., 136). This claim seems to reject not only an ontological status that precedes those acts, but the possibility of an alternative ontological status that follows from or inheres within the acts as well.[15]

The possibility that these practices leave ontological residues, as in my first reading, is obscured in order to assert the kind of contin-gency that is linked with agency. According to Butler, "[o]nly when the mechanism of gender construction implies the *contingency* of that construction does 'constructedness' *per se* prove useful to the political project to enlarge the scope of possible gender configura-tions" (ibid., 38). The significance of this claim should not be under-estimated; it is one of Butler's most important contributions to the project of reconfiguring the subject of feminism. However, given the rather strict opposition between the necessary and the contingent which helps to organize the analysis, the anti-ontological model tends to be coupled with a contingency that admits no necessity; that is, with a kind of absolute contingency. Thus, whereas discourse was seen to acquire some historical baggage—which accounted for its power to compel our conformity to conventional norms of gender identity—its effects do not seem to carry a comparable weight or manifest a similar density; even though a performance may be ritu-ally repeated, its effects do not necessarily accumulate in substantial form. Again, the subject's indeterminacy, its contingency and insta-bility, is secured by its underdeterminacy.

Standpoint theories, I believe, can build on some of the strengths without replicating the weaknesses of this project by offering an al-ternative account of the accumulated effects of these compulsory practices. In thinking about the process of gender construction, one can, taking a cue from Butler, recognize the importance of contin-gency without falling back into an opposition to necessity. In other words, I would like to pursue a specific version of the ontological model of the subject effect located in the first reading of Butler's project.

Whereas standpoint theory eschews natural and metaphysical models of subjectivity, models that posit being as the guiding force and telos of becoming, it also acknowledges the substantive effect of gender practices. These practices, these repetitions, leave complex marks or traces that produce something on the order of a second nature or a constructed, contingent necessity. This version of standpoint theory thus acknowledges a certain amount of inertia in the process of engendering that the theory of performativity tends to obscure. By this analysis, gender effects cohere with a certain weight and stability in subjective experience. The key point is that it is possible to recognize certain complex densities that accumulate over time without conceiving them in terms of an absolutely intractable depth or fixed interiority. To invoke one of Butler's central themes: construction need not imply determinism. The subject constituted in and through an accumulation of enactments, the subjectivity that coheres around the relative stability of practices and is manifest in the relative continuity of memories, habits, desires, and interests, is both limiting and enabling. Unlike the anti-ontological performative model, the laboring subject accumulates ontological weight without acquiring a transcendental stability.[16] To recall the earlier discussion of Butler's Nietzschean formula, the critique of a being *behind* the doing does not rule out the affirmation of a being *of* the doing; and it is this possibility of the being of becoming and, thus, of a contingency within necessity that will be affirmed as the subject of a feminist standpoint. In this conception of repetition, the accretions of past practices constitute the enabling ground of a feminist standpoint. As we will see in the next section, a feminist standpoint can be constructed from a selection of this identity effect.

For now the question is, what modes of agency does this model of subjectivity admit or foreclose? What kinds of opportunities are there to resist and reconstruct the norms and institutions that elicit our practices? If we recall, Butler linked agency to the contingency of socially constructed subjectivity. The possibility of subversive enactments was secured, if not by the subject's lack of history, then by its dearth of historical baggage. Resistance was conceived as an ability to interrupt the always incomplete processes of subjectivization.

Standpoint theory's rejection of this radical indeterminacy and absolute contingency, its insistence on the relative stability of identity effects, forces us to return to the original problematic: in Butler's words, "[i]f gender is not an artifice to be taken on or taken off at will and, hence, not an effect of choice, how are we to understand the constitutive and compelling status of gender norms without falling into the trap of cultural determinism?" (1993, x) In attributing a certain fixity and stability to the subject construction, is standpoint theory threatening to reinstall a disabling and rigidly exclusive determinism? I have examined Butler's antidote to determinism and found it wanting in some respects. In the next section I want to consider an alternative response to this problem of how to formulate an immanent resistance. Drawing on Nietzsche to locate an exit from this determinist dilemma, we will examine the process by which a feminist standpoint can be selected from the limiting and enabling ground of women's labor. To pose once more Butler's incisive formulation of our shared problematic: "The critical task is . . . to locate strategies of subversive repetition enabled by those constructions, to affirm the local possibilities of intervention through participating in precisely those practices of repetition that constitute identity and, therefore, present the immanent possibility of contesting them"(1990, 147). A standpoint, as we will see, is one such strategy for participating in the practices that constitute identity, one way to "do" the construction we are in, and to "do" it, moreover, as a politically efficacious construction.

From Ontology to Politics

Butler demonstrates the potential value for feminism of Nietzsche's critiques of free will (the doer behind the deed) and determinism (the elimination of will); I propose that we can also learn from Nietzsche's alternative to these models of subjectivity. Thus, before we move on from the discussions of the ontology of labor and its subject effect to the concept of a standpoint, I want to identify (and then later build on) some suggestive parallels between a feminist standpoint and the Nietzschean idea of the eternal return.

As interpreted by Deleuze, the eternal return teaches an alternative conception of subjectivity that incorporates at least two of Nietzsche's central observations. The first of these is that critique requires not only destruction but also creation—not only negation but also affirmation. However, to propose only the opposite of what has been affirmed hitherto—for example, to affirm pure becoming in the place of absolute being—is ultimately insufficient because it only preserves the original choices. Hence the second Nietzschean maxim is that we affirm not that which is opposite but that which is different, that we affirm in an active rather than a reactive mode. The eternal return, as an ethic that invites us to affirm actively what we can be, provides a guide for constructing a subject that lies beyond the opposition between voluntarism and determinism.

For my purposes here, what is important about Nietzsche's doctrine that everything recurs is that it reformulates the relationship between being and becoming in nonoppositional terms: "That *everything recurs* is the closest *approximation of a world of becoming to a world of being*" (Nietzsche 1968, 330). Deleuze explains that "[a]ll we need to do to think this thought is to stop believing in being as distinct from and opposed to becoming or to believe in the being of becoming itself. What is the being of that which becomes, of that which neither starts nor finishes becoming? *Returning is the being of that which becomes*" (1983, 48). With this thought, being is displaced from its transcendental foundations, but is not discarded: that which we continue to affirm in practice, that which returns, can become being. This notion of the being of becoming attests to the value Nietzsche places on a coherent and active willing subject. However, unlike traditional conceptions, Nietzsche formulates being as a moment in becoming rather than as its origin or telos.

This formulation suggests an alternative to models of feminist subjectivity founded upon an absolute essential being as well as to antiessentialist models of radically contingent becoming. To draw an analogy between this Nietzschean construction of being and the feminist project outlined here, a standpoint, as an ethic rather than a metaphysic, teaches us to select and affirm aspects of our past and present practices to serve as the enabling ground from which to construct a collectivity. This project of transforming subject positions into standpoints involves an active intervention, a conscious and concerted effort to reinterpret and restructure our lives. To recall my description of standpoint theory in the introductory chapter, a standpoint is a collective interpretation of a particular subject position rather than an immediate perspective automatically acquired by an individual who inhabits that position. A standpoint is derived from political practice, from a collective effort to revalue and reconstitute specific practices. Thus a standpoint constitutes a subject, but one which does not rely on a transcendental or natural essence. A standpoint is a project, not an inheritance; it is achieved, not given (see, for example, Hartsock 1983a, 288, 303). The collectivity, the "we" that coalesces around a particular standpoint, is a dynamic achievement rather than a static fact. Founded in neither a unitary identity nor a spontaneous expression of unity, there is nothing guaranteed, nothing inherently stable in these collective subjects, these group projects.

Three aspects of this formulation of a standpoint should be underscored. First, the subjects of these feminist standpoints are collective subjects. Here we build on the Marxist insistence, reiterated by Lukács, that collectives rather than individuals are the agents of social change and hence the appropriate units of analysis. Second, I want to emphasize that the focus here is on *feminist* standpoints, not women's standpoints. In other words, this project of constructing subjectivities is conceived—and this marks a departure from the Nietzschean model—as group projects of social transformation. Standpoint theory can be read, then, as an attempt to convert Nietzsche's ontological ethic into political projects dedicated to the construction of subversive collectivities. Third, marking a departure from the original feminist standpoint theories, the emphasis is on the plural. I do not posit a singular feminist subject and hence do not defend a unified feminist project. The different subject positions of women can be transformed into a multiplicity of feminist standpoints. Feminist standpoints are productive of multiple, subversive, collective subjects.

But if standpoints are fabricated and not given, the question is, how are they constructed? How can we proceed to devise a feminist standpoint? The answer is that we proceed selectively. As Hartsock explains it, "women's experience and activity as a dominated group contains both negative and positive aspects. A feminist standpoint picks out and amplifies the liberatory possibilities contained in that experience" (1983b, 232). Feminist standpoints are not based on an uncritical celebration of everything all women are or do. Instead, they are organized around a selective revalorization of specific practices and capacities that can then serve as a basis for what their participants can be and what they can do. What Nietzsche invites us to affirm is not the eternal return of *the identical* but the eternal return as a *principle of selection.* However, to claim that a feminist standpoint is selective is not to suggest that we can rummage through our collective interpretations of women's practices and simply choose an identity. This selection is not an act of "free will" or "self-determination," as if there were a will or a self that were radically free to determine who to will to be. Moreover, this selection is the work not of reflection but of practice; that is, we do not just think what to be, we enact it in word and deed. This process of selection must be conceived—as the process of subjectivization was conceived in Butler's account—as an ongoing process, an enactment, rather than as the product of a single decision or declaration. To build on the Nietzschean model, this selection is a process that is simultaneously *deconstitutive* and *constitutive*; specifically, we selectively will that which is active over that which is reactive, that which enables us to do and be more over that which would limit or separate us from what we can do or be, that which augments our power over that which detracts from it. To clarify this, for the remainder of this chapter I will describe two different kinds of selective practices that can be used to construct a feminist standpoint: irony and self-valorization, for which two kinds of laughter, one ironic and the other joyful, are symptomatic.

Deconstitutive Selections: Irony as Negation

The first selective mechanism that I consider is the practice of ironic laughter.[17] According to Kathy Ferguson's very useful analysis of the nature and value of irony for feminism, irony invokes a "doubleness of perspective" that can serve "as a way of problematizing the coherence and completeness of all beliefs, including (especially) one's own" (1993, xi). Ferguson presents examples of different reading and writing strategies, all of which reveal and promote rather than conceal and resist ambiguity, uncertainty, instability, and multiplicity. Irony is an important strategy for feminism in part because it can provoke a certain kind of laughter, one that can be subversive of the "categorical agreement with being" (ibid., 181). As Ferguson describes it, irony evokes a laughter that functions as the grain of salt that we take with our beliefs and commitments, a laughter that prevents us from holding them too tightly or too uncritically; ironic self-laughter slips among our different identities to disrupt their unity and "to serve as antidote to the longing for completion" (ibid., 30). In this way, ironic laughter signals the recognition of and the insistence on the force of difference.

Since I am specifically concerned with the question of how to renegotiate one's identity, the kind of ironic laughter proposed here as a mechanism of selection is more narrowly conceived as self-laughter. As such it shares a certain affinity with one form of Nietzschean laughter. Laughter is, for Nietzsche, a significant symbol and an important practice; but there are different kinds of laughter, or, as he suggests, different ranks of laughter (1966, 232). Self-laughter is the type he invokes most frequently. There are times, Nietzsche observes, when we need to laugh at ourselves in order to get a needed rest from ourselves (1974, 164). Self-laughter helps us to put the self in perspective; it is a sign of irreverence and a practice of destabilization that can serve, at least in this mode, as a force of negation or of deconstitution. More specifically, self-laughter can be seen as a means to disarm or neutralize aspects of the self without invoking ressentiment or bad conscience. "Not by wrath does one kill but by laughter" (Nietzsche 1954c, 153). Thus self-laughter can serve as a means to resist without denial; self-laughter is one of the tools that can help us to extricate ourselves from that which weakens us. In particular it can disengage us from the reactive forces that limit us, disable us, or, to echo a Deleuzian formula, separate us from what we can do.

I do not mean to suggest that ironic laughter is the only mechanism of disengagement, the only critical strategy, or the only technique of negation. Clearly its subversive power is very limited. Nor do I want to suggest that it is in every case an appropriate or productive practice. Indeed, in many cases it would be inconceivable. What interests me about this particular tool and the reason why I choose to privilege it in this account is the way that it manages to avoid many of the usual pitfalls of an *oppositional* stance. That is, these applications of irony seem to me to be exemplary of a mode of resistance or critical practice that, by refusing the path of denial, circumvents some of the typical problems of the reactive gesture. Thus, while irony is certainly not the only deconstitutive mechanism of selection that we can engage, it is instructive as a mechanism that can be characterized as antagonism without ressentiment.[18]

The following examples are illustrative of some of the different sorts of disengagements that ironic self-references can activate.[19] In each of these examples, the ironic gesture invokes doubleness or multiplicity in a way that highlights the tensions and slippages within that which Nietzsche describes as a "social structure composed of many souls" (1966, 26). Specific relations within this seemingly incompatible multiplicity are then accentuated in a way that raises questions about the self in its relation to conventional norms.

First, irony can be used to reveal the inadequacy of traditional ideas and images. Irony is thus one strategy by which culturally marginalized groups can struggle against the categories used to represent this marginality. In her study of the roles of irony and fantasy in contemporary fiction by women, Nancy Walker claims that, "[w]hat characterizes the contemporary novel by women . . . is not merely a fluidity of identity, but a consciousness of the ironic distance between the self as formulated externally, by cultural heritage, and the self as an internal process of redefinition and discovery" (Walker 1990, 78). Irony is often used in literature by women and people of color to disengage from degrading cultural categories; as Walker explains it, "irony is a way of negating the truth or validity of a received tradition and pointing to its incongruity or absurdity" (ibid., 22). Irony can thus be used to deactivate false, obsolete, or otherwise inapplicable cultural conventions by calling attention to one's difference. In this way, irony can help us to clear out specious stereotypes by pointing to their lack of force.

If in the first case irony is used against that which we are not, in the second case, irony is used against that which we are but do not want to be. That is, irony can also be employed to disarm ideals or images with constitutive force, those to which we may be more closely bound or in which we may be implicated; it is in this sense that irony can induce *self*-laughter. The ironic gesture can be used to insist on the complexity of subjectivity, its overdetermined constitution, by playing one plane of determination off against another in a way that helps us escape or rather exceed any simple determinism. I found this kind of doubleness within the self that could evoke ironic self-laughter in Sheila Rowbotham's recounting of her own development as a feminist in *Women's Consciousness, Man's World.* Consider, for example, Rowbotham's description of her relationship to cosmetics. According to Rowbotham, she decided at one point in her life that she wanted to stop wearing mascara because it was inconsistent with her emerging identification with feminism but found that it was not an easy thing to do. In describing her response to this situation, Rowbotham evokes a split within herself between the kind of feminist identity she was constructing and a traditional feminine identity she wanted to leave behind (1973, 44–45). Rowbotham thus conveys the constitutive force of these norms of femininity while at the same time suggesting that she cannot be reduced to or determined by them. To the extent that we can laugh at this doubleness within ourselves, we demonstrate that we are not fully or singularly determined by those conventions, while the laughter itself serves to loosen their hold even further without ever denying their constitutive impact. That is, we cannot simply deny that in which we are implicated; purity is not possible. We can, however, at least in *some* circumstances, laugh at ourselves insofar as we are not reduced to or determined by any specific attribute or norm and, by means of this laughter, render it even less effective. Thus irony can serve as one possible strategy for dealing with that which we are and do not want to be; self-laughter forces open a space for becoming different.

Whereas in the first case irony was used against that which we are not and in the second against that which we are and do not want to be, a third example shows how irony can be used to disengage from political strategies of polar opposition informed by the logic of *ressentiment* and the reactive conceptions of identity in which they are grounded. *On Our Backs*, a sex magazine for lesbians, presents one example of this use of irony. The title itself presumably pokes fun at the radical feminist journal *Off Our Backs* and particularly its association with certain tendencies within the feminist anti-porn movement. This kind of play against anti-porn feminism is not confined to the title. The inaugural issue of *On Our Backs*—billed as "Entertainment for the Adventurous Lesbian"—presents, among other contributions, a telling satire, "April 1, 1984," which reports a fictitious clash between a lesbian-feminist S/M support group and a group of lesbian-feminist anti-porn crusaders in England. Members of the anti-porn group, C.W.A.P.I. (Concerned Women Against Perverted Individuals), who carry signs bearing slogans like "Keep Minorities Small," insist that "a cup of tea is preferable to any sexual encounter." One of the leaders states that C.W.A.P.I. wanted to promote "a healthy atmosphere in which only the gentlest lovemaking would be tolerated." "It is time," declares another member, to "proclaim our lifestyle as the true and only valid form of feminist daily experience" (Knightly 1984, 23).

One of the effects of this kind of ironic humor is to suggest a doubleness—the feminist "on her back"—that problematizes stereotypical and one-dimensional conceptions of identity (as, in this case, an identity that is *either* politically committed *or* actively sexual). More importantly, these gestures serve to point out and contest the logic of ressentiment ("You are evil; I am not you, therefore I am good") and the asceticism ("You are [dangerously] sexual; I am not you, therefore I am not [dangerously] sexual") that animate certain segments of the anti-porn position.[20] This laughter helps to clear some space for *On Our Backs*'s affirmation of an expansive sexuality that is not defined as more true or correct than any other. In and through these techniques, *On Our Backs* manages to reveal the reactive logic that informs some anti-porn discourse without—and this is crucial—simply recreating the conventional pro-porn position: obviously they are not representing ideas, acts, and passions that conform to the acceptable range of female sexual practices; clearly they are not affirming themselves as objects of male desire. Indeed, the laughter arises from the recognition that they are beyond these traditional oppositions. Thus, *On Our Backs* takes aim at both conventional ideals of sexuality and a certain kind of opposition to these ideals, using irony as one of the tools with which to disengage from this reactive opposition between women's (good) and men's (evil) sexual practices. This form of irony highlights the problems with reactive oppositions in a way that leaves room for a more nuanced resistance.

One component of this process of constructing a feminist standpoint thus involves clearing away worn-out and dated ideals and images, recognizing without valorizing the scars that domination leaves, and disengaging from reactive oppositions. In each of these cases, the ironic self-reference serves, at least in part, as a means to disable that which cannot simply be refused. Ironic self-laughter is a mechanism of selection that enables us to renegotiate certain conventions or dimensions of subjectivity without assuming that an autonomous, self-constituting self can "just say No." Irony helps us disengage from that which makes us weak; it is one way to disarm those images, dimensions, or imputations of identity that could be disempowering. When laughter displaces denial in this way, we are better able to ward off the bad conscience and disavow a politics fueled by guilt. By means of a selective use of ironic self-laughter we can begin to neutralize the forces of ressentiment and extract ourselves from a moralizing politics beholden to ideals of purity.

However, although irony is an important resource for feminism, I am advocating that it play only a limited role. Whereas ironic laughter is an important way for some individuals or collectivities in certain circumstances to say "No," we must complement this work of negation with the practice of affirmation. For this reason I take issue with Ferguson's recommendation that we adopt a more general ironic sensibility and, in particular, with her suggestion that as feminists we sustain an ironic view of our commitments (1993, xi), thereby "giving doubt and partiality a place of honor within feminist theory," together with hope and certainty (ibid., 32). As a companion to our political commitments, Ferguson argues that irony can be "a vehicle for enabling political actions that resist the twin dangers of paralysis (nothing can be done because no final truth can be found) and totalization (there is one way to do things and it reflects the truth that has been found)" (ibid., 30–31). To translate Ferguson's claim into Nietzsche's terms, the ironic commitment is an alternative to nihilism, on the one hand, and the ascetic ideal, on the other. Ferguson argues that, as a kind of built-in reminder of the contingency and partiality of our commitments, the ironic stance can prevent our claims from ossifying into incontestable truths and disrupt a politics dependent on and impoverished by the ideal of unity.

While I agree that we must be selective in our reappropriations of women's experiences while mindful of their specificity, as well as that irony can play an important role in this process, I maintain that this use of irony constitutes a destructive rather than a constructive gesture and, for this reason, is a necessary but limited strategy. Ferguson's notion of an ironic affirmation is problematic because it collapses two moments, one that negates and one that affirms, in a way that unnecessarily limits the creative power of our collective practices. Her conception of affirming something ironically amounts to tempering one's commitment, as when one finds oneself unable to commit to a specific "Yes" and offers instead a universal "Maybe," a "Yes" that is always undercut. Rather than limit the quality of our commitments, I argue that we should be selective about their content and their range. In contrast to Ferguson's notion of an ironic affirmation, I would like to see a feminist standpoint constructed around a selective affirmation, as a product not of "Maybe" but of both "No" and "Yes." To return to Nietzsche's prescription: "I teach the No to all that makes weak—that exhausts. I teach the Yes to all that strengthens, that stores up strength, that justifies the feeling of strength" (1968, 33). In this way we can view negation and affirmation as separate moments serving distinct functions in the process of selection. Selection is a process of both disengaging and engaging; the goal is to move from this ironic laughter, the laughter that creates distance, that clears a space for difference, toward a joyful laughter—the laughter of affirmation.

Deconstituting Drag and Constituting Houses

To clarify the conceptual distinction between two mechanisms of selection, one deconstitutive (an example of which is described above) and the other constitutive (the focus of the next section), I want to pause to consider another aspect of Judith Butler's project. In *Gender Trouble*, Butler privileges drag performance as a potentially subversive practice. This kind of gender parody can provoke a response that is subversive of the very notion of natural identity: "As the effects of a subtle and politically enforced performativity, gender is an 'act', as it were, that is open to splittings, self-parody, self-criticism, and those hyperbolic exhibitions of 'the natural' that, in their very exaggeration, reveal its fundamentally phantasmatic status" (1990, 146–147). Drag is particularly instructive, Butler suggests, insofar as it can expose the performativity of heterosexual gender identities: *"In imitating gender, drag implicitly reveals the imitative structure of gender itself—as well as its contingency"* (ibid., 137). This parodic redeployment of gender can help to denaturalize gender identity by problematizing (that is, both disrupting and multiplying) the relationships among sex, gender, and desire. However, this is not to claim that parody is necessarily subversive, a point that Butler makes quite clear in *Bodies That Matter*: "I want to underscore that there is no necessary relation between drag and subversion, and that drag may well be used in the service of both the denaturalization and the reidealization of hyperbolic heterosexual gender norms" (1993, 125).[21] This indeterminacy is illustrated by reference to *Paris Is Burning*, a film by Jennie Livingston about the New York drag balls and the specific forms of community that develop around them. Butler suggests that, although in some respects the drag performances portrayed in the film have a certain subversive potential, they more often serve to reconsolidate rather than displace dominant race, class, and heterosexual gender norms.[22] What interests her more about the ball scene is the subversive potential of the alternative kinships arrangements, organized by "houses." Butler explains her interest in these terms: "These men 'mother' one another, 'house' one another, 'rear' one another, and the resignification of the family through these terms is not a vain or useless imitation, but the social and discursive building of community, a community that binds, cares, and teaches, that shelters and enables" (ibid, 137).

Now, to employ the scheme elaborated here, drag can be seen as an example of a gesture that could in some forms and in some circumstances denaturalize, and thereby problematize, specific norms. To the extent that it enables a disengagement from heterosexual gender norms, it can clear a space for alternative projects. The house structure encompasses a different kind of practice and poses a different kind of challenge. Although it makes use of certain parodic elements (combining the language of the traditional heterosexual, nuclear family under the sign of the house of fashion) the primary value of the project is—as Butler suggests but does not explain—

constructive rather than destructive. Both projects are at least potentially valuable, potentially subversive; but whereas one is possibly effective as a critique, as a way to disarm an existing sex–gender regime, the other is dedicated to affirmation, to the self-valorization of a collectivity. This difference is not, however, clearly registered in Butler's account; or rather, the analysis of why one strategy is more subversive than the other is not adequately developed. The vocabulary used to describe the drag performances is the same as that which is used to describe the house. The house is a resignification, a reelaboration of kinship relations just as drag is a reiteration of gender norms; in both cases the repetition is emphasized as that which entails a certain indeterminacy and a potential discontinuity. But it seems to me important to recognize and register the ways in which the second example exceeds these terms; that is, the language of repetition does not pick up on or do justice to the creative force, the constitutive power, the utopian thrust of these alternative kinship practices. The drag performance can be conceived as a way of talking back that is in itself an individual practice. A house, on the other hand, is potentially more than a reiteration (with a difference) of the traditional family: within these social spaces it enacts new modes of collectivity that more than an individual, can create and sustain alternative values, needs, and desires. The drag performances may help to challenge the norm, whereas the kinship networks carry the potential to enact a transvaluation on the site cleared by this deconstitutive practice.

Constitutive Selections: Self-Valorization as Affirmation

How, then, do we conceive the creative endeavor of affirmation? Just as the destructive dimension of the selection process was portrayed as an immanent resistance, a negation from the inside rather than a pure opposition, we can think of the creative dimension in similar terms. That is, we cannot affirm some utopian beyond or other but only that which we are and which enables us to be more. But let me be clear about my terms here: To affirm is not only to reflect positively on or to bestow a positive interpretation, but to adopt as a project, to will to develop further. Pure affirmation is selective, and it selects that which is active over that which is reactive: "To affirm is still to evaluate, but to evaluate from the perspective of a will which enjoys its own difference in life instead of suffering the pains of the opposition to life that it has itself inspired" (Deleuze 1983, 185). To affirm something is both to acknowledge and to practice it as a positive, empowering development. Affirmation is not acquiescence; affirmation is not a matter of mere adjustment to or compliance with that which exists: "To affirm is to create, not to bear, put up with or accept" (ibid., 185–186). In Deleuze's formulation,

> *To affirm is not to take responsibility for, to take on the burden of what is, but to release, to set free what lives.* To affirm is to unburden: not to load life with the weight of higher values, but *to create* new values which are those of life, which make life light and active. There is creation, properly speaking, only insofar as we make use of excess in order to invent new forms of life rather than separating life from what it can do. (ibid., 185)

Nietzsche teaches "not affirmation as acceptance, but affirmation as creation" (ibid., 185). We affirm that which we can be and that which can enable us to be "light and active"—joyful and expansive. But again, how do we envision this practice of affirmation? By what mechanism do we say "Yes"? How do we select, how do we engage that which can make us active collective subjects? How do we arrive at a laughter that is not ironic but joyful?

There are many possible mechanisms of selection that we could discuss here; but I want to propose self-valorization as a Marxist project that is comparable to the Nietzschean affirmation. This concept can, I believe, highlight and develop the most constructive political dimensions of standpoint theory. Self-valorization, then, as a political project of affirmation, is a second mechanism of selection around which a feminist standpoint can be constructed.

Marx's concept of self-valorization, developed by Antonio Negri, is presented most clearly in *Marx beyond Marx: Lessons on the Grundrisse* (1991).[23] Negri's preoccupations in this text foreshadow my own: Negri turns to the *Grundrisse*, one of the few texts in which Marx deals with the role of the working class in the transition to communism, to find a theory of revolutionary subjectivity beyond the voluntarism and determinism to which much of traditional Marxism, and often Marx himself, succumbs (Negri 1991, 8, 11). Negri is interested in the possibilities of a Marx beyond Marx: beyond the vulgar determinism that links our fate to the independent machinations of structural forces and the romantic voluntarism that would will us toward a humanist utopia (see ibid., 153–154). The concept of self-valorization is part of this attempt to conceive an immanent resistance to capitalist relations on the part of antagonistic subjects.[24]

Negri presents two strategies of immanent subversion, one essentially destructive, the other constructive. The first destructive strategy, or set of strategies, is summarized as the "refusal of work." Included under this heading are those practices designed to negate capitalist valorization, and specifically those struggles that seek to subvert the capitalist exploitation of wage labor, including strikes, work slowdowns, and sabotage. The second constructive strategy or set of strategies focuses on creating alternatives—on selecting and cultivating the seeds of the future. These are projects of self-valorization. Self-valorization designates not the valorization of the self, but autonomous and collective projects of value-creating practices. These projects of self-valorization are linked with the development of new ontological possibilities; projects of self-valorization are conceived as alternative processes of constitution, as the means by which collective counter-subjectivities are composed. Harry Cleaver describes the concept of self-valorization as that which designates the constructive power of self-constitution made possible through the refusal of capitalist relations: "Alongside the power of refusal or the power to destroy capital's determination, we find in the midst of working-class recomposition the power of creative affirmation, the power to constitute new practices" (1992, 129). Revolution is thus conceived as a practice that involves "the simultaneous overthrow of capital and the *constitution of a new society: communism*" (Cleaver 1991, xxvii).

The affirmative dimension of Marxist praxis is possible once we excise from Marx's historical materialism residues of the Hegelian dialectic. In Negri's distillation of Marx's method in the *Grundrisse,* the abstract and teleological logic of dialectical contradiction is replaced by the concrete and contingent logic of antagonism. According to Negri's characterization of this "method of antagonistic tendency," the antagonisms are not regulated by the dialectical logic of opposition nor will they terminate in dialectical synthesis; rather than posing as inverted mirror images of one another, antagonistic forces develop within separate spaces: "The separation, from the workers' point of view, is the consolidation of a historically given reality; it is the productive power of the free subject which dominates on this terrain" (1991, 133). A resistance that is active rather than merely reactive requires a space, a moment of separation, a process of (relatively) autonomous constitution that the reactive and "all-resolving" logic of thesis, antithesis, and synthesis cannot admit. Negri argues that

> [w]e must immediately underline that in this light the antagonistic logic ceases to have a binary rhythm, ceases to accept the fantastical reality of the adversary on its horizon. *It refuses the dialectic* even as a simple horizon. *It refuses all binary formulae....* It is only on this terrain that we will be able to begin to speak of new categories: not of capital but for the overthrow of capital. (ibid., 189)

By replacing the logic of reactive opposition with that of active antagonism, we open a space for affirmation as well as negation. The separation of the antagonists provides the creative space for the cultivation of subversive difference. This reading of Marx's method can be summarized in two of Negri's key formulas: not contradiction but antagonism, not inversion but separation.

Negri elaborates the concept of self-valorization through a reconsideration of the antagonism between necessary labor, the labor necessary to reproduce the worker as possessor of labor power, and surplus labor. Negri takes us back to Marx's analysis of the struggle over the workday, where capital seeks to increase the proportion of surplus labor over necessary labor while the working class struggles to increase the proportion of necessary labor—what Negri characterizes as the sphere of labor as "not-capital" or "not-work" (ibid., 72). Negri argues that we must extend Marx's analysis of the "antagonistic dynamism" within this division of the social workday to an ontological plane. This is possible once we view these two modes of labor as developing within relatively autonomous social spaces. According to Negri, we should be able to discern and promote within these two social spaces different forms of practice, different configurations of subjectivity, and antagonistic modes of valorization (ibid., 93). That is, these different processes of valorization constitute potentially separate libidinal, symbolic, and production economies that create subjects with separate needs, desires, pleasures, and capacities. Negri proposes these projects of self-valorization as part of a strategy to expand and recompose the sphere of necessary labor. By these means, the workers multiply and increase their requirements, passions, and abilities in ways that cannot be satisfied within the limits of capitalist production. These projects of self-valorization consist of value-creating practices that are incompatible with capitalist valorization: the workers try "continually to broaden *the sphere of non-work*, that is, the sphere of their own needs, the value of necessary labor" (ibid., 71).[25] Capital seeks to restrict the scope of necessary labor, to contain and to control—to profit from—the production of new needs, new pleasures, and new practices. The workers seek to expose and to exceed these limits, to destroy them, and to replace them with alternatives. The struggle can be conceived as a struggle over labor itself, with capital struggling to restrain and confine the productive force of labor and workers striving to exceed these constraints on the constitutive force of labor.

By posing self-valorization as a mechanism of selection that constructs a standpoint, I believe that we can highlight and extend the strategic impetus and political potential of standpoint theory. Conceived as movements of self-valorization, feminist standpoints are ongoing, collective projects that cultivate the antagonistic potential and constructive possibilities of women's value-creating practices. We can think, for example, of the value of the relational labor involved in caring for children or in creating and sustaining kinship networks and the modes of subjectivity linked to those forms of labor, which standpoints constructed around different modes of caring labor attempt to affirm and promote. Feminist standpoints can thereby be constituted by and productive of collective subjects with values and needs, dreams and desires that are incompatible with present conceptions of what is necessary for social reproduction.[26] Thus leisure practices, parenting practices, and the building of kinship networks may all require, as value-creating practices that are arguably necessary for human reproduction, more in the way of social recognition and economic support than weekends, wages, tax credits, AFDC, or national holidays presently provide. In other words, by altering the content and expanding the scope of necessary labor, these projects of self-valorization create standpoints that are subversive of dominant modes of cultural and socioeconomic valorization. The subject effects of women's labor are thus transformed into feminist standpoints: achieved, selective, and, most importantly, politically engaged collective projects.

This version of a feminist standpoint is, then, the product of two mechanisms of selection: irony and self-valorization. Irony, as a deconstitutive mechanism, helps us disengage from that which weakens and disables us; self-valorization, as a constitutive mechanism, is a means by which we engage what we can do. Whereas the laughter that accompanies the destructive dimension of this project was characterized as an ironic laughter, as a laughter that signals an active rather than reactive negation, the laughter that accompanies the constructive dimension of the project can be conceived as a joyful laughter, as the laughter that affirms our creative powers. Despite their different functions, the deconstituting and constituting mechanisms serve the same general goal: to construct subversive feminist collectivities. That is, irony and projects of self-valorization are deployed in order to select and to cultivate *effective* standpoints. The project's critical power and transformative capacity are the true tests of its merit.

To develop this version of standpoint theory, I carved a path from ontology through subjectivity to politics: the ontology of labor served as a point of entry into a process of subjectification, selected elements of which were then transformed into the political project of a standpoint. The immanent, creative, and strategic dimensions of this ontology of labor and the modes of subjectivity to which it gives rise form the basis of a standpoint that is achieved, selective, and politically engaged. By this reading, a feminist standpoint is both created and creative: it is simultaneously the product and the ground of a feminist politics. The subject of this particular standpoint—a collective feminist subject created through irony (self-laughter) and self-valorization, a subject that *we will to return*—stands on a ground now distant from the problems of voluntarism and determinism. Posed in these terms, in terms that should emphasize some of its nonessentialist possibilities, I contend that feminist standpoint theory, this remnant of the past, can serve us well as a tool for the future.

Beyond the Paradigm Debate

The preceding analysis is only a beginning. It is intended as a contribution to what I conceive as a Marxist or socialist feminist project dedicated to theorizing the collective constitution of feminist subjectivities.[1] My version of this project is indebted to two different theoretical traditions. First, a tradition that extends—though, as we have seen, not always directly or uniformly—from Nietzsche through Foucault to Butler provided useful tools for conceiving a gendered subject as a construction. The similarities between Nietzsche's and Foucault's work emphasized their common critique of humanist models of subjectivity, while the contrasts between their accounts brought Nietzsche's alternative model of subject construction into sharper relief. Elements of Butler's work were then used to develop these critical tools further and adapt them to a feminist project. For my purposes, the most valuable aspect of Butler's work is its rigorous antiessentialism, its challenge to view the subject of feminism always as an effect or construction even when it is also posited as a cause or agent. This has been particularly useful to me in confronting the lingering essentialism one can find within certain Marxisms and socialist feminisms. Butler's answer to the strategic political question that she poses, however—how to "do" this construction—reveals the weaknesses of the performative model of the subject. To elaborate a more powerful model of subversive subjectivity, I drew on an alternative theoretical tradition.

This second tradition, which in my account extended from a specific trajectory of Marxist thought through socialist feminism to standpoint theory, provided useful tools for conceiving of collective feminist subjects situated within and potentially against a field of socioeconomic forces. The investigation of selected Marxist theories and socialist feminist theories generated certain methodological precepts for developing nontotalized models of social systems, models of the totality of social relations not beholden to the ascetic ideal, the systematicity of which does not render them deterministic. Chapter 4 then attempted to bring specific aspects of these two traditions together in order to work through one possible account of how the multiplicity of *subject positions* within this social totality could generate antagonistic collectivities or standpoints, how these shared spaces could be transformed into *subjects*. That is, the objective of Chapter 4 was to imagine how the structural positions within the socioeconomic totality, how these *passive* subject positions, could be crafted into *active*, collective subjects.

The problem with structural analyses that conceive the subject only in terms of an effect of socioeconomic forces—socialist feminist systems theories provide one example of this—is that they neglect to account for the potentially autonomous force of subjectivity; here, to use another vocabulary, we find subject positions but no subjects. In an account like Butler's, in contrast, subjects are conceived in active terms but are not situated clearly in a socioeconomic context. Consequently, the analysis risks lapsing into individualistic and even voluntaristic models of resistance. My project is an attempt to bring these two elements together in the form of a collective subject both constituted by socioeconomic structures and capable of subverting them. Labor serves as the particular link in this account between system and subject; as conceived here, the structural divisions of labor organize various laboring practices upon which standpoints, conceived as active collective subjects, can be constructed.

This model of a feminist standpoint is predicated on a particular conception of labor gleaned from certain socialist feminist and Marxist traditions. Socialist feminists and standpoint theorists have furthered our understanding of these laboring practices by expanding our notion of what is to be included. By focusing on traditional forms of women's labor like caring labor and kin work, socialist feminists and standpoint theorists have helped to move the concept of labor away from narrow conceptions of wage labor. The alternative to economistic models of labor that was presented here, the conception of labor as value-creating practices that was derived from an alternative Marxist tradition, is designed to affirm the constitutive force of certain practices as well as to politicize the question of their value. My interest in labor stems from the conviction that the divisions of labor (including those based on gender and race) play a crucial role in the construction of social hierarchies and that the laboring practices they impose could be tapped as a potential force for their subversion. Thus, by focusing specifically on laboring practices as opposed to other kinds of practice, we are reminded not to neglect the role of economic forces in sustaining systems of domination.

In promoting the importance of the divisions of labor and laboring practices, however, I am not arguing for the priority of the economic over the cultural, as if to comply with the formulas of some Marxist orthodoxy. On the contrary, the laboring practices discussed here, particularly those identified by socialist feminists and standpoint theorists, are constitutive practices that cut across the economic and cultural divide: laboring practices produce both economic and cultural forms, the value of which are both economically and culturally determined.

The particular model of a standpoint presented here is forged from these laboring practices, from the desires, values, needs, and interests they can engender. A feminist standpoint is a constructed collectivity; it designates a project that transforms a potential group, a structural position, into a subversive collective subject. As a model of collective subjectivity, the standpoint offers what I think is an important alternative to the individual as the unit of feminist analysis.[2] In some cases, important and productive critiques of false generalizations, of ascetic conceptions of unity and of the potential for "identity politics" to naturalize identities, rather than instigate a reconsideration of the collective, both as an intellectual category and a social and political practice, have had the effect of shifting the focus of analysis from the collective to the individual. That is, in some accounts, the valorization of difference has been translated into an affirmation of the irreducibility of individual difference, and in such cases crucial questions about the fate of difference in our thinking and in our practices are reduced to yet another reinsertion of liberal individualism. But the individual, while obviously real and worthy of attention, is not (as both Marx and the history of social movements have taught us) the primary agent of social change—hence standpoint theory's preference for the group as the unit of analysis. This is not to suggest, of course, that the category of the collective is either straightforward or unproblematic. On the contrary, the challenge is to conceive of and construct group subjects that do not replicate some of the homogenized and unified, purely functionalist or overly romantic, naturalized or naturalizing models of the past. While I believe this model of a feminist standpoint moves in the right direction, there are obviously many questions left unanswered and much work left to do.

This Marxist or socialist feminist project, at least as it is conceived here, cannot proceed while the terms of the modernist–postmodernist paradigm debate still govern our thinking. For one thing, it poses difficulties for attempts like this to recognize and build on potential affinities between the Nietzschean and Marxist traditions. One of my goals, not only in chapter 2 but throughout the book, was to free current conceptions of our theoretical and practical possibilities from the confines of this either/or proposition so that we would be better able to consider alternative approaches, hybrid accounts, on their own terms.

I would have predicted that, in the time elapsed since I started this project several years ago, this critique of the modernist–postmodernist paradigm debate would have become outdated. Instead I am struck by the persistence of this debate, in political theory and especially in feminist theory. Despite what I perceive as widespread disenchantment with the dispute, its terms continue to be reproduced, sometimes formally, as in analyses figured explicitly within its terms, but more often as a trope employed occasionally in the course of an argument to frame an issue or to dismiss an opponent. That these modernist–postmodernist paradigm formulas continue to be reinvoked at this point is, I would argue, not a testament to their ongoing utility but rather a symptom of the stagnation of our thinking.

The problems with this debate—namely, the reductions it enables, the innovations it suppresses and, increasingly, the animosity it fosters—are especially evident in contemporary feminist theory. A specific pair of arguments, one presented by Jane Flax and the other by Teresa Ebert, two of the more thoughtful and provocative feminist theorists writing today, exemplify for me both the analytical limitations and the acrimonious style of the more recent theoretical work inspired by the modernist–postmodernist paradigm formulas. In the first example I want to consider, Flax identifies a variety of feminist theories with what she characterizes as the Enlightenment discourse of truth, claims that postmodernism is threatening to those who subscribe to this Enlightenment ideal, and then suggests that some of the emotional intensity with which some feminists repudiate the postmodernist challenge can, "[s]ince the projects of postmodernism and of women of color do overlap," be attributed to a defense of these white feminists' race privilege (1993, 146).[3] In a parallel formulation written from the perspective of the other camp, Ebert presents a critique of a variety of poststructuralist feminist theories, which she combines under the category of ludic feminism and then describes as a theory that serves to defend the class privileges of its proponents. Ludic feminism is posed in sharp contrast to the particular version of Marxist-socialist feminism that Ebert advocates as the only discourse willing and able to challenge patriarchal capitalism.[4]

Both arguments are deeply problematic. As I understand it, the logic behind Flax's argument goes something like this: Postmodernism and antiracism "overlap," postmodernism is antiracist, hence anti-postmodernism must be racist, hence feminists who are anti-postmodernist take this position in part in order to protect their race privilege.[5] Ebert relies on a comparable logic: Marxism (and, indeed, by Ebert's account, only a rather orthodox form of Marxism) is anti-classist, whatever is not Marxist is classist, hence "ludic" feminist theories that are antiMarxist or even non-Marxist serve to protect the privileges of those whom she describes as "upper-middle-class ludic theorists" (1996, 33).[6] There is no evidence to support any claims about the motives of their opponents. Neither, I believe, is there sufficient evidence that, setting aside questions of authorial intention, the arguments themselves always serve these interests.

It seems to me that, given the dearth of evidence, the real force of these arguments (beyond the satisfaction one may experience upon hearing one's enemies maligned) depends largely on the oppositional logic of paradigm debate: there are two alternatives, and one is the antithesis of the other; you are either with me or against me. The kinds of specious syllogism that underpin these arguments have been normalized, I believe, by means of the modernist–postmodernist paradigm debate which authorizes the conflation and occlusion of specific important differences and habituates us to the logic of guilt by association. In other words, the modernist–postmodernist paradigm debate creates the conditions of possibility for these arguments, which, I maintain, are thereby rendered less able to advance feminism, antiracism, and class struggle.

As I suggested earlier, I think it is time to dismantle the modernist–postmodernist paradigm debate in political theory and feminist theory and abandon these camps. The paradigmatization of poststructuralist thought served some important purposes in the 1980s: by avoiding poststructuralism's simple assimilation into dominant modes of discourse by those who did not recognize its difference and recruiting those who did into a common project, postmodernism established new agendas and provoked constructive debates in these fields. But what may be productive in one historical moment can prove unproductive and even counterproductive in another. Now that poststructuralist and poststructuralist feminist thought have achieved a certain legitimacy as independent forces, we are in a position to explore the possibilities of a more complex field of alternatives.

This dismantling of the paradigm debate would require the refusal of what I call postmodernism; that is, a paradigm of theoretical discourse that is based on or credited to a particular reading of poststructuralist texts and that is defined in terms of its opposition to a homogeneous model of modernist discourse. This particular conception of postmodernism both nullifies the many important differences among poststructuralist theories and obscures the specificity of their challenges to modern traditions. Dismantling the paradigm debate also means rejecting the assumption of a unified model of modernist thought. For example, recognizing the affinities between Marxist and liberal discourses should not blind one to their profound and, I would argue, still-compelling differences. To find an exit from this debate, we need to unpack these paradigm formulas and insist, wherever possible, on more specific references to particular texts or arguments from the poststructuralist or modern traditions.[7] Of course those who want to move beyond postmodernism's antimodernism, must refuse anti-postmodernism as well; that conception only serves at this point to reproduce the terms of the old debate, to call one's opponent into being. Rather than ally with or oppose these mutually exclusive paradigm options, this reactive pair, rather than risk re-creating what has evolved into a standoff, I believe that it is time to advance more nuanced views of our theoretical options.

Those of us interested in thinking through the potential utility of Marxist theories for feminist projects should be particularly wary of participating in the debate and reproducing these paradigm formulas. We should be wary, first, because this debate has played a role in discrediting Marxism within the fields of political theory and feminist theory; and, second, because, as I have tried to demonstrate, there are some potentially productive engagements between certain elements of Marxist and poststructuralist theories that the modernist–postmodernist paradigm formula disallows.[8]

My point is not that we should all be nice and try to get along. This is not a plea for civility, but rather a call to conceive more productive lines of debate and to pursue more compelling conflicts. Again, I do not claim that the disputes between, for example, feminists grounded in a Marxist tradition and feminists who draw on poststructuralist frameworks are unimportant; I only want to propose that the modernist–postmodernist paradigm formulas no longer help us identify and advance those disputes. The points of agreement and lines of conflict between these discourses are by now more complex and fragmentary than the oppositional scheme is equipped to register. For example, it seems to me that one potentially useful question that should be considered is not the question that was posed within the terms of the modernist-postmodernist paradigm debate about whether it is the economy or culture that is more fundamental to contemporary constructions of gender but rather how to rethink the categories of the economic and the cultural in ways that can better account for the complexity of their intersections and thus call them into question as clearly distinct realms.[9] We will be better able to engage this and other important questions, I am convinced, once we finally consign the terms of the modernist–postmodernist paradigm debate—with its reductive models and reactive reversals—to their rightful place as once timely and creative but now outdated and ineffectual historical categories.[10]

As I said, this analysis is only a beginning. Part of what I have hoped to accomplish in this book is to clear a space, propose some tools, and suggest a framework for theorizing feminist subjects. Although there are many avenues of inquiry developed here that require further exploration, two of the problematics—one centered on the theme of labor and the other on the question of collectivity—stand out for me as particularly important areas of continuing investigation. First, how can we view women's labor in a way that can better register the complexity of systems and subjectivities constituted in part on the basis of the divisions of labor by class, race, gender, ethnicity, and across national boundaries? A great deal of theoretical and empirical research is needed if we are to continue to advance our understanding of what different women do, how it is valued, and the possible connections between new forms of exploitation and new modes of activism. Second, what are some of the different ways to conceive a collective subject, ways that move beyond the liberal model, according to which the individual is primary and authentic, the group is a "mere" secondary construction, and a legitimate group is posed as a consensual aggregation of individuals?[11] Given the pervasiveness of liberal individualism and its stubborn grip on our thinking in late capitalist societies, this remains a difficult task indeed.[12] What are some of the possible ways of regarding collectivities not only as determined subject positions but also as active subjects—how can these subject positions be transformed into relatively autonomous agents capable of social change? Having reached the end of this analysis, I have a new appreciation of just how important it is, and just how difficult it will be, to address adequately these problematics of labor and collectivity. These remain, for me, among the most compelling and challenging ongoing projects of contemporary feminist theory and practice.

NOTES

Introduction

1. Feminist standpoint theory is, like any other label applied ex post facto to a group of theoretical projects, a rather dubious category. To characterize these heterogeneous texts as part of a coherent school of thought is to run roughshod over the substantial differences in their methods, contents, and goals. At least one of these standpoint theorists, Dorothy Smith, has expressed her aversion to being "caged" by this label, claiming that her work is now read through the filter of these interpretations—which, in Smith's estimation, often distort her arguments (1992, 91; see also 1997, 392–393). Of course, one should never confuse an ideal type constructed from a variety of texts with the specific arguments in the texts themselves. Categories are constructed to highlight certain similarities among particular phenomena at the expense of other elements that are different. The value of such a classificatory category lies in its ability to underscore important affinities among these texts that can suggest distinctive and productive lines of inquiry, and I continue to deploy the label of standpoint theory, problematic though it may be, for that reason.

2. Indeed, in some cases I may take the work of the authors on whose work I build in directions they did not wish to pursue. I am thinking here in particular of Dorothy Smith, whose project, while a source of inspiration and instruction in many respects, is ultimately quite different from mine (for example, see note 13 to this section).

3. Useful overviews of feminist standpoint theories can be found in Ferguson 1993; Harding 1986a, 1986b, 1991, and Jaggar 1983.
4. Here I anticipate a Lukácsian formulation developed by Fredric Jameson that will be discussed in Chapter 3.
5. See Rosemary Hennessy 1993 for an excellent argument for systemic analyses of social totalities within feminism.
6. There are other attempts to rework standpoint theory that do not privilege these accounts of women's labor in the same way. Sandra Harding, for example, focuses on the epistemological dimensions of standpoint theories, grounding them in the more general conditions of women's lives (including but not confined to laboring practices) and the position of marginality (see 1991, 119–134). Similarly, Patricia Hill Collins (1991) grounds Black feminist thought in Black women's experience, of which labor is one determinant among many. Nancy Hirschmann (1992), to cite yet another important example, takes up and develops the psychological focus of those standpoint projects that draw on feminist theories of psychosexual development.
7. The category of women's labor (which is deployed here to examine the practices of women in Western capitalist social formations) is posed as an abstract, unmarked category of gender analysis that can be further specified. For example, the concept of the gender division of labor has been rendered more complex and nuanced by authors detailing how it is simultaneously organized along racial lines. See, for example, Amott and Matthaei 1991, Glenn 1992, and Malveaux 1990. Collins (1991) incorporates some of these insights into her analysis of a Black women's standpoint.
8. This account is drawn from Rose (see 1983, 83).
9. See Ruddick 1989. Ruddick identifies maternal labor, the focus of her study, as one of the specific forms of caring labor (1989, 46–47).
10. The term is from Micaela di Leonardo 1987.
11. See, for example, Hartsock's (1983a; 1983b) account of the sexual division of labor.
12. See Smith 1987. As Smith explains it, women "do those things that give concrete form to the conceptual activities. They do the clerical work, giving material form to the words or thoughts of the boss. They do the routine computer work, the interviewing for the survey, the nursing, the secretarial work. At almost every point women mediate for men the relation between the conceptual mode of action and the actual concrete forms on which it depends" (83).
13. It should be noted that this marks a clear departure from the work of Dorothy Smith, who conceives a standpoint in other terms and uses it for a different purpose. Smith proposes what she calls a women's

standpoint as the centerpiece of a proposed method of social inquiry: the standpoint of women directs our research to the local and everyday worlds of our subjects. One could characterize my version of standpoint theory as an attempt to incorporate specific elements of Smith's sociological work combined with certain aspects of Hartsock's and Rose's political project. The category of standpoint is also conceived differently in the work of Patricia Hill Collins. Collins employs the term "standpoint" to refer to the immediate perspective of a group, in this case, of African American women. The term "Black feminist thought," on the other hand, is used to designate a conscious reworking of some of the themes located in this standpoint or immediate perspective (1991, 22). Again, I reserve the term "standpoint" for a mediated construction rather than a spontaneous development.

14. It is worth noting that this focus on epistemology in the original standpoint theories was consistent with a more general interest in questions of knowledge and method among feminist theorists at the time.

15. As I use the terms here, humanism is a type of essentialism. There are, however, other forms of essentialist thinking about subjectivity beyond the classic humanist variety. For example, theories that locate the essence of women in some biological core have been described as essentialist. For a useful discussion of some of the different meanings of essentialism in feminist theory, see Ferguson 1993, 81–83.

Chapter 1. Nietzsche, Foucault, and the Subject of the Eternal Return

1. See the volumes edited by Allison 1985, O'Hara 1985, Koelb 1990, and Patton 1993 for illustrative examples and critical discussions of this new Nietzsche scholarship.

2. There are at least three general positions on this issue. Walter Kaufmann offers one approach with his reading of Nietzsche as a fundamentally antipolitical thinker whose scattered political pronouncements should be dismissed in favor of his more purely philosophical discussions. Today, however, many are skeptical of this kind of depoliticized interpretation and tend to organize instead around at least two other possible approaches to Nietzsche's politics. Representing one alternative, Bruce Detwiler insists that Nietzsche's undemocratic politics are consistent with and even required by his philosophy of power (1990, 5, 13); representing another approach, Mark Warren ar-

gues that Nietzsche's philosophy underdetermines and is even at odds with his politics (1988, 209).

3. For a different attempt to develop a Nietzschean critique of postmodernism, see Higgins 1990.

4. Nietzsche describes this immanent perspective as a *"new world-conception"*: "The world exists; it is not something that becomes, not something that passes away. Or rather: it becomes, it passes away, but it has never begun to become and never ceased from passing away—it maintains itself in both.—It lives on itself: its excrements are its food" (1968, 548). Joan Stambaugh, who disputes the Heideggerian interpretation of the will to power as a metaphysical category, also affirms the immanence of Nietzsche's perspective. As she describes it, the will to power constitutes a claim about existence or the "givenness" of the world (what is *there*) rather than its essence (*what* is there) (1972, 101). Gilles Deleuze's characterization of the will to power as "a principle of internal genesis" is also designed to emphasize the immanence of Nietzsche's perspective (see 1983, 91). Finally, Mark Warren contributes to this reading of Nietzsche's project an apt description of the will to power as a critical (and materialist) ontology of practice (1988, 111).

5. It should be noted that Deleuze develops this distinction between the active and the reactive in the context of a far more detailed and nuanced discussion than is necessary for my purposes here (1983, 39–72). See also Michel Haar 1985, 11, and Elizabeth Grosz's (1993) excellent discussion of the active and reactive.

6. Deleuze describes the immanence of Nietzsche's values in these terms: "Evaluations, in essence, are not values but ways of being, modes of existence of those who judge and evaluate, serving as principles for the values on the basis of which they judge. This is why we always have the beliefs, feelings and thoughts we deserve given our way of being or our style of life." (Deleuze 1983, 1).

7. This diagnosis, and the concept of power/knowledge with which it is facilitated, is developed most clearly in the work of Foucault's "middle period," particularly in his genealogies of the asylum, the clinic, the prison, and the *dispositif* of sexuality, as well as in the interviews of that period, several of which were published in *Power/Knowledge* (1980a).

8. Similarly, Nietzsche's rejection of the doctrine of objectivism and the "pure, will-less, painless, timeless knowing subject" that it presumes (1969, 119) does not lead him to endorse relativism—or, as Nietzsche describes it, the idea that "everything is *merely* subjective" (1968, 545)—as its opposite. The doctrine of perspectivism, which Nietzsche presents as an alternative conception of objectivity, an objectivity for the future, is an epistemology that does not claim either that truths

are absolute, incontestable, and disinterested, or that they reflect "merely" relative opinions. A life-affirming perspectivism is constructed in response to the either/or choice between a life-denying objectivism and a life-degrading relativism.

9. Similarly, Foucault's Nietzschean disavowal of the faith in transcendental truth and rejection of the doctrine of scientific objectivity is not accompanied by a refusal to entertain any distinction between the true and the false. In an interview Foucault characterizes the choice between accepting the dominant understanding of rationality and falling prey to irrationality as a kind of blackmail. According to Foucault, instead of "isolating the form of rationality presented as dominant, and endowed with the status of the one-and-only reason, in order to show that it is only one possible form among others," this either/or choice "operates as though a rational critique of rationality were impossible" (1988, 27). To reject the dominant form of reason enshrined in current conceptions of objectivity is not to oppose alternative proposals for more inclusive models of rationality.

10. Nietzsche insists that his interest in questions of epistemology is secondary to his focus on the ontology of subjectivity. According to Nietzsche, philosophy reduced to the "theory of knowledge" is philosophy in its last throes: "an end, an agony, something inspiring pity" (1966, 123). Despite this, Nietzsche scholars—following the lead of Walter Kaufmann—have traditionally interpreted nihilism as a primarily epistemological crisis. More recently, consistent with Heidegger's, or, along different lines, with Deleuze's reading of Nietzsche, the ontological dimensions of the crisis have been emphasized (see, for example, chapter 10 of the Expanded Edition of Tracy Strong's book on Nietzsche (1988) in which the author reconsiders his earlier understanding of Nietzsche's perspectivism and argues that it has more to do with an adequate theory of the subject than with a theory of knowledge). Mark Warren, in his provocative study of Nietzsche, makes the strongest case for this reading of Nietzsche's central problematic (see, for example, 1988, 4). As for Foucault, his primary concern is clear: the constitution of subjectivity or, more specifically, the processes of subjectification.

11. Although it is beyond the scope of this study, Foucault is, of course, also critical of "scientific Marxism"; that is, of those versions of Marxist discourse constructed around certain "laws of history" and beholden to an ideal of absolute and uncontested truth as well as any Marxism that makes claims to an ideal of orthodoxy.

12. For an interesting analysis of the normative inadequacies of Foucault's work, see Nancy Fraser 1989, 17–66.

13. Peter Dews argues that "Foucault, in his unwillingness to abandon

entirely his critical stance towards power, and his simultaneous suspicion of any normative standpoint, is obliged to cling to an elusive, residual naturalism, which he himself realizes is philosophically untenable" (1987, 169). See also Fraser 1989, 55–66; and Poster 1984, 36–37.

14. While Foucault's emphasis on the negative, destructive moment, as opposed to the positive, constructive moment, of critique is a limitation from the perspective of my project, this may not pose a problem for other purposes. For example, perhaps it is the lack of a constructive project that enables Foucault to oppose certain aspects of the present configuration of power in such a radical and thoroughgoing fashion.

15. For a critique of this interpretation of the eternal return as a cosmology, see Alexander Nehamas 1985, 142–153.

16. In addition to Deleuze 1983, the following analysis also draws on or shares affinities with specific dimensions of a number of excellent discussions of the eternal return. Particularly important are Michel Haar 1985, Kathleen Marie Higgins 1987, Pierre Klossowski 1985, Alexander Nehamas 1985, Joan Stambaugh 1972, Tracy Strong 1988, and Mark Warren 1988.

17. See also Deleuze 1983, 68–71, and Strong's discussion of the selective, "filtering," and transformative effect of the eternal return (1988, 270–271). Given Nietzsche's refusal to privilege the role of consciousness, many commentators insist that this process of selection depends more on an active affirmation in practice than on a conscious affirmation in thought. Strong emphasizes this connection to activity in his reading of the eternal return, a teaching that he distinguishes from a categorical imperative (see, for example, 1988, 268). Warren 1988 also highlights the centrality of practice.

18. As Warren explains it: "Thus Nietzsche's 'revaluation of values' stems from his removal of the categories of agent-unity that lie behind the ideals of Western culture—especially the notions of autonomy, individuality, and free will—out of the realm of the metaphysically given (where they serve as assumptions divorced from practices) and into the realm of human morals or goals (where they can be conceived as projects)" (1988, 157).

19. As Haar describes it, "[t]hat will is strong which can harmonize its own forces, forces in themselves divergent, and can dominate their constant development" (1985, 11).

20. Deleuze also insists on the dual nature of Nietzsche's critique and formulates the positive moment in these terms: "Critique is not a reaction of *re-sentiment* but the active expression of an active mode of existence; attack and not revenge, the natural aggression of a way of being. . . . This way of being is that of the philosopher precisely be-

cause he intends to wield the differential element as critic and creator and therefore as a hammer" (1983, 3). See also Schacht's (1973) argument that Nietzsche creates as well as destroys values.

21. There are two ways in which this aspect of Nietzsche's project is typically misunderstood. First, this construction of reverse values is often misinterpreted as an end in itself, rather than as a technique of devaluation. Walter Kaufmann is critical of this misreading, insisting that Nietzsche's reversals should be seen as polemical antitheses against current prejudices rather than perverse valorizations: "Nietzsche's writings are rich in such antitheses; and his polemics frequently obscure his own position" (1974, 265). Thus, for example, Nietzsche's devaluation of slave morality was misrepresented by Nazi ideologues as a simple valorization of master morality. Kaufmann, however, misrepresents Nietzsche's project in a second way. Perhaps to further discredit the Nazis' claim to have found a precursor in Nietzsche, he also denies that Nietzsche offers new values in the place of those he destroys: "In other words, the `revaluation' means a war against accepted valuations, not the creation of new ones" (ibid., 111). Kaufmann's refusal to affirm the positive moment of Nietzsche's critical project is puzzling, but should, I believe, be understood in the context of his efforts to discredit the link that had been made between Nietzsche and fascism. That is, this claim that Nietzsche did not legislate new values is presented as part of Kaufmann's response to the claim that Nietzsche is a "prophet" of something on the order of a new religion.

22. For example, by focusing on Nietzsche's descriptions of the will to power as a will to dominate others, Bruce Detwiler stresses the antidemocratic thrust of his teachings. Warren, in contrast, by highlighting the extent to which Nietzsche expresses the constitutive, creative, and empowering dimensions of the will to power, emphasizes the potentially democratic implications of Nietzsche's thought.

23. See, for example, James H. Read 1989. Read attempts an internal critique of Nietzsche's theory of power which he uses to defend a nonoppressive description of the will to power.

24. See Warren 1988, 242–246, for further development of this point.

Chapter 2. Modernism, Postmodernism, and the Logic of Paradigm Debates

1. Foucault himself, it should be noted, rejected the label of postmodernism and refused to be pulled into this paradigm debate, claiming at one point that he did not understand the kinds of problems that the terms modernity and postmodernity are supposed to capture (1988, 34).

2. In a postscript Kuhn attempts to remedy this lack of precision by distinguishing between two different definitions of the term "paradigm." Here, I employ Kuhn's more global conception of a paradigm as a "disciplinary matrix" (see Kuhn 1970, 182). It should be noted, however, that Kuhn's analysis of paradigm construction and change focuses on developments in the natural sciences rather than in the social sciences or philosophy. By his criteria, these latter disciplines would seem to find themselves in a permanent pre-paradigm period during which several competing schools of thought coexist. Certainly there are significant differences in the nature and function of paradigms in the natural sciences and the human sciences. For one thing, paradigms in the human sciences do not require the rather strict allegiance that those in the natural sciences demand. Moreover, there is an important difference of scale here; modernism and postmodernism are probably better described as "metaparadigms." Despite these limitations, I believe that Kuhn's descriptions of the processes of paradigm building, competition, and change can provide useful insights into certain features of the modernism–postmodernism debate as it was constructed in the 1980s.

3. It should be noted that while both Connolly and Bové suggest that Nietzsche and Foucault effect a significant rupture within the tradition of political thought on the order of a new paradigm, they do not formulate it in terms of a postmodernist break from that tradition. By Connolly's account, for example, poststructuralism is a late modern phenomenon. My point is not that Connolly, Bové, or any of the other theorists discussed here constructed, on the basis of these efforts, the modernist–postmodernist paradigm debate. My claim is that, in defending Foucault from Taylor's critique, Connolly and Bové deploy many of the classic techniques of paradigm building and competition outlined by Kuhn. These contributions to the construction of a postmodernist paradigm—an intellectual construct that far exceeds the contribution of any handful of authors—need not be intentional or self-conscious. Nor, of course, was it unwarranted: the elaboration of a successor paradigm is in many respects a productive intellectual practice.

4. At one point Taylor attributes Foucault's refusal of a normative project to his "official Nietzschean stance" (1984, 163). Based on the analysis of Foucault's reworking of Nietzsche's thought in the previous chapter, I would argue that Taylor falsely accuses Nietzsche: it is Foucault, not Nietzsche, who refuses normative criteria. By my account Foucault's limitations in this regard should be attributed not to an overly strict allegiance to Nietzsche but rather to an appropriation of Nietzsche's thought that is insufficiently attentive to its construc-

tive possibilities. It should be noted that in the second part of his argument Taylor makes a passing reference to another "yea-saying" Nietzsche that Foucault seems to neglect (1985, 384).

5. These terms do, of course, appear in other accounts: yet another of Foucault's defenders claims that these criticisms "reflect a misunderstanding of Foucault's enterprise" credited to the fact that "they take him as a modern when he is finally a postmodern" (Hoy 1988, 34).

6. "This passage," Foucault explains, "quotes a `certain Chinese encyclopedia' in which it is written that `animals are divided into: (a) belonging to the Emperor, (b) embalmed, (c) tame, (d) sucking pigs, (e) sirens, (f) fabulous, (g) stray dogs, (h) included in the present classification, (i) frenzied, (j) innumerable, (k) drawn with a very fine camelhair brush, (l) *et cetera*, (m) having just broken the water pitcher, (n) that from a long way off look like flies'" (1970, xv).

7. Hoy also claims that "[w]hat may worry philosophers today . . . is that somehow a paradigm shift is occurring which will leave some behind" (1988, 12).

8. Habermas reveals a similar frustration over these standard techniques of paradigm legitimation, or by what he tends to characterize as an antidisciplinarian rebellion against received standards of argumentation. These successors to Nietzsche, he claims, refuse to follow "the rules" of academic discourse. These discourses "unsettle the institutionalized standards of fallibilism; they always allow for a final word, even when the argument is already lost: that the opponent has misunderstood the meaning of the language game and has committed a category mistake in the *sorts* of responses he has been making" (1987, 337).

9. One can thus find nuanced analyses of specific modernist and poststructuralist arguments, on the one hand, and references to paradigmatic formulations of modernism and postmodernism, on the other, and can sometimes find them together in the same argument.

10. See also Ansell-Pearson's (1990) critique of Warren's inattention to the specificity of Marxist thought.

11. It should be noted that when Warren is less explicitly concerned with maintaining the modernist–postmodernist framework, his occasional discussions of the relationship between Nietzsche and Marx are more finely calibrated.

12. This decision to let an orthodox version of Marxism represent the whole tradition is commonplace in the postmodernist feminist literature. For example, in another attempt to construct a postmodernist feminist critique, Jane Flax reduces Marxism to another derivation of the "Enlightenment" belief in Reason; in this case, a belief in the teleological, law-governed, and ultimately rational progress of History, the purpose of which is human perfection (1993, 134).

13. Diamond and Quinby employ a similar strategy. They defend the postmodern turn in feminist theory on the grounds that both liberalism and Marxism "partake of the Enlightenment's uncritical acceptance of science and reason as the sole means for discovering truth and knowledge" (1988, 194–195). Flax, too, insists that Marxism and liberalism share the "Enlightenment" dream of "innocent knowledge" (1993, 134).

14. Flax comes to the same conclusion on the basis of a similar logic: either we can accept the Enlightenment ideal of universal reason which exists independently of the self and is unaffected by bodily, historical, and social experiences or interests, and which provides an objective, neutral, and universal foundation from which to recover the underlying truth about the "laws of nature," or, as postmodernists, we can craft historically specific theories of subjects constituted in and through relations of power (1987, 624–625, 642–643). See also Tress's (1988) critique of the false choice that Flax presents.

15. I find it interesting to note how frequently the term "eclectic," used pejoratively, is employed in analyses indebted to the modernist–postmodernist paradigm debate. Though the term itself is neutral, designating merely the use of a diversity of approaches, in the context of these accounts it carries a purely negative connotation, implying the presence of incoherence or lack of rigor. Certainly I agree that eclectic arguments can be both careless and incoherent, but from what perspective would one presume that they are all necessarily so? From what perspective would one assume that because an argument is crafted from a combination of theoretical sources one could then label it inadequate? The critical force of the term, I believe, depends in these cases on the conceptual framework of the modernist–postmodernist debate, which posits a mutual opposition between paradigms. From this perspective, those arguments that mix elements from the modernist and postmodernist traditions, those that do not honor the boundaries between these paradigms, are necessarily problematic; that is, given the supposed opposition between paradigms, we can presume their incoherence.

16. This lack of nuance and reactive logic are evident in the way that certain categories are deployed in the context of the modernist–postmodernist debate. For example, in Hekman's analysis, the Cartesian, autonomous, constituting subject is universalized and then represented as "the subject" in a way that tends to deny the existence of other modernist subjects (specifically, the gendered laboring subject of feminist standpoint theories). To cite another example, Nancy Hartsock describes how Richard Rorty refuses to specify further the term

"Epistemology," as if there is only one modernist theory of knowledge. Rorty then reasons that since this is the only modernist alternative, it must be rejected entirely; or, as Hartsock concludes in a parody of this logic, "if one cannot see everything from nowhere, one cannot really see anything at all" (Hartsock 1989–1990, 21). By this logic a "subject" is necessarily naturalized, "systems" are uniformly universalizing, "totality" is a code word for Hegelian teleology, and "epistemology" is inevitably absolutist. General terms are reduced to a narrow content and then dismissed on principle.

17. Connolly finds an alternative to theoretical postponism, an alternative to this very limited conception of the poststructuralist problematic, in the work of Foucault: "Foucault offers rudiments of a constructive general theory, I think, when he writes about 'disciplinary society' and when he speaks of a new subjectivity and the cultivation of care for difference through strategies of critical detachment from the identities that constitute us" (1991, 57). Since I find Foucault's ethic of self making less compelling than Nietzsche's ethic of the eternal return, I would argue that these elements of a constructive alternative can be found more readily in the work of Nietzsche than in the work of Foucault.

18. Indeed, in the essay entitled "What Is Enlightenment?" Foucault refuses the terms of this paradigm debate, denouncing what he calls the blackmail of being either for or against the Enlightenment (1984, 45).

Chapter 3. The Aspiration to Totality

1. See also Martin Jay's 1984 study of varied conceptions of totality within the Marxist tradition.
2. This review of the historical and conceptual development of socialist feminism is a highly selective foray into the tradition, not an exhaustive summary.
3. For useful critiques of Dalla Costa, see Hartmann 1981a, Tong 1989, and Vogel 1981.
4. I owe this insight to Michael Hardt.
5. I take the label unified-systems theory from Rosemarie Tong, who also presents a useful description of Young's analysis (1989, 183–186).
6. It should be noted that Young has since moved her work in different directions. For her own critical reflections on the socialist feminist unified systems project, see the "Introduction" to Young 1990.

7. As Young notes, she is not the first to propose this approach: "in arguing for gender division of labor as a central category of feminist historical materialism I believe I am making explicit a characteristic of socialist feminist theory which already exists" (1981, 50). See, for example, Zillah Eisenstein 1979.

8. Hennessy 1993 makes a strong case for the importance of extending the focus beyond the boundaries of a given social formation in order to situate particular analyses within the global relations of multinational capitalism.

9. Even Young, although she insists that capitalism and patriarchy are historically and analytically distinct systems, she emphasizes the historical inevitability and functional character of the relationship. See, for example, Young 1981, 62. For a dual-systems model that attempts to focus more consistently on the dynamic and contradictory dimensions of the relationship between patriarchy and capitalism, see Ferguson and Folbre 1981.

10. Jean Bethke Elshtain also notes the relevance of Foucault's analysis in her critique of socialist feminism (1984, 25).

11. For an interesting critique of instrumentalist theories of power in radical feminism, see Cocks 1989, 174–194.

12. In another essay, "The Family as the Locus of Gender, Class, and Political Struggle: The Example of Housework" (1981c), Hartmann focuses more on certain tensions or contradictions between capitalism and patriarchy.

13. Hartsock takes the title of one of her articles and the subtitle of her book from Young's call for the development of a specifically feminist historical materialism (1983a, 305n).

14. Note, however, the implicit references in this statement to "true" human needs. The problems with this kind of essentialism, which can be found in both systems theory and standpoint theory, will be addressed below.

15. Bertell Ollman's theory of internal relations resonates in many ways with Lukács's account. According to Ollman's reading of the Marxist dialectic, which, like Lukács he presents as an alternative to economic determinism, the real focus of Marxist inquiry is not relations between things but things as Relations (1971, 66). Just as Lukács seeks to replace facts with processes, Ollman argues that Relations, not things, constitute the basic unit of reality (ibid., 71).

16. In a claim reminiscent of Lukács's description of the whole as more than the sum of its (distinct) parts, Hartsock argues that "[a] mode of life is not divisible. It does not consist of a public part and a private part, a part at the workplace and a part in the community—each of which makes up a certain fraction, and all of which add up to 100 per-

cent. A mode of life, and all the aspects of that mode of life, take meaning from the totality of which they form a part" (1979, 63).

17. Unlike Lukács, however, I am more interested in the potential practical power of these collective subjects than in their epistemological authority.

18. It is in this class-as-totality formula that we find the clearest example of the logic of "expressive causality"—by which each of the parts contain within themselves and thereby express the whole—that Althusser critiques.

19. For a reading of Lukács that contests this claim about a residual humanism, see Feenberg 1986.

20. More recently, proponents of standpoint theory have discarded the earlier emphasis on a single feminist standpoint ("the" feminist standpoint) in favor of a multiplicity of feminist (and other) standpoints. See, for example, Harding 1991; Hartsock forthcoming; Hirschmann 1992; and Stanley and Wise 1990.

21. Althusser's model is presented in polemical opposition to "Hegelian Marxism," a tradition within which Lukács is presumed to be included. Although it is not my intention to sort through Althusser's debate with Lukács, it should be noted that his critiques do not always match Lukács's work. Although Althusser presents his project as a break with and critique of the so-called Hegelian Marxist tradition, I find Jameson's insistence that there are important continuities among their contributions to be more credible (see Jameson 1981).

This is not, however, to deny the applicability of Althusser's critiques of Hegelian Marxism to Lukács's work; there are certainly occasions when Lukács draws on such formulas. For example, there are instances where, despite his formal objections to it, Lukács resorts to an expressive causality, asserting a simple identity between different forces of determination in lieu of working through a more complex and specific analysis (see, for example, Lukács 1971, 170).

22. For example, in her work on systems theory, Young argues in favor of the ultimate priority of the structure over the superstructure (1980, 185).

23. "'Man' is a myth of bourgeois ideology: Marxism-Leninism cannot *start* from 'man'. It starts 'from the economically given social period'; and, at the end of its analysis, when it 'arrives', *it may find real men*" (Althusser 1976, 52).

24. Here I am following Althusser's critique of John Lewis (see ibid., 40–53).

25. As Althusser explains: "For when you begin with man, you cannot avoid the idealist temptation of believing in the omnipotence of liberty or of creative labor—that is, you simply submit, in all 'freedom,'

to the omnipotence of the ruling bourgeois ideology, whose function is to mask and to impose, in the illusory shape of man's power of freedom, another power, much more real and much more powerful, that of capitalism" (ibid., 205).

26. In a claim reminiscent of these earlier versions of socialist feminism, Barbara Epstein insists that the concept of alienation, grounded in some conception of human nature, is crucial to feminism and progressive theory more generally: "If there is no human nature outside social construction, no needs or capacities other than those constructed by a particular discourse, then there is no basis for social criticism and no reason for protest or rebellion" (1995, 114). Again, while I appreciate the importance of critical ideals and alternative values, it is not clear to me why they must be located outside history, why these needs or capacities must be conceived—in a way that is, I believe, both mystifying and potentially conservative—as pre-existing in order to generate resistance.

Chapter 4. Labor, Standpoints, and Feminist Subjects

1. An earlier version of this chapter was published as "Subject for a Feminist Standpoint," in *Marxism beyond Marxism*, ed. Saree Makdisi, Cesare Casarino, and Rebecca Karl, 89-118 (New York: Routledge, 1996)

2. For alternative attempts to reconfigure feminist subjects along nonessentialist lines, see, for example, Gloria Anzaldúa's "new mestiza" (1987), Judith Butler's "performative subject" (1990), Teresa de Lauretis's "eccentric subject" (1990), Kathy Ferguson's "mobile subjectivities" (1993), and Chela Sandoval's "differential mode of consciousness" (1991).

3. For this reason I exclude Mary O'Brien's (1981) often provocative version of standpoint theory. Her account of the ontological and epistemological possibilities available to those who bear and raise children is too dependent on biological determinations. Even though she insists on the *social* relations of reproduction, she does not succeed in distinguishing her analysis from a discourse on the effects of transhistorical biological difference. Thus, despite her insights into the ways in which culture always mediates our experience with nature, her emphasis on the biological dimensions of childbearing renders her work incompatible with the nonessentialist version of standpoint theory that I am interested in pursuing.

4. Note that nature plays a very minor role in this story: nature poses certain needs that we attempt to meet; beyond that, human existence is a social affair.

5. Diane Elson reads this passage to claim that labor "is a fluidity, a potential, which in any society has to be socially 'fixed' or objectified in the production of particular goods, by particular people in particular ways" (1979, 128).

6. These are the terms that Deleuze (1983, 91) and Warren (1988, 111) used to describe the will to power.

7. This notion of labor as value-creating activity is developed by Michael Hardt and Antonio Negri (1994, 7–11).

8. The first sustained presentation of the theory of performativity appeared in *Gender Trouble* (1990). It was subsequently elucidated and to some extent reworked in *Bodies That Matter* (1993). In this discussion I take the second book to be a clarification and expansion of the basic lines of the argument presented in the first book rather than a departure from them.

9. A number of authors have identified this as a weakness in Butler's account. See, for example, Di Stefano 1991, 17; Ebert 1992–93, 38–39; and Jones 1993, 9–11.

10. Teresa Ebert develops a similar critique of Butler (1992–1993, 35–39) and, in the same essay, presents a materialist feminist analysis of gender and sexuality as effects of labor that is in some ways comparable to the one I defend here. See also the conclusion where I discuss other aspects of Ebert's work.

11. Again, I am presuming Jameson's formulation of Marxism as a problematic.

12. This is not to suggest that I present a materialist as opposed to an idealist framework, as if laboring practices and signifying practices operate on mutually exclusive planes of determination. Rather, by focusing on labor, we can open up a particular line of vision that can highlight some links between economic and political institutions, on the one hand, and daily practices, on the other.

13. According to Butler's argument, even if we do not intend to invoke these discredited models, the danger is that this link will be made for us by the sheer force of conventional gender discourse. Any analysis that takes the subject as a starting point, as the subject of the story, regardless of whether that subject is presented as a transcendental a priori or an immanent social product, risks participating in the further reification of normalizing gender categories. Thus Butler's presentation of these potentially quite different ontological alternatives as just so many versions of the expressive model is justified in part by the

claim that this same conflation is inevitable given the force of the hegemonic discourse of natural differences. Given the seemingly inevitable reification of identity terms, Butler suggests that identity should be not the ground, but rather the object, of feminist critique and struggle. Hence, the ontological alternative is foreclosed in part to maintain a vigilant focus on the processes by which this identity is constructed. Although I do not take up this particular argument, for an interesting version of this debate over the status of identity categories, see the essay by Susan Bordo (1992) and the responses to it printed in *Hypatia* (1992).

14. Others have similarly noted the reductive basis of Butler's critique. Christine Di Stefano argues that "Butler has overdrawn her target, pulling together a number of theoretical errors that might still be usefully distinguished" (1991, 7). Kathy Ferguson claims that Butler (together with many of her critics) tends to reduce the subject(s) of feminism to the modern juridico-legal subject, when, in fact, "[j]uridico-legal subjects are not the only agents in town" (1993, 134).

15. This appears to be the strategy at work in the many descriptions of this effect of gender discourse as a fiction or an illusion. The practice of gender produces the *"appearance of substance"* which we "come to believe and to perform in the mode of belief" (Butler 1990, 141). We can also see this approach in Butler's frequent insistence on a certain nondialectical historical formula: "this repetition is not performed *by* a subject; this repetition is what enables a subject and constitutes the temporal condition for the subject" (1993, 95).

16. This echoes Jaqueline Zita's reservations about analyses in which the body is conceived as a product of discourse and with her own insistence on the "historical gravity of the sexed body." In Zita's words: "Postmodernism is right in bringing into focus the contingency of sex identity imposed on and incorporated into the body's soma but wrong in supposing these to be lightweight and detachable" (1992, 125, 126).

17. Much of this discussion was inspired by Kathy Ferguson's (1993) insightful inquiry into the character and value of irony. It should be noted that Ferguson proposes a more expansive notion of irony and hence a more varied set of practices. I am also indebted to Darko Suvin for challenging me to clarify my argument in this section.

18. Like Ferguson, I am interested in irony as a complement to rather than a substitute for other strategies, but not—and here I believe that I part company with Ferguson—as an accompaniment to all of our strategies. This point will be taken up later.

19. My conception of irony departs somewhat from the traditional use of the term, which involves a figure of speech in which the intended

meaning of what is said is the *opposite* of the apparent meaning. Following Ferguson, I use the term more broadly to grasp certain forms of doubleness of expression (Ferguson 1993, 30). More specifically, I focus on irony as a form of self-undercutting, where one meaning calls into question but does not necessarily contradict another. Thus, in contrast to the standard definition of irony, what interests me about many of these kinds of ironic self-references is the way that they evoke a disjuncture, a tension, rather than a strict opposition between two simultaneous meanings. With the persistence of this tension rather than a simple reversal, the two meanings remain in conflict with one another. "the key to the sense of doubleness in irony . . . is that the integrity of the 'literal' layer is retained to some extent" (Seery 1990, 174).

20. For an interesting analysis of the role of *ressentiment* in certain forms of feminist politics, see Joan Cocks 1991.

21. See also Di Stefano's (1991) critical assessment of the subversive force of drag.

22. See also bell hooks's critical analysis of the film (1992, 145–156).

23. For further clarification of the concept of self-valorization in Negri's work, see Cleaver 1991 and 1992, Hardt 1994, Ryan 1982, 204–212, and Virno and Hardt 1996, 264.

24. Negri asks a question that Butler also poses: "is it necessary to reject not only substantialist ontology but every type of ontology in order to prevent fetishism (revolutionary or otherwise), taking the place of critical reasoning?" However, Negri, in contrast to Butler, responds in the negative: "On the contrary, I believe that the subjective point of view is basically constitutive and that this constitutive process can be interpreted in ontological terms according to an hermeneutic of real determinations" (1989, 128).

25. According to Marx's analysis, "the determination of the value of labour-power contains a historical and moral element" (Marx 1977, 275). That is, judgments about what is to be considered necessary—which needs and pleasures must be satisfied in order to reproduce the worker—are culturally specific. Negri thus focuses on these determinations as an important locus of class struggle (see also Hardt and Negri 1994, 9).

26. Again, I want to emphasize that my analysis is cast within (or at least begins within) an ontological rather than an epistemological register. My primary interest here is not in the possibility of alternative modes of knowing and the inculcation of an alternative "consciousness" with antagonistic "interests," but rather in the possibility of alternative modes of subjectivity and the creation of alternative "desires," "habits," "wills," etc. The potential epistemological effects are

of less concern in this version of standpoint theory than the ontological artifacts.

Conclusion: Beyond the Paradigm Debate

1. Although I do not consider these labels to be of much consequence, I prefer to describe my project as Marxist feminist or socialist feminist rather than materialist feminist simply because those names effectively highlight one of the project's most distinctive features: its anticapitalist focus. When used to mark a contrast to idealist approaches, the term "materialism" strikes me as too broad; when the label "materialist" is used to distance the project from orthodox Marxism, I think it concedes too much to orthodoxy.

2. Hartsock, following a certain tradition of Marxist thought, notes that "the subjects who matter are not individual subjects but collective subjects, or groups" (1997, 371). Collins 1997 also emphasizes the centrality of the group as opposed to the individual in her conception of the project of standpoint theory. Hartsock then insists, in a formulation that I also support, that "[t]hese groups must not be seen as formed unproblematically by existing in a particular social location and therefore seeing the world in a particular way. My effort to develop the idea of a feminist standpoint, in contrast to 'women's viewpoint,' was an effort to move in this direction" (1997, 371–372).

3. An alternative explanation for the intensity of some feminists' antipostmodernism—an explanation that could also account for the vehemence of some postmodernist feminists' anti-modernism—is that they are by this time exasperated by the misrepresentations of their arguments.

4. Both Flax and Ebert are aware that the categories they use to describe their opponents, the Enlightenment and ludic feminism, are reductive, that as general categories they make one theory out of many (see, for example, Flax 1993, 30; Ebert 1996, 184–186). Presumably they choose to enlist them because they find them useful. My point is not that we should avoid general categories, but rather that these particular categories no longer advance our thinking in this particular field at this particular time.

5. Flax's final claim that feminist anti-postmodernists are propelled by racist motives is presented in the "innocent" form of a question: "Since the projects of postmodernism and of women of color do overlap, I wonder whether there is a racial subtext at work that requires more attention. Directly attacking women of color or voicing our re-

sentment of them (in public) would be politically unthinkable. Is it easier and more acceptable for white women to express our discomfort with difference discourses and the politics of knowledge claims by categorically rejecting postmodernism and branding it politically incorrect?" (1993, 146)

6. In one formulation of this charge, Ebert focuses on the consequences of the theories rather than the motives of the authors: "Ludic feminism becomes—in its *effects*, if not in its intentions—a theory that inscribes the class interests of what bourgeois sociology calls the upper middle class." Ludic feminism is, then, "in *effect*, a theory for property holders" (1996, 26). Although I believe that she does not offer adequate support for this thesis, the claim is potentially interesting. In other sections of the text, however, she does not make this clear distinction between effects and intentions. In a later passage, for example, Ebert suggests that an intentional class bias is behind ludic feminism's inattention to the economic basis of gender construction and hierarchy: "Such a separation of gender and sex from economic practices legitimates the class interests of ludic feminists, who would, for the most part, like to see some measure of gender equality but who argue for it within the existing class relations so as not to disturb their own class privileges" (ibid, 47). There is no attempt to support this charge. Thus my problem with the argument is that when Ebert describes ludic theory as a theory of the ruling class (ibid., 86), not only does she fail to specify in every case whether it is a theory *by* the "ruling class" or *for* "the ruling class," but she also does not always present adequate support for either possibility.

7. Again, the vocabulary itself is not at issue here. The terms "postmodernism" and "modernism" have been defined in a variety of ways; their use in a particular context does not mean that the argument is necessarily implicated in the modernist–postmodernist paradigm debate as I describe it here. On the other hand, the term "postmodernism," with its suggestion of an *after* to modernism that could be read as an absolute opposition, together with the category of the Enlightenment, have been so often deployed in arguments framed in terms of the paradigm debate that they are by now, to my mind, too closely associated with the reductive and reactive logic of the modernist versus postmodernist formula to be particularly useful.

8. For just a few of the most interesting examples of how to work through the potential affinities between Marxism and poststructuralism with consequences for feminism, see Brown 1995; Callari and Ruccio 1996; Corlett 1996; Gibson-Graham 1996; Hardt and Negri 1994; Hennessy 1993; Jameson 1988b and 1991; and Spivak 1987, 1990.

9. See Nancy Fraser (1997) for an excellent attempt to address this question and propose alternatives.

10. It is important to emphasize that my argument is directed only to the fields of political theory and feminist theory; I leave open the question of the continued productivity of the modernist–postmodernist paradigm debate in other fields.

11. Young 1994 presents an interesting attempt to deal explicitly with this issue.

12. Collins also notes the obstacles posed by the dominance of liberal models (1997, 375).

REFERENCES

Allison, David B., ed. 1985. *The New Nietzsche: Contemporary Styles of Interpretation*. Cambridge: MIT Press.

Althusser, Louis. 1971. *Lenin and Philosophy and Other Essays*. Trans. Ben Brewster. New York: Monthly Review Press.

———. 1976. *Essays in Self-Criticism*. Trans. Grahame Lock. London: NLB.

———. 1990. *For Marx*. Trans. Ben Brewster. London: Verso.

Althusser, Louis, and Étienne Balibar. 1979. *Reading Capital*. Trans. Ben Brewster. London: Verso.

Amott, Teresa L., and Julie A. Matthaei. 1991. *Race, Gender, and Work: A Multicultural Economic History of Women in the United States*. Boston: South End Press.

Ansell-Pearson, Keith. 1990. "Nietzsche: A Radical Challenge to Political Theory?" *Radical Philosophy* 54: 10–18.

Anzaldúa, Gloria. 1987. *Borderlands/La Frontera: The New Mestiza*. San Francisco: Spinsters/Aunt Lute.

Arato, Andrew, and Paul Breines. 1979. *The Young Lukács and the Origins of Western Marxism*. New York: Seabury Press.

Bordo, Susan. 1992. "Feminist Skepticism and the 'Maleness' of Philosophy." In *Women and Reason*, ed. Elizabeth Harvey and Kathleen Okruhlik, 143–162. Ann Arbor: University of Michigan Press.

Bové, Paul. 1988. "The Foucault Phenomenon: the Problematics of Style." Foreword to Gilles Deleuze, *Foucault*. Minneapolis: University of Minnesota Press.

Brown, Wendy. 1995. *States of Injury: Power and Freedom in Late Modernity*. Princeton: Princeton University Press.

Burris, Barbara. 1973. "The Fourth World Manifesto." In *Radical Feminism*, ed. Anne Koedt, Ellen Levine, and Anita Rapone, 322–357. New York: Quadrangle/ New York Times Book Company.

Butler, Judith. 1990. *Gender Trouble: Feminism and the Subversion of Identity*. New York: Routledge.

——. 1991. "Imitation and Gender Insubordination." In *Inside/Out: Lesbian Theories, Gay Theories*, ed. Diana Fuss, 13–31. New York: Routledge.

——. 1992. "Contingent Foundations: Feminism and the Question of 'Postmodernism'." In *Feminists Theorize the Political*, ed. Judith Butler and Joan W. Scott, 3–21. New York: Routledge.

——. 1993. *Bodies That Matter: On the Discursive Limits of Sex*. New York: Routledge.

Callari, Antonio, and David F. Ruccio. 1996. "Introduction: Postmodern Materialism and the Future of Marxist Theory." In *Postmodern Materialism and the Future of Marxist Theory: Essays in the Althusserian Tradition*, ed. Antonio Callari and David F. Ruccio, 1–48. Hanover: Wesleyan University Press.

Cleaver, Harry. 1991. Introduction. to Antonio Negri, *Marx Beyond Marx: Lessons on the Grundrisse*, xix-xxvii. New York: Autonomedia.

——. 1992. "The Inversion of Class Perspective in Marxian Theory: From Valorisation to Self-Valorisation." In *Open Marxism, vol. 2: Theory and Practice*, ed. Werner Bonefeld, Richard Gunn, and Kosmas Psychopedis, 106–144. London: Pluto Press.

Cocks, Joan. 1989. *The Oppositional Imagination: Feminism, Critique, and Political Theory*. New York: Routledge.

——. 1991. "Augustine, Nietzsche, and Contemporary Body Politics." *Differences* 3 (1): 144–158.

Collins, Patricia Hill. 1991. *Black Feminist Thought: Knowledge, Consciousness, and the Politics of Empowerment*. New York: Routledge.

——. 1997. "Comment on Hekman's 'Truth and Method: Feminist Standpoint Theory Revisited': Where's the Power?" *Signs* 22 (2): 375–381.

Comay, Rebecca. 1986. "Excavating the Repressive Hypothesis: Aporias of Liberation in Foucault." *Telos* 67: 111–119.

Combahee River Collective. 1979. "A Black Feminist Statement." In *Capitalist Patriarchy and the Case for Socialist Feminism*, ed. Zillah Eisenstein, 362–372. New York: Monthly Review Press.

Connolly, William E. 1985. "Taylor, Foucault, and Otherness." *Political Theory* 13 (3): 365–376.

———. 1988. *Political Theory and Modernity*. Oxford: Basil Blackwell.

———. 1991. *Identity/Difference: Democratic Negotiations of Political Paradox*. Ithaca: Cornell University Press.

Corlett, William. 1996. "Containing Indeterminacy: Problems of Representation and Determination in Marx and Althusser." *Political Theory* 24 (3): 464–492.

Dalla Costa, Mariarosa. 1972. "Women and the Subversion of the Community." In *The Power of Women and the Subversion of the Community*. Bristol: Falling Wall Press.

De Lauretis, Teresa. 1990. "Eccentric Subjects: Feminist Theory and Historical Consciousness." *Feminist Studies* 16 (1): 115–150.

Deleuze, Gilles. 1983. *Nietzsche and Philosophy*. Trans. Hugh Tomlinson. New York: Columbia University Press.

Detwiler, Bruce. 1990. *Nietzsche and the Politics of Aristocratic Radicalism*. Chicago: University of Chicago Press.

Dews, Peter. 1987. *Logics of Disintegration: Post-structuralist Thought and the Claims of Critical Theory*. London: Verso.

Diamond, Irene, and Lee Quinby. 1988. "American Feminism and the Language of Control." In *Feminism and Foucault: Reflections on Resistance*, ed. Irene Diamond and Lee Quinby, 193–206. Boston: Northeastern University Press.

Di Leonardo, Micaela. 1987. "The Female World of Cards and Holidays: Women, Families, and the Work of Kinship." *Signs* 12 (3): 440–453.

Di Stefano, Christine. 1991. "Am I That Performance? Vicissitudes of Gender." Paper presented to the American Political Science Association, Washington, D.C.

Ebert, Teresa L. 1992–1993. "Ludic Feminism, the Body, Performance, and Labor: Bringing *Materialism* Back into Feminist Cultural Studies." *Cultural Critique* 23: 5–50.

———. 1996. *Ludic Feminism and After: Postmodernism, Desire, and Labor in Late Capitalism*. Ann Arbor: University of Michigan Press.

Ehrenreich, Barbara. 1984. "Life Without Father: Reconsidering Socialist-Feminist Theory." *Socialist Review* 73: 48–57.

Eisenstein, Zillah. 1979. "Developing a Theory of Capitalist Patriarchy and Socialist Feminism." In *Capitalist Patriarchy and the Case for Socialist Feminism*, ed. Zillah Eisenstein, 5–40. New York: Monthly Review Press.

Elshtain, Jean Bethke. 1984. "Reclaiming the Socialist-Feminist Citizen." *Socialist Review* 74: 21–27.

Elson, Diane. 1979. "The Value Theory of Labour." In *Value: The Representation of Labour in Capitalism*, ed. Diane Elson, 115–180. New Jersey: Humanities Press.

Epstein, Barbara. 1995. "Why Poststructuralism Is a Dead End for Progressive Thought." *Socialist Review* 25 (2): 83–119.

Feenberg, Andrew. 1986. *Lukács, Marx, and the Sources of Critical Theory*. Oxford: Oxford University Press.

Feminists, The. 1973. "The Feminists: A Political Organization to Annihilate Sex Roles." In *Radical Feminism*, ed. Anne Koedt, Ellen Levine, Anita Rapone, 368–378. New York: Quadrangle/ New York Times Book Company.

Ferguson, Ann, and Nancy Folbre. 1981. "The Unhappy Marriage of Patriarchy and Capitalism." In *Women and Revolution*, ed. Lydia Sargent, 313–338. Boston: South End Press.

Ferguson, Kathy. 1993. *The Man Question: Visions of Subjectivity in Feminist Theory*. Berkeley: University of California Press.

Flax, Jane. 1987. "Postmodernism and Gender Relations in Feminist Theory." *Signs* 12 (4): 621–643.

———. 1993. *Disputed Subjects: Essays on Psychoanalysis, Politics, and Philosophy*. New York: Routledge.

Foucault, Michel. 1970. *The Order of Things: An Archeology of the Human Sciences*. New York: Vintage.

———. 1977. *Language, Counter-Memory, Practice: Selected Essays and Interviews*. Trans. Donald F. Bouchard and Sherry Simon. Ithaca: Cornell University Press.

———. 1980a. *Power/Knowledge: Selected Interviews and Other Writings, 1972–1977*. New York: Pantheon Books.

———. 1980b. *The History of Sexuality, vol. 1: An Introduction*. Trans. Robert Hurley. New York: Vintage.

———. 1983. "The Subject and Power." In *Michel Foucault: Beyond Structuralism and Hermeneutics*, 2d ed., Hubert L. Dreyfus and Paul Rabinow, 208–226. Chicago: University of Chicago Press.

———. 1984. "What Is Enlightenment?" In *The Foucault Reader*, ed. Paul Rabinow, 32–50. New York: Pantheon.

———. 1986. *The Use of Pleasure: The History of Sexuality, vol. 2*: Trans. Robert Hurley. New York: Vintage.

———. 1988. *Politics, Philosophy, Culture: Interviews and Other Writings by Michel Foucault, 1977–1984*, ed. Lawrence D. Kritzman. New York: Routledge.

———. 1991a. *Remarks on Marx: Conversations with Duccio Trombadori*. Trans. R. James Goldstein and James Cascaito. New York: Semiotext(e).

———. 1991b. "Questions of Method." In *The Foucault Effect: Studies in Governmentality*, ed. Graham Burchell, Colin Gordon, and Peter Miller, 73–86. Chicago: University of Chicago Press.

Fraser, Nancy. 1989. *Unruly Practices: Power, Discourse, and Gender in*

Contemporary Social Theory. Minneapolis: University of Minnesota Press.

——. 1997. *Justice Interruptus: Critical Reflections on the "Postsocialist" Condition*. New York: Routledge.

Fraser, Nancy, and Linda Nicholson. 1990. "Social Criticism without Philosophy: An Encounter between Feminism and Postmodernism." In *Feminism/Postmodernism*, ed. Linda Nicholson, 19–38. New York: Routledge.

Freedman, Carl. 1990. "The Interventional Marxism of Louis Althusser." *Rethinking Marxism* 3 (3–4): 309–328.

Gibson-Graham, J.K. 1993. "Waiting for the Revolution, or How to Smash Capitalism While Working at Home in Your Spare Time." *Rethinking Marxism* 6 (2): 10–24.

——. 1996. *The End of Capitalism (As We Knew It): A Feminist Critique of Political Economy*. Oxford: Blackwell.

Glenn, Evelyn Nakano. 1992. "From Servitude to Service Work: Historical Continuities in the Racial Division of Paid Reproductive Labor." *Signs* 18 (1): 1–43.

Grosz, Elizabeth. 1993. "Nietzsche and the Stomach for Knowledge." In *Nietzsche, Feminism, and Political Theory*, ed. Paul Patton, 49–70. New York: Routledge.

Haar, Michel. 1985. "Nietzsche and Metaphysical Language." In *The New Nietzsche*, ed. David Allison, 5–36. Cambridge: MIT Press.

Habermas, Jürgen. 1981. "Modernity versus Postmodernity." *New German Critique* 22: 3–14.

——. 1987. *The Philosophical Discourse of Modernity*. Trans. Frederick Lawrence. Cambridge: MIT Press.

Harding, Sandra. 1986a. *The Science Question in Feminism*. Ithaca: Cornell University Press.

——. 1986b. "The Instability of the Analytical Categories of Feminist Theory." *Signs* 11 (4): 645–664.

——. 1991. *Whose Science? Whose Knowledge? Thinking from Women's Lives*. Ithaca: Cornell University Press.

Hardt, Michael. 1994. "Toni Negri's Practical Philosophy." In *Body Politics: Disease, Desire, and the Family*, ed. Michael Ryan and Avery Gordon, 225–228. Boulder: Westview.

Hardt, Michael, and Antonio Negri. 1994. *Labor of Dionysus: A Critique of the State-Form*. Minneapolis: University of Minnesota Press.

Hartmann, Heidi. 1981a. "The Unhappy Marriage of Marxism and Feminism: Towards a More Progressive Union." In *Women and Revolution: A Discussion of the Unhappy Marriage of Marxism and Feminism*, ed. Lydia Sargent, 1–41. Boston: South End Press.

——. 1981b. "Summary and Response: Continuing the Discussion." In

Women and Revolution, ed. Lydia Sargent, 363–373. Boston: South End Press.

———. 1981c. "The Family as the Locus of Gender, Class, and Political Struggle: The Example of Housework." *Signs* 6 (3): 366–394.

Hartsock, Nancy. 1979. "Feminist Theory and the Development of Revolutionary Strategy." In *Capitalist Patriarchy and the Case for Socialist Feminism*, ed. Zillah Eisenstein, 56–77. New York: Monthly Review Press.

———. 1981. "Fundamental Feminism: Process and Perspective." In *Building Feminist Theory: Essays from Quest a Feminist Quarterly*, ed. Quest Staff. New York: Longman.

———. 1983a. "The Feminist Standpoint: Developing the Ground for a Specifically Feminist Historical Materialism." In *Discovering Reality: Feminist Perspectives on Epistemology, Metaphysics, Methodology, and Philosophy of Science*, ed. Sandra Harding and Merrill Hintakka, 283–310. Dordrecht: D. Reidel Publishing.

———. 1983b. *Money, Sex, and Power: Toward a Feminist Historical Materialism*. Boston: Northeastern University Press.

———. 1989–1990. "Postmodernism and Political Change: Issues for Feminist Theory." *Cultural Critique* 14: 15–33.

———. 1997. "Comment on Hekman's 'Truth and Method: Feminist Standpoint Theory Revisited': Truth or Justice?" *Signs* 22 (2): 367–374.

———. Forthcoming. "The Feminist Standpoint Revisited." In *The Feminist Standpoint Revisited and Other Essays*. Boulder: Westview Press.

Hekman, Susan J. 1990. *Gender and Knowledge: Elements of a Postmodern Feminism*. Boston: Northeastern University Press.

Hennessy, Rosemary. 1993. *Materialist Feminism and the Politics of Discourse*. New York: Routledge.

Higgins, Kathleen Marie. 1987. *Nietzsche's Zarathustra*. Philadelphia: Temple University Press.

———. 1990. "Nietzsche and Postmodern Subjectivity." In *Nietzsche as Postmodernist: Essays Pro and Contra*, ed. Clayton Koelb, 189–215. Albany: State University of New York Press.

Hirschmann, Nancy J. 1992. *Rethinking Obligation: A Feminist Method for Political Theory*. Ithaca: Cornell University Press.

Honneth, Axel. 1994. "History and Interaction: On the Structuralist Interpretation of Historical Materialism." In *Althusser: A Critical Reader*, ed. Gregory Elliott, 73–103. Cambridge: Blackwell.

hooks, bell. 1992. *Black Looks: Race and Representation*. Boston: South End Press.

Hoy, David Couzens. 1988. "Foucault: Modern or Postmodern?" In *After Foucault: Humanistic Knowledge, Postmodern Challenges*, ed. Jonathan Arac, 12–41. New Brunswick: Rutgers University Press.

Hypatia. 1992. "Symposium on Susan Bordo's 'Feminist Skepticism and the 'Maleness' of Philosophy'." *Hypatia* 7 (3): 155–207.

Jaggar, Alison M. 1983. *Feminist Politics and Human Nature.* Totowa, N.J.: Rowman and Allanheld.

Jameson, Fredric. 1981. *The Political Unconscious: Narrative as a Socially Symbolic Act.* Ithaca: Cornell University Press.

——. 1988a. "*History and Class Consciousness* as an 'Unfinished Project'." *Rethinking Marxism* 1 (1): 49–72.

——. 1988b. *The Ideologies of Theory: Essays, 1971–1986, vol. 2.* Minneapolis: University of Minnesota Press.

——. 1991. *Postmodernism, or The Cultural Logic of Late Capitalism.* Durham: Duke University Press.

——. 1993. "Actually Existing Marxism." *Polygraph* 6/7: 170–195.

Jay, Martin. 1984. *Marxism and Totality: The Adventures of a Concept from Lukács to Habermas.* Berkeley: University of California Press.

Jones, Kathleen B. 1993. *Compassionate Authority: Democracy and the Representation of Women.* New York: Routledge.

Joseph, Gloria. 1981. "The Incompatible Menage A Trois: Marxism, Feminism, and Racism." In *Women and Revolution,* ed. Lydia Sargent, 91–107. Boston: South End Press.

Kaufmann, Walter. 1974. *Nietzsche: Philosopher, Psychologist, Antichrist.* Princeton: Princeton University Press.

Klossowski, Pierre. 1985. "Nietzsche's Experience of the Eternal Return." In *The New Nietzsche: Contemporary Styles of Interpretation,* ed. David B. Allison, 107–120. Cambridge: MIT Press.

Knightly, Gladys Fewkes. 1984. "April 1, 1984." *On Our Backs* 1:23.

Koedt, Ann. 1973. "Women and the Radical Movement." In *Radical Feminism,* ed. Anne Koedt, Ellen Levine, and Anita Rapone, 318–321. New York: Quadrangle/ New York Times Book Company.

Koelb, Clayton, ed. 1990. *Nietzsche as Postmodernist: Essays Pro and Contra.* Albany: State University of New York Press.

Kolakowski, Leszek. 1978. *Main Currents of Marxism: Its Origins, Growth and Dissolution, vol. 3: The Breakdown.* Oxford: Oxford University Press.

Kuhn, Thomas. 1970. *The Structure of Scientific Revolutions,* 2d ed. Chicago: University of Chicago Press.

Love, Nancy. 1986. *Marx, Nietzsche, and Modernity.* New York: Columbia University Press.

Lukács, Georg. 1971. *History and Class Consciousness: Studies in Marxist Dialectics.* Trans. Rodney Livingstone. Cambridge: MIT Press.

——. 1972. *Tactics and Ethics: Political Essays, 1919–1929.* Trans. Michael McColgan. New York: Harper and Row.

Malveaux, Julianne. 1990. "Gender Difference and Beyond: An Economic Perspective on Diversity and Commonality among Women." In *Theoretical Perspectives on Sexual Difference,* ed. Deborah L. Rhode, 226–238. New Haven: Yale University Press.

Marx, Karl. 1964. *Economic and Philosophic Manuscripts of 1844.* Trans. Martin Milligan. New York: International Publishers.

———. 1973. *Grundrisse.* Trans. Martin Nicolaus. New York: Vintage Books.

———. 1977. *Capital,* vol. 1. Trans. Ben Fowkes. New York: Vintage Books.

Marx, Karl, and Friedrich Engels. 1978. *The German Ideology.* In *The Marx-Engels Reader,,* 2d ed., ed. Robert Tucker. New York: Norton.

McNay, Lois. 1992. *Foucault and Feminism: Power, Gender, and the Self.* Boston: Northeastern University Press.

Megill, Allan. 1985. *Prophets of Extremity: Nietzsche, Heidegger, Foucault, Derrida.* Berkeley: University of California Press.

Mészáros, István. 1970. "Lukács' Concept of Dialectic." In *Georg Lukács: The Man, His Work, and His Ideas,* ed. G.H.R. Parkinson, 34–85. London: Weidenfeld and Nicolson.

Negri, Antonio. 1989. *The Politics of Subversion: A Manifesto for the Twenty-First Century.* Trans. James Newell. Cambridge: Polity Press.

———. 1991. *Marx beyond Marx: Lessons on the Grundrisse.* Trans. Harry Cleaver, Michael Ryan, and Maurizio Viano. New York: Autonomedia.

Nehamas, Alexander. 1985. *Nietzsche: Life as Literature.* Cambridge: Harvard University Press.

Nietzsche, Friedrich. 1954a. *Twilight of the Idols.* In *The Portable Nietzsche.* Trans. Walter Kaufmann. New York: Penguin.

———. 1954b. *Thus Spoke Zarathustra.* In *The Portable Nietzsche,* ed. Walter Kaufmann. New York: Penguin.

———. 1966. *Beyond Good and Evil: Prelude to a Philosophy of the Future.* Trans. Walter Kaufmann. New York: Vintage.

———. 1968. *The Will to Power.* Trans. Walter Kaufmann and R. J. Hollingdale. New York: Vintage.

———. 1969. *On the Genealogy of Morals.* Trans. Walter Kaufmann. New York: Vintage.

———. 1974. *The Gay Science.* Trans. Walter Kaufmann. New York: Random House.

O'Brien, Mary. 1981. *The Politics of Reproduction.* Boston: Routledge and Kegan Paul.

O'Hara, Daniel, ed. 1985. *Why Nietzsche Now?* Bloomington: Indiana University Press.

Ollman, Bertell. 1971. *Alienation: Marx's Conception of Man in Capitalist Society.* Cambridge: Cambridge University Press.

Patton, Paul, ed. 1993. *Nietzsche, Feminism, and Political Theory.* New York: Routledge.

Poster, Mark. 1984. *Foucault, Marxism, and History: Mode of Production versus Mode of Information.* Cambridge: Polity Press.

Rajchman, John. 1985. *Michel Foucault: The Freedom of Philosophy.* New York: Columbia University Press.

Read, James H. 1989. "Nietzsche: Power as Oppression." *Praxis International* 9 (1/2): 72–87.

Resnick, Stephen, and Richard Wolff. 1993. "Althusser's Liberation of Marxian Theory." In *The Althusserian Legacy,* ed. E. Ann Kaplan and Michael Sprinker, 59–72. London: Verso.

Rose, Hilary. 1983. "Hand, Brain, and Heart: A Feminist Epistemology for the Natural Sciences." *Signs* 9 (1): 73–90.

———. 1986. "Women's Work: Women's Knowledge." In *What Is Feminism?,* ed. Juliet Mitchell and Ann Oakley, 161–183. Oxford: Basil Blackwell.

Rowbotham, Sheila. 1973. *Woman's Consciousness, Man's World.* New York: Penguin Books.

Ruddick, Sara. 1989. *Maternal Thinking: Toward a Politics of Peace.* New York: Ballantine Books.

Ryan, Michael. 1982. *Marxism and Deconstruction: A Critical Articulation.* Baltimore: Johns Hopkins University Press.

Said, Edward W. 1988. "Michel Foucault, 1926–1984." In *After Foucault: Humanistic Knowledge, Postmodern Challenges,* ed. Jonathan Arac, 1–11. New Brunswick: Rutgers University Press.

Sandoval, Chela. 1991. "U.S. Third World Feminism: The Theory and Method of Oppositional Consciousness in the Postmodern World. *Genders* 10: 1–24.

Schacht, Richard. 1973. "Nietzsche and Nihilism." In *Nietzsche: A Collection of Critical Essays,* ed. Robert C. Solomon, 58–82. Garden City: Anchor Press.

Schutte, Ofelia. 1984. *Beyond Nihilism: Nietzsche without Masks.* Chicago: University of Chicago Press.

Seery, John Evan. 1990. *Political Returns: Irony in Politics and Theory from Plato to the Antinuclear Movement.* Boulder: Westview.

Shaw, Brian J. 1990. "Totality, Realism, and the Type: Lukács' Later Literary Criticism as Political Theory." *Philosophical Forum* 21 (4): 412–441.

Smith, Dorothy E. 1987. *The Everyday World as Problematic: A Feminist Sociology.* Boston: Northeastern University Press.

———. 1990. *Texts, Facts, and Femininity: Exploring the Relations of Ruling*. New York: Routledge.

———. 1992. "Sociology from Women's Experience: A Reaffirmation." *Sociological Theory* 10 (1): 88–98.

———. 1997. "Comment on Hekman's 'Truth and Method: Feminist Standpoint Theory Revisited'." *Signs* 22 (2): 392–398.

Smith, Steven B. 1984. *Reading Althusser: An Essay on Structural Marxism*. Ithaca: Cornell University Press.

Spivak, Gayatri Chakravorty. 1987. *In Other Worlds: Essays in Cultural Politics*. New York: Routledge.

———. 1990. *The Post-Colonial Critic: Interviews, Strategies, Dialogues*, ed. Sarah Harasym. New York: Routledge.

Stambaugh, Joan. 1972. *Nietzsche's Thought of Eternal Return*. Baltimore: Johns Hopkins University Press.

Stanley, Liz, and Sue Wise. 1990. "Method, Methodology, and Epistemology in Feminist Research Processes." In *Feminist Praxis: Research, Theory, and Epistemology in Feminist Sociology*, ed. Liz Stanley, 20–60. New York: Routledge.

Strong, Tracy B. 1988. *Friedrich Nietzsche and the Politics of Transfiguration*, expanded edition. Berkeley: University of California Press.

Surin, Kenneth. 1993. " 'The Continued Relevance of Marxism' as a Question: Some Propositions." *Polygraph* 6/7: 39–71.

Taylor, Charles. 1984. "Foucault on Freedom and Truth." *Political Theory* 12 (2): 152–183.

———. 1985. "Connolly, Foucault, and Truth." *Political Theory* 13 (3): 377–385.

Tong, Rosemarie. 1989. *Feminist Thought: A Comprehensive Introduction*. Boulder: Westview Press.

Tress, Daryl McGowen. 1988. "Comment on Flax's 'Postmodernism and Gender Relations in Feminist Theory'." *Signs* 14 (1): 196–200.

Van Allen, Judith. 1984. "Capitalism without Patriarchy." *Socialist Review* 77: 81–91.

Virno, Paolo, and Michael Hardt, eds. 1996. *Radical Thought in Italy: A Potential Politics*. Minneapolis: University of Minnesota Press.

Vogel, Lise. 1981. "Marxism and Feminism: Unhappy Marriage, Trial Separation or Something Else?" In *Women and Revolution*, ed. Lydia Sargent, 195–217. Boston: South End Press.

Walker, Nancy A. 1990. *Feminist Alternatives: Irony and Fantasy in the Contemporary Novel by Women*. Jackson: University of Mississippi Press.

Walzer, Michael. 1986. "The Politics of Michel Foucault." In *Foucault: A Critical Reader*, ed. David Hoy, 51–68. Oxford: Basil Blackwell.

Warren, Mark. 1988. *Nietzsche and Political Thought*. Cambridge: MIT Press.

Young, Iris. 1980. "Socialist Feminism and the Limits of Dual Systems Theory." *Socialist Review* 50/51: 169–188.

—— 1981. "Beyond the Unhappy Marriage: A Critique of Dual Systems Theory." In *Women and Revolution*, ed. Lydia Sargent, 43–69. Boston: South End Press.

——. 1990. *Throwing Like a Girl and Other Essays in Feminist Philosophy and Social Theory*. Bloomington: Indiana University Press.

——. 1994. "Gender as Seriality: Thinking about Women as a Social Collective." *Signs* 19 (3): 713–738.

Zita, Jacqueline N. 1992. "Male Lesbians and the Postmodernist Body." *Hypatia* 7 (4): 106–127.

INDEX

Allison, David, 163n1
Althusser, Louis, 14, 93; and determinism, 108–109; on Hegel, 103–105, 115; on ideology, 107–108; on Lukács, 103, 173n18, 173n21; compared to Negri, 115–116; on overdetermination, 104–106; on relative autonomy, 106–108; anti-humanism of, 111–115; on totality, 71, 103–111
Aristotle, 62
Amott, Teresa, and Julie Matthaei, 162n7
Ansell-Pearson, Keith, 169n10
Anzaldúa, Gloria, 174n2
Arato, Andrew, and Paul Breines, 94

Balibar, Étienne, 109, 112, 114
Bordo, Susan, 176n13
Bové, Paul, 50, 52–57
Brown, Wendy, 179n8
Burris, Barbara, 74
Butler, Judith, 3, 177n24; on drag, 143–145; on performativity, 15, 125–134, 152–153, 174n2; on post-modernism, 65–66

Callari, Antonio, and David Ruccio, 179n8
Cleaver, Harry, 147, 177n23
Cocks, Joan, 172n11, 177n20
Collins, Patricia Hill, 162n6, 162n7, 163n13, 178n2, 180n12
Comay, Rebecca, 37
Combahee River Collective, 84
Connolly, William, 16, 50, 52–57, 66–67
Corlett, William, 179n8

Dalla Costa, Mariarosa, 14, 86, 91; compared to dual-systems theory, 79–80; on single-system theory, 75–77, 85
De Lauretis, Teresa, 174n2
Deleuze, Gilles, 165n10, 166–167n20; on the active and reactive, 21–22, 146; on eternal return, 40–42, 134–135, 166n17; on will to power, 164n4, 175n6
Detwiler, Bruce, 163n2, 167n22
Dews, Peter, 165–166n13
Diamond, Irene, and Lee Quinby, 170n13

Di Leonardo, Micaela, 162n10
Di Stefano, Christine, 175n9, 176n14,
 177n21

Ebert, Teresa, 129, 156–157, 175n9,
 175n10
Eclecticism, 64–65, 67, 170n15
Ehrenreich, Barbara, 88–89
Eisenstein, Zillah, 74, 77, 113, 172n7
Elshtain, Jean Bethke, 89, 172n10
Elson, Diane, 175n5
Engels, Friedrich, 75, 77, 122
Epistemology, 9–10, 177n26; and
 Althusser, 106; and Lukács, 97–98,
 173n17; in modernist–postmod-
 ernist paradigm debate, 57, 62–63,
 65, 171n16; and Nietzsche,
 164–165n8, 165n10
Epstein, Barbara, 174n26
Essentialism, 1, 10, 121–122, 163n15,
 172n14

Feenberg, Andrew, 173n19
Feminism: materialist, 178n1; radical,
 73–74, 78, 172n11; socialist, 73–75.
 See also feminist systems theories;
 standpoint theory
Feminist systems theories, 75–86; critiques of, 86–89
Feminists, The, 74
Ferguson, Ann, and Nancy Folbre,
 172n9
Ferguson, Kathy, 162n3, 163n15,
 174n2, 176n14; on irony, 137–138,
 142–143, 176n18, 176–177n19
Flax, Jane, 156–157, 169n12, 170n13,
 170n14
Foucault, Michel, 3, 88; Connolly and
 Taylor readings of, 52–57; and
 critique, 44–45; on genealogy of
 sexuality, 36–39; on Marx and
 Marxism, 17, 28–29, 35, 165n11;
 and Nietzsche, 17–18; as postmodernist, 57–58, 67–68, 167n1; on
 power/knowledge, 22–23; on rationality, 165n9; on the subject, 34–39;
 on subjectification, 20; on totality,
 27–31, 71–72
Fraser, Nancy, 60, 165n12, 166n13,
 180n9; and Linda Nicholson, 72
Freedman, Carl, 105, 109

Gibson-Graham, J. K., 105, 179n8
Glenn, Evelyn Nakano, 162n7
Grosz, Elizabeth, 164n5

Haar, Michel, 20, 42, 164n5, 166n16,
 166n19
Habermas, Jürgen, 60, 169n8
Harding, Sandra, 162n3, 162n6,
 173n20
Hardt, Michael, 171n4, 177n23; and
 Antonio Negri, 175n7, 177n25,
 179n8
Hartmann, Heidi, 14, 74, 91–92, 107;
 on Dalla Costa, 76, 171n3; on dual-
 systems theory, 78–81, 88, 172n12;
 compared to unified-systems theory, 82–86
Hartsock, Nancy, 8, 108, 113,
 136–137, 172n13, 173n20, 178n2;
 and Lukács, 98–99; on Rorty,
 170–171n16; on women's labor, 5–6,
 162n11
Hegel, G. W. F. *See* Althusser, Louis:
 on Hegel; Lukacs, Georg: on Hegel;
 Negri, Antonio: on Hegel
Hekman, Susan, 62–65, 67, 170n16
Hennessy, Rosemary, 107–108, 162n5,
 172n8, 179n8
Higgins, Kathleen Marie, 164n3,
 166n16
Hirschmann, Nancy, 162n6, 173n20
Honneth, Axel, 115
hooks, bell, 177n22
Hoy, David Couzens, 16, 60, 64,
 169n5, 169n7
Humanism and antihumanism:
 Lukács and 96, 101; in standpoint
 theory, 113–114. *See also* Althusser,
 Louis: on the subject; Foucault,
 Michel: on the subject; Negri,
 Antonio: on the subject; Nietzsche,
 Friedrich: on the subject

Irony, 137–143, 176–177n19

Jaggar, Alison, 162n3
Jameson, Fredric, 97–98, 106, 109–110,
 173n21, 179n8
Jay, Martin, 171n1
Jones, Kathleen, 175n9
Joseph, Gloria, 80–81

Kant, Immanuel, 16, 24, 60
Kaufmann, Walter, 26, 27, 163n2,
    165n10, 167n21
Klossowski, Pierre, 166n16
Knightly, Gladys Fewkes, 141
Koedt, Ann, 74
Koelb, Clayton, 163n1
Kolakowski, Leszek, 71
Kuhn, Thomas, 50–52

Labor: gender division of, 5, 82–84, 90;
    Marx's conception of, 121–125;
    compared to signifying practices,
    129; women's, 5–7, 91–92, 153–154,
    159. *See also* self-valorization
Liberalism, 8, 61, 63, 71, 180n12
Livingston, Jennie, 144
Love, Nancy, 27
Lukács, Georg, 14; on Hegel, 94, 97,
    103–104; on identical subject-object
    of history, 100–103, 112–113; on to-
    tality, 93–100
Lyotard, Jean-François, 57, 72

Malveaux, Julianne, 162n7
Marx, Karl, 95, 99; feminists on, 75,
    77, 90, 99, 113; on labor, 122–124;
    as modernist, 60, 63. *See also*
    Foucault, Michel: on Marx and
    Marxism; Negri, Antonio
Marxism, 11; humanist, 35, 111–114,
    122, 124; in the modernist-
    postmodernist paradigm debate, 11,
    59–65, 69; orthodox, 17, 28, 60–62,
    75, 165n11.
McNay, Lois, 38
Megill, Allan, 60
Mészáros, István, 102
Modernist–postmodernist paradigm
    debate, 1–2, 13–14, 49–50; construc-
    tion of, 50–59; limitations of,
    59–69, 155–159

Negri, Antonio, 11, 14, 15, 93; on
    Hegel, 116–118, 147; on self-
    valorization, 146–149; on the sub-
    ject, 117–118; on totality, 115–117
Nehamas, Alexander, 166n15, 166n16
Nietzsche, Friedrich, 3, 12, 143,
    168n4; and aphorism, 25–26; on the
    ascetic ideal, 25, 34; and critique,

43–44; on the eternal return, 40–43,
    47, 134–135; on laughter, 138; on
    nihilism, 19–21; on perspectivism,
    164–165n8; on *ressentiment*, 34; on
    the subject, 32–34, 139; on systems
    theory, 24–27, 71–72; on will to
    power, 20–22, 44, 45–46, 123. *See
    also* Deleuze, Gilles

O'Brien, Mary, 174n3
Off Our Backs, 140
O'Hara, Daniel, 163n1
On Our Backs, 140–141
Ollman, Bertell, 172n15

Paradigm, definition of, 51. *See also*
    Kuhn, Thomas; modernist-
    postmodernist paradigm debate
Paris Is Burning, 144
Patton, Paul, 163n1
Plato, 24, 62, 64
Poster, Mark, 166n13
Postmodernism, definition of, 49, 157.
    See also modernist–postmodernist
    paradigm debate
Postmodernity, definition of, 48–49
Poststructuralism, definition of, 49

Race, 156, 178–179n5; and racial divi-
    sion of labor, 5, 162n7; in systems
    theories, 80–81, 83–85
Rajchman, John, 27
Reactive reversal, 44, 66, 68, 159
Read, James, 167n23
Resnick, Stephen, and Richard Wolff,
    106
Rorty, Richard, 57, 170n16
Rose, Hilary, 5, 6, 8, 91, 162n8
Rowbotham, Sheila, 140
Ruddick, Sara, 162n9
Ryan, Michael, 177n23

Said, Edward, 18
Sandoval, Chela, 174n2
Schacht, Richard, 21, 167n20
Schutte, Ofelia, 26
Seery, John Evan, 177n19
Self-valorization, 15, 146–150
Shaw, Brian, 98
Smith, Dorothy, 90–91, 99, 122–123,
    161n2; on standpoint theory, 161n1,

Smith, Dorothy (*cont.*)
162–163n13; on structure and su-
perstructure, 110–111; on women's
labor, 5, 162n12
Smith, Steven, 115
Spivak, Gayatri, 179n8
Stalin, Joseph, 71
Stambaugh, Joan, 164n4, 166n16
Standpoint theory (feminist), 3–11,
90–92, 98–99, 102, 132–137. *See
also* Hartsock, Nancy; Rose, Hilary;
Smith, Dorothy
Stanley, Liz, and Sue Wise, 173n20
Strong, Tracy, 165n10, 166n16, 166n17
Surin, Kenneth, 12
Suvin, Darko, 176n17

Taylor, Charles, 50, 52–57, 64
Tong, Rosemarie, 171n3, 171n5
Totality, 4–5, 14, 70–71, 119; and antagonism, 115–118; dangers of,
71–72; dialectical, 93–99; feminist
critiques of, 72; structural, 103–111.
See also feminist systems theories;

Foucault, Michel: on totality;
Nietzsche, Friedrich: on systems
theory; standpoint theory
Tress, Daryl McGowen, 170n14

Van Allen, Judith, 87
Virno, Paolo, and Michael Hardt,
177n23
Vogel, Lise, 171n3

Walker, Nancy, 139
Walzer, Michael, 50, 52–57
Warren, Mark, 61, 163–164n2, 165n10,
166n17, 167n24; on eternal return,
42, 166n16; on will to power, 20,
22, 164n4, 167n22, 175n6
Williams, Raymond, 12

Young, Iris, 14, 180n11; and dual-
systems theory, 80, 81; on unified-
systems theory, 82–86, 87, 89, 90,
172n9, 173n22

Zita, Jacqueline, 176n16